SHAKESPEARE THE PROFESSIONAL
AND RELATED STUDIES

Shakespeare the Professional

and Related Studies

by

KENNETH MUIR

King Alfred Professor of
English Literature,
University of Liverpool

HEINEMANN
LONDON

Heinemann Educational Books Ltd

LONDON   EDINBURGH   MELBOURNE   TORONTO
SINGAPORE   JOHANNESBURG   NEW DELHI
AUCKLAND   IBADAN   HONG KONG
NAIROBI

ISBN 0 435 18579 9
© Kenneth Muir 1973
First published 1973

Published by Heinemann Educational Books Ltd
48 Charles Street, London W1X 8AH
Printed in Great Britain by
Butler & Tanner Ltd, Frome and London

Preface

These studies of Shakespeare as a professional writer have all appeared, in earlier versions, during the last ten years. All have been revised and half of them have been enlarged. As some of them were published in Japan, India, Poland, France and Switzerland, as well as in the United States and England, it seemed to be worthwhile to collect them, especially as they are linked in various ways. The first three chapters are concerned with the relationship between the poet, the dramatist and the actor; the next six discuss the way in which the poet's imagery was used for essentially dramatic purposes; and the last three show that in the alternative profession open to him, as a narrative poet, Shakespeare tried out, more skilfully and dramatically than in his earliest plays, some of the themes and images he was to use in his mature work.

K.M.

NOTE

The line references to the plays refer to the *Complete Works* edited by Peter Alexander. There are a few places, however, where I have preferred my own reading.

Acknowledgements

I am indebted to the Cambridge University Press and to the Editor of *Shakespeare Survey* for permission to include, in a revised form, articles which constitute Chapters 1, 2, 4 and 8. Chapter 1 was delivered at the International Shakespeare Conference at Stratford-on-Avon in 1970. Chapter 3 appeared in the *Rudolf Stamm Festschrift* and I am grateful to the editors and the publishers (Francke Verlag) for permission to republish. Chapter 5 was published in the *Bulletin of John Rylands Library*, Chapter 6 in *The Literary Half-Yearly*, Chapter 7 in *Etudes Anglaises*; parts of Chapter 8 appeared in *The Cambridge Journal* and *Különlenyomat a Filológiai Közlöny* and parts of Chapter 1 in *Filološki Pregled*; Chapter 9 was published in *Kwartalnik Neofilologiczny*, Chapter 10 in *Shakespearean Essays* (University of Tennessee Press), Chapter 11 in *Anglica*, and Chapter 12 in *Shakespeare 1564–1964*, ed. E. Bloom (Brown University Press). I am grateful to editors and publishers for permission to reprint.

Contents

To Clifford Leech

I Shakespeare the Professional

A conference on the theme of Shakespeare, theatre poet, encourages the reiteration of commonplaces: and, if my argument is familiar, two sentences which, according to Boswell, were deleted from *The Vicar of Wakefield*, may serve as an apology. 'When I was a young man, being anxious to distinguish myself, I was perpetually starting new propositions. But I soon gave this over, for I found that generally what was new was false.'[1]

Shakespeare's greatness as a poet has never been in doubt in English-speaking countries; the critics and actors have always paid lip-service to his greatness as a dramatist. Yet it is only during the last hundred years that we have known enough about the conventions of the Elizabethan theatre to judge Shakespeare's technical competence. Early this century, Robert Bridges, reacting against Bradley, wrote his famous attack on Shakespeare's carelessness and incompetence. He had the excuse that Victorian productions, however brilliantly acted, were merely adaptations. This was brought home to me very forcibly by Sir Donald Wolfit's production of *Cymbeline* in which he made precisely the same cuts as Irving had done half a century earlier. As a result the last act was completely unintelligible to those who had not read the play. Memories of the Irving production seduced Bernard Shaw into rewriting the last act for a production at the Stratford Memorial Theatre; but when he re-read Shakespeare's fifth act he frankly confessed that it was better than his own.

Actor-managers in the nineteenth century, despite their avowed bardolatry, believed they could improve on his plays and therefore assumed that he was not really a competent dramatist. Part of the trouble, but only part, was the difficulty of adapting the plays for a different kind of stage. One early production of *As You Like It* at Stratford, to judge from the prompt book, divided the play into three acts, the first ending with the line

So this is the forest of Arden!

The curtain fell and rose again on a tableau of Rosalind, Celia and Touchstone, shading their eyes as they gazed into the distance. Even worse than this, the Arden scenes were all run together, instead of alternating with the court scenes.

It is not surprising that when Thomas Hardy was asked to contribute to a Shakespeare memorial in the shape of a national theatre, he replied that he did not think

that Shakespeare appertains particularly to the theatrical world nowadays, if ever he did. His distinction as a minister of the theatre is infinitesimal beside his distinction as a poet, man of letters, and seer of life, and that his expression of himself was cast in the form of words for actors and not in the form of books to be read was an accident of his social circumstances that he himself despised.[2]

Hardy went on to hazard a guess that Shakespeare's plays 'would cease altogether to be acted some day, and be simply studied'.

There was some slight excuse for Hardy's anti-theatrical bias in 1908 and we are told that when he did go to see Shakespeare performed his eyes were riveted not to the stage but to the text of the play. It is, moreover, arguable, even if the *Sonnets* are not autobiographical, that Shakespeare was sometimes uneasy in his profession. He confesses that he has made himself 'a motley to the view'; and even if this is only metaphorical, in the next sonnet (111) he blames Fortune.

That did not better for my life provide
Than public means which public manners breed.
Thence comes it that my name receives a brand,
And almost thence my nature is subdued
To what it works in, like the dyer's hand.

The two sonnets together suggest that Shakespeare was thinking of his profession as an actor rather than his work as a dramatist, though in both capacities he could be described as making 'old offences of affections new'. In any case, if the *Sonnets* were not wholly fictional, he was involved in a situation where he was bound to feel socially inferior.

But the feelings expressed in these sonnets were probably momentary and there was perhaps an element of that self-dramatization for which Othello has been wrongly blamed. Shakespeare must have been aware that his dramatic, as well as non-dramatic, verse would outlive the monuments of princes. All the poets he depicted in his plays were foolish, ineffective or time-serving, but no one would deduce from that that he had a low opinion of his own profession as poet, so one would expect similar ironies in his references to his other profession as actor. For Shakespeare had the advantage, shared by few dramatic poets, of being intimately concerned with every aspect of the theatre; as shareholder, actor, dramatist and perhaps even as director, he was entirely professional. Racine had an intimate acquaintance with the theatre — or at least with actresses — but he was no actor. Ibsen had worked in the theatre, but not while he was writing his masterpieces. Strindberg, likewise, had little experience of acting, although he wrote detailed instructions to the company which performed his plays. Chekhov's leading lady became his wife; but he declared that fiction was a lawful wife, while drama was 'a showy, noisy, impertinent and tiresome mistress' and the theatre 'a serpent that sucks your blood'.[3] Shaw had been the greatest of all dramatic critics; he had affairs, like Racine, with a number of actresses; and he directed a number of his own plays.

But of the great dramatists, only Molière and Shakespeare were professional in every sense of the word.

There are, of course, dangers involved. The actor, particularly the actor in a repertory theatre, knows what tricks will enable him to get by; his work is often hurried and makeshift; he aims sometimes at immediate applause rather than the praise of the judicious. And, as Hamlet implies, though not necessarily with the poet's concurrence, the judicious will always be in a minority.

The actor-dramatist, writing for a stable company, is apt to rely on the talents of his fellow actors to bring to life imperfectly realized characters; he will be tempted to repeat effects which have paid off before; he will, for example, disguise yet another heroine as a boy; and he will certainly rely on his knowledge that the audience simply won't notice minor discrepancies and improbabilities. He will, in other words, be writing for the present and not for posterity. But those who write for posterity have never reached their audience.

It was considerations like these which led Robert Bridges to denounce Shakespeare's audience whose low standards and bad taste prevented the greatest of poets from becoming a great artist. Bridges was doubtless reacting against bardolatry, but he seems to have been ignorant of the real nature of Shakespeare's audience, and, much more seriously, of the conventions of the Elizabethan theatre. If one examines the attempts of the best nineteenth-century poets to write plays, one will take leave to doubt whether the absence of an audience is conducive to the production of great drama, and whether it is a disadvantage to write for a particular theatre and a particular company. *The Borderers*, *The Cenci*, and the plays of Tennyson, Browning and Bridges were never clapper-clawed by the palms of the vulgar, yet many of them sacrifice character to situation in ways which the better Elizabethan dramatists would have avoided. The advantages of being a professional theatre poet can be seen from the failures of these amateurs. But perhaps the most telling example is afforded by the great poet of our day, whose dramatic experiments extended over thirty years from *Sweeney Agonistes* to *The Elder Statesman* and whose interest in the problems of the dramatist can be seen in his dialogue on dramatic poetry at the beginning of his career and his lecture on poetry and drama near the end. Mr Martin Browne's recent book,[4] with its lavish quotations from early drafts of Eliot's plays, reveals only too clearly that in some respects he remained an amateur who leaned heavily on Browne's advice. The last and weakest of the plays, *The Elder Statesman*, underwent some radical revisions. Between the performances at the Edinburgh festival and its opening in London some weeks later, many changes were made. Actors found it difficult to speak some lines naturally, and these were altered or cut. Eliot was dissatisfied with the reactions of the audience and he felt that some passages were too 'poetical'. These were eliminated. The final scene between the young lovers had gone badly and Eliot reduced it to a third of its length. What is more significant, he transferred words spoken by the man to the woman. This is surely an indication that the characters had never come alive.

Eliot was a poet who had invaded the professional theatre rather later in life – at about the age when Shakespeare retired to Stratford – and despite his prestige as a poet, as a dramatist he never left off his L-plates. He did not know instinctively what lines would be effective in the theatre; he found it difficult to vary his style to suit different characters; and too many of his characters are either caricatures or mouthpieces for himself. He was not writing for a particular company, so he did not know how effective his speeches would be in the mouths of the actors who were afterwards chosen to speak them.

Shakespeare, of course, acquired his mastery only by degrees. In his earliest plays the characters are differentiated not by how they say it, but only by what they say. Often indeed, they are not distinguished at all. Here, for example, are three speeches from *Henry VI*:

> (i) Why stand we like soft-hearted women here,
> Wailing our losses, whiles the foe doth rage,
> And look upon, as if the tragedy
> Were play'd in jest by counterfeiting actors?
> Here on my knee I vow to God above
> I'll never pause again, never stand still,
> Till either death hath clos'd these eyes of mine
> Or fortune given me measure of revenge.

> (ii) I will stir up in England some black storm
> Shall blow ten thousand souls to heaven or hell;
> And this fell tempest shall not cease to rage
> Until the golden circuit on my head,
> Like to the glorious sun's transparent beams,
> Do calm the fury of this mad-bred flaw.

> (iii) I cannot weep, for all my body's moisture
> Scarce serves to quench my furnace-burning heart;
> Nor can my tongue unload my heart's great burden,
> For self-same wind that I should speak withal
> Is kindling coals that fires all my breast,
> And burns me up with flame that tears would quench.
> To weep is to make less the depth of grief –
> Tears then for babes; blows and revenge for me!

These three speeches are by York, Gloucester and Warwick, but it would be difficult to say which was which.

By the time he wrote *Romeo and Juliet* Shakespeare was able to differentiate between the speech of Mercutio, Capulet and the Nurse, besides that of the lovers: but in the years that followed (as Granville-Barker pointed out) the most vital characters speak mainly in prose – Shylock, Falstaff, Rosalind, Beatrice. Prose, of course, is nearer to the colloquial than verse is likely to be; but no one who has read Brian Vickers's book[5] will imagine that Shakespeare eschewed rhetoric when writing prose. Indeed Kenneth Hudson has shown[6] that Shakespeare's prose was never as close to the ordinary talk of the time as Middleton's, Dekker's or even Jonson's. By the time Shakespeare had finished *2 Henry IV*, the verse itself had acquired a new flexibility and subtlety, so that one could say, with pardonable exaggeration, that Shakespeare taught himself to write his mature dramatic verse by experimenting with dramatic prose.[7]

Alleyn and Burbage were both praised for their naturalness; but it is clear that between 1587 and 1597 the style of acting became increasingly subtle. It is unnecessary to discuss whether the change was caused by the fact that the better dramatists had begun to write in a more colloquial style, or whether the dramatists were driven by the actors to write parts in which their new techniques could be manifested – unnecessary both because the question cannot be resolved, and because Shakespeare, as I have emphasized, was an actor as well as a playwright, an actor before he was a playwright.

The new verse style reached its early perfection in *Hamlet*. I need only recall a few of its characteristics. The style varies according to the character and even according to the situation. The formal oration by Claudius in the second scene with its suavely balanced phrases differs radically from the speech in which he attempts to pray and likewise from the deviousness of his temptation of Laertes, though all three are acceptable as the utterances of the same man. Hamlet's speech goes through numerous mutations: courtly formality, savage parody of Laertes, parody of Osric, antic disposition with Polonius, ratiocination on the drunkenness of the court or on the Senecal man, literary and dramatic criticism in the scenes with the players, and, lastly, the four major soliloquies, all different. Superficially, indeed, the first and the third are concerned with the temptation of suicide, and the second and the fourth with self-reproaches because his task is still unfulfilled; but the differences are equally obvious. Yet behind all these manifestations is a coherent personality, not Everyman, as C. S. Lewis perversely argued. One other example may be given – the Ghost. As Bernard Shaw said, 'the weird music of' the

Ghost's 'long speech which should be the spectral wail of a soul's bitter wrong crying from one world to another in the extremity of its torment', should not be given to 'the most squaretoed member of the company'.

The second point about the style of Hamlet is equally important. There are nearly 3,000 lines of verse in the play and over 1,000 lines of prose. But, unless one's attention is called to it, one is unlikely to notice which medium is being used at any particular moment. Eliot expressed the hope that the audience would not be aware during a performance of one of his later plays that it was written in verse, and he avoided the alternation of verse and prose because he thought the audience would thereby become more conscious of the verse. Shakespeare, being himself without this kind of embarrassment, does not embarrass us. We forget we are listening to poetry: we seem rather to be listening to men and women talking. The different levels of reality provided by the Dido play and *The Mousetrap* make Hamlet's intervening soliloquies seem perfectly natural speech.

Another aspect of Shakespeare's professionalism is his use of imagery. Critics have differed about the extent to which he knew what he was doing. That he deliberately inserted a score of sickness images into *Hamlet* strains one's credulity; but that he was completely unconscious of them strains it more. Nor is it possible to accept Pasternak's view, which he advanced after translating the play, that the repetition of such images was due to carelessness or haste. It may be worth while to suggest that the main groups of images take their origin in plot and situation. The war imagery, for example – which most critics have tended to overlook – arose naturally from the military operations of Fortinbras, as well as from the struggle between Hamlet and his uncle. What Richard Altick calls 'the odour of corruption' could have been suggested by the dead bodies and skulls, as well as by the thing which is rotten in the state of Denmark, the rank smell of sin; and since Shakespeare in many of his plays had associated disorder in the state with sickness and sickness with sin, it is not surprising that it should pervade the world of Elsinore. The sickness images, of course, if considered in their contexts, apply to the guilt of Claudius and Gertrude, and only once to Hamlet himself.[8] The poisoning of Gertrude, Laertes, Gonzago, Hamlet and his father naturally spills over into the imagery of the play. The theatrical imagery arises naturally from the scenes connected with *The Mousetrap* and even the imagery related to cosmetics springs from the hypocrisy of Claudius (who himself refers to the harlot's cheek), from the frailty of women, which sets a blister on 'the fair forehead of an innocent love', and perhaps from the reiterated idea that Fortune is a strumpet – for Hamlet, as critics have suggested, moves from this idea to an acceptance of the fact that he is guided by Providence.

It does not greatly matter where Shakespeare derived his images, whether from his sources or from his imagination setting to work on the sources. As Professor Bradbrook suggested long ago, the breast-feeding images in *Macbeth* may have been prompted by the account given in the *Chronicles* of the way in which Scottish women preferred to nurse their own babies; or it may rather be prompted by the subject proposed for debate before James I, whether a man's character was influenced by his nurse's milk – or, indeed, by a combination of the two.

Shakespeare was professional, too, in his method of composing his plays. All the evidence would seem to show that he hunted for plots rather than for themes. He would not have decided to write a play about Justice and Mercy, or about Jealousy, or Ingratitude or Ambition; but he would read *Promos and Cassandra* or the old play of *King Leir* and decide how best to dramatize the material, what theme he could extract from it. It is possible to deduce why Shakespeare made the alterations he did – why he linked the Lear story with that of the Paphlagonian King, why he rejected the marriage of Promos and Cassandra, and substituted Mariana for Isabella. Reading the story of Disdemona and the Moorish captain, he would see the need for raising the status of the Moor, for eliminating the months of happiness before the voyage to Cyprus, for altering the motive of the villain, for making the Moor alone responsible for the murder of Desdemona, and for making him commit suicide when he learns that Desdemona is innocent. But these changes alone would not turn the sordid *novella* into a satisfactory scenario. Shakespeare, we may surmise, saw the opportunities afforded by three details of the tale. After the murder, the Moor suffers from a deep melancholy because he 'had loved the lady more than his very eyes'. He had killed the thing he loved. Then there was the marriage of black and white with the possibilities involved of paradox, antithesis and symbol; and as the Devil was depicted as black, whereas the demi-devil of the play is white, this would suggest the diabolic imagery analysed by Leslie Bethell.[9] But perhaps the detail which most attracted Shakespeare was the contrast between the Ensign's fine appearance and his secretly depraved nature. This fitted in with one of Shakespeare's persistent obsessions — from Tarquin to Angelo and Claudius — of the difficulty of distinguishing seeming from being.[10] Perhaps this was a question of professional interest to an actor — as we can see from the stage references in *Richard III* and *Macbeth*. If an actor can take the part of angel or devil, male or female, how can one tell (when all the world's a stage) that any man is not acting a part? At the end of the third book of *Paradise Lost*, Satan, journeying to Eden to encompass the Fall of Man, encounters Uriel,

> The sharpest sighted spirit of all in Heav'n.

He does not recognize Satan, but directs him to Paradise. Milton comments:

> For neither Man nor Angel can discern
> Hypocrisie, the onely evil that walks
> Invisible, except to God alone,
> By his permissive will, through Heav'n and Earth:
> And oft though wisdom wake, suspicion sleeps

> At wisdoms Gate, and to simplicitie
> Resigns her charge, while goodness thinks no ill
> Where no ill seems.

Most hypocrites in literature succeed only in deceiving some people some of the time. Tartuffe and Pecksniff don't succeed with everyone. But Shakespeare seems to have shared Milton's view on the impenetrability of evil: and this is surely the answer to those who regard Othello as excessively stupid. Othello is deceived like everyone else in the play, and like the Archangel Uriel.

Despite numerous caveats on the danger of treating characters in a poetic play as characters in a novel or even as living human beings, there are still too many critics and some directors who continue the practice. We are told that Othello becomes jealous in only five minutes after the beginning of Iago's temptation, as though playing time could be equated with real time. It may be true, as Una Ellis-Fermor argued in her British Academy lecture,[11] that 'the genuine dramatic mode of thought, the fundamental quality which reveals the innate dramatic genius', and which 'distinguishes the essentially dramatic from all other kinds of genius' is the power of the dramatist to identify himself with each of his characters, each in turn and simultaneously. It is easy to see that Bernard Shaw can speak through Barbara and Cusins as well as through Undershaft; that Millamant, Mirabell, Lady Wishfort, Witwoud, Sir Wilfull and Marwood are magnificently realized; and that Eliot, who lacked this power, could create a Celia Copplestone but is less successful with the Chamberlaynes. Yet one cannot accept Professor Ellis-Fermor's formulation without certain qualifications. In several of Marlowe's plays only one or two characters are fully realized, yet one would hesitate to say that he lacked innate dramatic genius; while, on the other hand, Browning who possessed a remarkable power of identifying himself with a wide variety of characters, wrote only unsuccessful plays. The power of self-identification is clearly not sufficient.

Then perhaps it should be stressed that the dramatist – the professional dramatist – relies on the actors to embody his characters, adding to them the physical presence of Burbage, Garrick, Mrs Siddons or Sir John Gielgud. A character on the page needs to be incarnated in a character on the stage. In *Measure for Measure* Barnadine is given only seven speeches, Juliet seven and Froth eight, with a total of only 232 words between the three characters. But Shakespeare knew that all three could be made into unforgettable figures.

The third qualification, or clarification, which needs to be made is that every good dramatist, especially the poetic dramatist, eschews the methods of naturalism. Ibsen said of *Emperor and Galilean* that he wanted to give the reader the impression that what he was reading was something that had really happened. But he was continually stressing that 'in the realm of art there is no place for pure reality, but only for illusion'.[12]

Yet there are still some critics who apply prosaic methods of analysis to Shakespeare's characters and arrive inevitably at absurd results. Part of the trouble is due to the fact that for the last 250 years the novel has been the dominant literary form; and during the last 100 years we have been urged to wring the neck of rhetoric. So we get the dramatic critic of the *Daily Telegraph* assuring us that Congreve was a bad dramatist; and the dramatic critic of the *Sunday Times* asserting on successive Sundays that a single line in Pinter's one-act play, *Landscape*, expresses love more successfully than anything in *Antony and Cleopatra*, instancing from the latter the lines:

> Now boast thee, Death, in thy possession lies
> A lass unparallel'd.

Dame Peggy Ashcroft spoke the Pinter line in question – 'Oh my true love I said' – in a way that enraptured Mr Hobson along with the rest of the audience. Here, he thought, was the true voice of feeling, as opposed to the rhetorical artifice of Shakespeare's lines. I admire Pinter 'on this side idolatry' as much as any, but it need hardly be said that he, too, indulges in rhetoric. He departs from the colloquial order of words to obtain poetic effects. The line admired by Mr Hobson is at the very end of the play; but, if it is read in its context, Pinter's rhetorical artifice will be apparent:

> He lay above me and looked down at me.
> He supported my shoulder . . .
> So tender his touch on my neck.
> So softly his kiss on my cheek . . .
> My hand on his rib . . .
> So sweetly the sand over me.
> Tiny the sand on my skin . . .
> So silent the sky in my eyes.
> Gently the sound of the tide . . .
> Oh my true love I said.[13]

Here are nice examples of anaphora and assonance; and the passage as a whole is as far removed from the colloquial speech of today as Shakespeare's lines were from the speech of Jacobean England.

This same fear of rhetoric has bedevilled a large number of recent productions of Shakespeare. David Warner is an excellent actor and he gave us an unforgettable portrait of Henry VI; but he tried to make the great Towton speech sound as colloquial as prose by inserting medial pauses and by pretending that the lines were not end-stopped. This was obviously wrong-headed, not merely because the poetry was ruined, but because the following passage in which the son-killing father and father-killing son bewail the evils of civil war appeared to be absurd instead of emblematic. Another example of the same fear of rhetoric is the treatment of rhymed verse. We have heard in recent years a Beatrice who tried to conceal the fact that she was speaking a six-line stanza; a Romeo and Juliet who seem ashamed to be sharing a sonnet on their first meeting; and, worst of all, a Titania who guyed her instructions to the fairies about the entertainment of Bottom, by pronouncing *dewberries* as though it rhymed with *eyes* rather than *bees*:

> Hop in his walks and gambol in his eyes;
> Feed him with apricocks and dewberries,
> With purple grapes, green figs, and mulberries;
> The honey-bags steal from the humble-bees,
> And for night-tapers crop their waxen thighs.

This amused many of the audience, but it could not but make the judicious grieve.

Shakespeare's original audience has often been criticized, but at least they were willing to respond to poetry. I have touched on the fruitful interaction of Shakespeare with his fellow actors, who gave as well as demanded; but I have implied the collaboration of what must have been a magnificent audience. Whatever their defects, their favourite play was *Hamlet*: whatever the virtue of modern audiences, their favourite play is *The Mousetrap*.

It is often said that Shakespeare learnt more from the theatre itself and from the plays in which he performed than he did from books, and certainly the playwright's job can be learnt more effectively in the theatre than outside it. He quickly learnt to bombast out a blank verse as the best of his predecessors. But perhaps some recent critics have over-emphasized this aspect of his apprenticeship. It did not take him long to pick up everything that Marlowe, Lyly and Kyd could teach him. From his predecessors Shakespeare learnt a lesson every bit as valuable: he learnt what to avoid. But from treading the boards and experiencing the response of an audience he acquired a knowledge, which soon became a sixth sense, of how to play on them as on a pipe, how to surprise their laughter or their tears, or as Louis MacNeice put it, how to try their heart-strings in the name of mirth; how to point an epigram or make an effective exit; when to use music or the lyrical poetry which requires no accompaniment; the variation of pace, the use of gesture, of silence; the contrast of voices; even the use of slapstick.

But acting, it may be suggested, does not merely teach a playwright the tricks of the trade: it is also a stepping-stone to that more fundamental quality of a dramatist of making his characters live by living in them. Coleridge explained this ability 'to paint truly and according to the colouring of nature, a vast number of personages' by suggesting that Shakespeare 'had only to imitate certain parts of his own character, or to exaggerate such as existed in possibility'. Coleridge, again, said in a letter to Sotheby that Shakespeare alone reveals the ability 'to send ourselves out of ourselves, to *think* ourselves into the thoughts and feelings of beings in circumstances wholly and strangely different from our own'.[14] This, no doubt, is true as far as it goes; but it is an ability likely to be developed by acting.

We are all familiar with those passages in Keats's letters in which he describes the poetic character, which is more the character of the dramatic poet than of the poet *per se*:

> When I am in a room with people, if I ever am free from speculating on creations of my own brain, then not myself goes home to myself; but the identity of every one in the room begins to press upon me that I am in a very little time annihilated.[15]

In the same way Shakespeare's identity is annihilated by his characters. In all his plays, we are never conscious of the presence of the dramatist. He is completely lost in his characters. As early as *Love's Labour's Lost*, the Curate who plays Alisander in the pageant of the Nine Worthies makes a complete fool of himself through stage-fright. The audience on the stage rag him unmercifully; and the audience in the auditorium roar with laughter. But at this point we are suddenly reminded of his humanity: the Clown, Costard, describes him for us:

> a foolish mild man; an honest man, look you, and soon dash'd. He is a marvellous good neighbur, faith, and a very good bowler; but for Alisander – alas! you see how 'tis – a little o'erparted.

When Falstaff is recruiting in Gloucestershire, after Feeble, the woman's tailor, has been chosen, the least suitable of all the candidates, and the more suitable ones are bribing Bardolph to get them off, Feeble surprises us by saying:

> By my troth, I care not; a man can die but once: we owe God a death: I'll ne'er bear a base mind: an't be my destiny, so; an't be not, so: no man is too good to serve's prince; and let it go which way it will, he that dies this year is quit for the next.

Astonishingly, but convincingly, Feeble has attained to the stoical resignation of Hamlet: 'If it be now, 'tis not to come; if it be not to come, it will be now; if it be not now, yet it will come: the readiness is all'.

Or take Barnadine who is introduced into *Measure for Measure* as a condemned murderer whose one function is to be executed instead of Claudio. All goes well until the moment comes when he is told that he is to die. He says: 'Friar, not I; I have been drinking hard all night, and I will have more time to prepare me, or they shall beat out my brains with billets. I will not consent to die this day, that's certain.' The Duke says: 'O, Sir, you must.' Barnadine retorts: 'I swear I will not die to-day for any man's persuasion.' He wins his point; and at the end of the play, although he is a drunken murderer, he is pardoned.

When the caddish and cowardly Parolles is exposed for what he is in *All's Well that Ends Well*, he is given a short soliloquy:

> If my heart were great,
> 'Twould burst at this. Captain I'll be no more;
> But I will eat, and drink, and sleep as soft
> As captain shall. Simply the thing I am
> Shall make me live.

Although some commentators on the last sentence have made a good deal more of it than Shakespeare intended, we can see at least the poet allows his coward to speak for himself.

Or take two contrasted characters in *King Lear*. The Captain who agrees to murder Cordelia acquiesces with the words:

> I cannot draw a cart, nor eat dried oats;
> If it be man's work, I'll do it.

In a line and a half, it has been said, Shakespeare gives us a biography, a philosophy of life, and a character. Earlier in the play, one of Cornwall's servants intervenes in the blinding of Gloucester. At the end of the scene, two of Cornwall's other servants, who have not had the courage to rebel while the blinding was being carried out, comment on Cornwall and Regan:

> I'll never care what wickedness I do,
> If this man come to good.

> If she live long,
> And in the end meet the old course of death,
> Women will all turn monsters.

The two servants do their best to help the blinded Gloucester. They are not sentimentalized, but they express the horror of ordinary people at the brutal deed we have seen enacted. It is worth mentioning that in a recent production of the play at Stratford, this scene was cut, because the director thought he could improve on Shakespeare by eliminating this touch of humanity.

Hazlitt, like Keats, described Shakespeare's ability to identify himself with his characters:

> The striking peculiarity of Shakespeare's mind was its generic quality, its power of communication with all other minds – so that it contained a universe of thought and feeling within itself, and had no one peculiar bias, or exclusive excellence more than another. He was just like any other man, but that he was like all other men. He was the least of an egotist that it was possible to be. He was nothing in himself; but he was all that others were, or that they could become. He not only had in himself the germs of every faculty and feeling, but he could follow them by anticipation, intuitively, into all their conceivable ramifications, through every change of fortune or conflict of passion or turn of thought ... There was no respect of persons with him. His genius shone equally on the evil and on the good, on the wise and foolish, the monarch and the beggar ... He had only to think of anything in

order to become that thing, with all the circumstances belonging
to it . . . That which, perhaps, more than anything else, distinguishes the dramatic productions of Shakespeare from all
others, is this wonderful truth and individuality of conception.
Each of his characters is as much itself, and as absolutely inde-
pendent of the rest, as well as of the author, as if they were living
persons, not fictions of the mind. The poet may be said, for the
time, to identify himself with the character he wishes to represent,
and to pass from one to another, like the same soul successively
animating different bodies. By an art like that of the ventriloquist,
he throws his imagination out of himself, and makes every word
appear to proceed from the mouth of the person in whose name
it is given . . . One might suppose that he had stood by at the time,
and overheard what passed.[16]

This power, which Keats and Hazlitt agreed that Shakespeare possessed to a supreme degree, is one which is
encouraged by acting. One has only to talk with any competent actor, even with amateurs, to recognize that to play
any role successfully one has to identify oneself with the
character. You cannot play Goneril or Regan successfully if
you do not, for the time being, look at the situation from
their point of view. But, of course, it is the business of the
director to see that the proper balance of the play is maintained. We don't want another production in which the
villains are excused. I suppose everyone who has taken part
in a production of a play, either as an actor or as a director,
would agree that one emerges from rehearsals with an in-
creased understanding not merely of the play but of human
beings; but if an actor has as much delight in playing Iago
as Imogen, a poet will take as much delight in conceiving
one as the other. The same power is present to some degree
in the greater novelists, most noticeably in Dickens, who was
an actor of genius and whose public readings enabled him to
portray a wide range of characters.

Shakespeare, then, extended his powers of empathy by the
practice of his profession as actor, and also by his profession
as playwright. So that if we read the plays written between

1590 and 1608 we find an ever-increasing subtlety of characterization. Richard III and Macbeth commit much the
same crimes; but despite the fact that Shakespeare uses his
knowledge of acting in depicting Richard, he remains outside the character. Macbeth, on the other hand, is depicted
from within. By the time he came to write the great
tragedies, Shakespeare could imagine himself as Hamlet and
Claudius, Othello and Iago, Antony and Cleopatra. This
imaginative identification went far beyond asking himself
such a question as: 'If I were in Hamlet's position what
would I do?' – though this is a salutary question for critics to
ask themselves – it was more like a case of possession. One
could almost say that though Shakespeare created Hamlet,
Hamlet returned the compliment.

Although I have been stressing Shakespeare's professionalism, it would be a mistake to imagine that when we
have analysed the skills of Shakespeare the Craftsman (as
Professor Bradbrook calls him in her excellent Clark
lectures[17]) we have plucked out the heart of his mystery. If
he is distinguished from most other poetic dramatists by
being fully professional, he is likewise distinguished from
most professionals by the way he proved axioms – the great
commonplaces – on his pulses; by the fact (as he admitted)
that he had made old offences of affections new; and by the
sense he gives us that each individual work illuminates all
the rest, though each work

> Is a new beginning, a raid on the inarticulate.[18]

With *The Winter's Tale* and *The Tempest* in mind one cannot
continue the Eliot quotation:

> With shabby equipment always deteriorating
> In the general mess of imprecision of feeling.

Nor, after *The Tempest*, if the Circus Animals deserted him,
can we imagine Shakespeare like Yeats, lying down

> where all the ladders start
> In the foul rag-and-bone shop of [his] heart.[19]

I began by excusing Hardy and Bridges for their failure to appreciate that Shakespeare's plays were satisfactorily constructed for the Elizabethan theatre, because of the adaptations then in vogue. The wheel is come full circle. Adaptations are once again the fashion; and if one were to give advice to a young director, who had not yet made a name for himself, one might suggest that the quickest way to acquire a reputation would be to play Shakespeare straight, without cuts and without gimmicks.

More than sixty years have elapsed since Hardy said there was no future for Shakespeare in the theatre. It is surely strange that we are still without a theatre which approximates to the Globe or the Blackfriars, where we could see whether his stage-craft – on which so many critics have written eloquently – is successful in practice. I am not, of course, suggesting that all productions of Shakespeare should be on a replica of the Globe. They would seem very dull to those international audiences which have only a smattering of English; and in the theatre standardization is death. I am not even opposed to some adaptations: for, however much we may admire the Granville-Barker style of production, we have to admit that change is desirable lest one good custom should corrupt the world of the theatre. I am merely suggesting that among the experiments Shakespeare's own method is worth trying.

I began by quoting Boswell, and it will be appropriate to end with a well-known passage in the *Life of Johnson*:

BOSWELL: I remember many years ago, when my imagination was warm, and I happened to be in a melancholy mood, it distressed me to think of going into a state of being in which Shakespeare's poetry did not exist. A lady whom I then much admired, a very amiable woman, humoured my fancy, and relieved me by saying, 'The first thing you will meet in the other world will be an elegant copy of Shakespeare's works presented to you.' Dr. Johnson smiled benignantly at this, and did not appear to disapprove of the notion.[20]

It is to be hoped that besides being elegant the celestial edition would be purged of those errors in the text committed by careless compositors and over-confident editors. But one wonders whether even so this would be a fitting reward for a lover of Shakespeare. One would like, besides the elegant edition, a Playhouse in Paradise where his works would be performed by angelic actors, who would be able to resist Satanic temptations to cut, bowdlerize or improve the original scripts.

2 Shakespeare's Poets

It has been observed by more than one critic that the poets depicted, and the references to poetry, in Shakespeare's plays seem to be by a man who regarded the art and its practitioners with irony, satire or contempt. But it is never safe to assume that Shakespeare shared the views of his characters, even of his virtuous characters; and the opinions expressed in his plays on the subject of poetry are all, in their various ways, suspect, because they are appropriate to the characters who speak them.

The earliest reference is in *The Two Gentlemen of Verona*, where Proteus instructs Thurio how to win Silvia. It must be remembered that Proteus is playing a double game since he wishes to win Silvia for himself. He is already false to Valentine and his advice to Thurio is insincere:

> But you, Sir Thurio, are not sharp enough;
> You must lay lime to tangle her desires
> By wailful sonnets, whose composed rhymes
> Should be full-fraught with serviceable vows.

(III. ii. 67–70)

The Duke backs up Proteus' words with the remark:

> Much is the force of heaven-bred poesy. (iii. ii. 72)

But the poetry advocated by Proteus is hardly heaven-bred: it is strictly utilitarian. Its object is the winning of Silvia, although Proteus does not wish it to succeed:

> Say that upon the altar of her beauty
> You sacrifice your tears, your sighs, your heart;
> Write till your ink be dry, and with your tears
> Moist it again, and frame some feeling line
> That may discover such integrity.

(III. ii. 73–7)

Thurio, who is clearly incapable of genuine passion, is not really expected to weep, or even to be sincere in what he writes. He merely has to seem to be sincere, to give the illusion of 'such integrity'. Written at a time when scores of second-rate poets were turning out Petrarchan sonnets, the lines indirectly satirize the fashion. Yet Sir Sidney Lee, in one of his periodic attempts to show that Shakespeare did not express a genuine love or friendship for the recipient of the Sonnets, but was simply attempting to extort money by flattery, used Proteus' lines in support of his argument. Apparently Lee believed that time-serving insincerity would be less of a blot on Shakespeare's reputation than the faintest suspicion of homosexuality. He was writing after the trial of Oscar Wilde. But the sonnets Thurio is urged to write are the kind of poems that Shakespeare accused the Rival Poets of writing — the 'strained touches' of rhetoric and 'their gross painting'.

Proteus proceeds to advise Thurio to serenade Silvia

> With some sweet consort; to their instruments
> Tune a deploring dump.

(III. ii. 84–5)

Thurio says he has 'a sonnet that will serve the turn'; but the song in praise of Silvia is hardly a 'deploring dump' and far too good to be supposed to come from Thurio's pen. Shakespeare, perhaps, could not resist the temptation of writing a good song. The same thing happens at the end of *Love's Labour's Lost*. The exquisite songs in praise of the owl and the cuckoo are supposed to be written by the two learned men, Holofernes and Nathaniel. But Holofernes' other poetic effusions are deliberately absurd and Nathaniel, though more modest, belongs to the same school of poetry. In one recent production of the play at Stratford-on-Avon, the director tried to conceal the beauty of the words by a deliberately feeble performance of a poor setting, thus effectively ruining one of Shakespeare's most exquisite endings.

In *Love's Labour's Lost*, which is, amongst other things, a play upon words, there are appropriately no less than eight amateur poets. Even Moth tries his hand at composition; and Armado, his master, who is drunk on figures of rhetoric, exclaims when he falls in love with Jaquenetta:

> Assist me, some extemporal god of rhyme, for I am
> sure I shall turn sonneter. Devise, wit; write,
> pen; for I am for whole volumes in folio.
>
> (I. ii. 177–81)

But we are given only six lines of Armado's composition, a postscript to his bombastic epistle.

The four poems by the King and his lords vary in quality. The King's own, being the weakest, was wisely omitted from *The Passionate Pilgrim*. Longaville's opens splendidly –

> Did not the heavenly rhetoric of thine eye –

but fails to live up to its promise. Berowne's, like the first sonnet in *Astrophel and Stella*, is in neatly turned alexandrines. But of the four poems Dumain's ode is the only one which is entirely charming and successful.

Berowne comments satirically on his fellow poets, but it is left to Holofernes to pronounce magisterially on Berowne's own poem: that it is not as good as Ovid's.

> Here are only numbers ratified; but, for the elegancy,
> facility, and golden cadence of poesy, *caret*. Ovidius
> Naso was the man.
>
> (IV. ii. 113–16)

Later in the scene he tells Nathaniel that he

> will prove those verses to be very unlearned, neither
> savouring of poetry, wit, nor invention.
>
> (lines 146–7)

What Holofernes understood by elegancy, facility and golden cadence, we can judge from his own extemporal verses on the death of the deer. Whereas the four lords are writing in the style of the nineties, Holofernes harks back to an earlier manner. He tells Nathaniel that he 'will something affect the letter, for it argues facility'.

> The preyful Princess pierc'd and prick'd a
> pretty pleasing pricket.
>
> (IV. ii. 54)

The poem depends, like a riddle, on an absurd conceit – adding L to sore to make sorel; but even more absurd than the poem is the author's complacent conviction, overlaid with mock modesty, that he is a genius:

> This is a gift that I have, simple, simple; a foolish
> extravagant spirit, full of forms, figures, shapes,
> objects, ideas, apprehensions, motions, revolutions.
> These are begot in the ventricle of memory, nourish'd
> in the womb of pia mater, and delivered upon the
> mellowing of occasion. But the gift is good in those
> in whom it is acute, and I am thankful for it.
>
> (IV. ii. 63–9)

Holofernes has one devoted admirer. The Curate speaks of his 'rare talent', declaring

> I praise the Lord for you, and so may my parishioners.
>
> (IV. ii. 70–1)

Shakespeare's best-known reference to the poet is in the speech of Theseus in the last act of *A Midsummer-Night's Dream*. Ever since Pollard pointed out the significance of the mislineation of these lines, it is generally accepted that they were a marginal insertion; but there is nothing to indicate whether they were written five minutes or five years after the rest of the speech:

> The lunatic, the lover and the poet
> Are of imagination all compact.
> One sees more devils than vast hell can hold;

B

That is the madman. The lover, all as frantic,
Sees Helen's beauty in a brow of Egypt.
The poet's eye, in a fine frenzy rolling,
Doth glance from heaven to earth, from earth to heaven;
And as imagination bodies forth
The forms of things unknown, the poet's pen
Turns them to shapes and gives to airy nothing
A local habitation and a name.

(V. i. 7–17)

Shakespeare's original intention was to make Theseus compare the lover and the lunatic. Then he inserted the lines about the poet, lines which are much more powerful than the surrounding ones.[1] At first sight, the association of poets with lunatics and equally frantic lovers seems to have a satirical purpose and this, doubtless, is Theseus' purpose. The 'fine frenzy' and the rolling eye recall the divine fury of which Plato, Sidney and others had spoken. The poet gives 'A local habitation and a name' to nothing. His creations, being the result of imagination, have no more connection with the real world than the delusions of the madman or the lover who cannot see his beloved as she really is. Theseus is ignoring Sidney's conjuration, at the end of his *Apology*, 'no more to scorn the sacred mysteries of poesy; no more to laugh at the name of poets, as though they were next inheritors to fools; no more to jest at the reverend title of a rhymer'. Theseus, in spite of his maturity compared with the young lovers in the play, should not be taken as Shakespeare's spokesman. He is, in fact, a bit of a Philistine. One has only to read the sonnets about the Dark Lady to realize that Shakespeare did not see Helen's beauty in a brow of Egypt.

Theseus is wrong, even about the lovers. He thinks their story is untrue; but as Hippolyta properly points out:

All the story of the night told over,
And all their minds transfigur'd so together,
More witnesseth than fancy's images,

> And grows to something of great constancy;
> But, howsoever, strange and admirable.
>
> (V. i. 23–7)

The strange story of the lovers is, in the world of the play, true.

There is, I think, an additional irony. In his previous plays – historical, comical, tragical – Shakespeare had kept reasonably close to real life. The audience had to swallow plenty of improbable fictions – from the two pairs of identical twins severed by shipwreck to the methods used to tame the Shrew – but there had been no impossibilities. When Mercutio discourses on Queen Mab no one imagines that his account is meant to be taken seriously. But in *A Midsummer-Night's Dream* Shakespeare, as it were, took a leaf out of Mercutio's book and exhibited fairies on the stage; and even if many of his audience believed in fairies, *his* fairies were notoriously different. Not merely were they different from those of folk lore, but they varied in size from those able to wear bats' wings as coats or hide in acorn-cups to Titania herself who is large enough to embrace an ass. The audience, moreover, is asked to accept the magical effects of Oberon's juice and the transformation of Bottom; and, side by side with such things, there is placed the earthy absurdity of the amateur actors. Shakespeare had distanced *The Taming of the Shrew* by presenting it before Christopher Sly, who imagines for a few hours that he is not a drunken tinker but a lord. In *A Midsummer-Night's Dream* Shakespeare relies only on his poetry to create the wood near Athens and what happens in it. He 'gives to airy nothing / A local habitation and a name'. What Theseus intends as a gibe against poetry is a precise account of Shakespeare's method in this play. But what Theseus did not appreciate was that the poet who creates

> Forms more real than living man,
> Nurslings of immortality

may yet be making a valid comment on real life.

There is a poet called Lodowick in the anonymous
Edward III. Many critics believe that the second act, in
which he appears, was written by Shakespeare; but Swinburne, who did not, referred to Lodowick as a pimp. He is
employed by the King to write a poem to the Countess, as a
means of seducing her; and he announces her arrival when
she comes for her last interview with the King – in which
virtue triumphs over adulterous passion. But there is nothing
in Lodowick's part to suggest that he approves of the King's
adulterous designs, nor even that he assists them. At the
beginning of the act he describes how the King has fallen in
love with the Countess. It is clear from the language he uses
that he admires the Countess and deplores the King's
adulterous love:

> If she did blush, 'twas tender modest shame,
> Being in the sacred presence of a King:
> If he did blush, 'twas red immodest shame,
> To vaile his eyes amisse, being a king:
> If she lookt pale, 'twas silly womans feare,
> To beare her selfe in presence of a king:
> If he lookt pale, it was with guiltie feare,
> To dote amisse, being a mighty king.

The King enters and orders Lodowick, who 'is well read in
poetrie', to fetch ink and paper. He asks him to 'inuocate
some golden Muse' and bring 'an enchanted pen'. Lodowick asks to whom he should write, though he presumably
guesses that it is the Countess despite the fact that the King
does not name her.

The technique of the scene is interesting. We hear only a
line and a half of Lodowick's poem; but the King's instructions to him are like the rough draft of a poem, more poetical,
indeed, than anything Lodowick writes. The King tells him:

> Better than bewtifull thou must begin,
> Devise for faire a fairer word than faire . . .
> For flattery feare thou not to be convicted;
> For, were thy admiration ten tymes more,

> Ten tymes ten thousand more the worth exceeds
> Of that thou art to praise, thy praises worth.

While Lodowick is composing his poems, the King peruses the Countess in his thoughts. He cannot compare her voice to music because

> To musicke every sommer leaping swaine
> Compares his sunburnt lover when she speaks.

Nor can he compare it to the nightingale, who sings of adulterate wrong,

> For sinne, though synne, would not be so esteemed,
> But rather, vertue sin, synne vertue deemd.

He then thinks of similes for her hair:

> far softer than the silke wormes twist,
> Like to a flattering glas, doth make more faire
> The yelow Amber.

He decides that the phrase *Like to a flattering glas* 'comes in too soon' because he wants to use it about her eyes. The King's speech gives a fair impression of a man composing a poem, accepting some similes and rejecting others, and thus suggests the silent process of Lodowick's composition.

Lodowick's first line —

> More faire and chast then is the Queen of Shades —

is criticized by the King on two grounds: that his love should not be compared to 'the pale Queene of night' and for the epithet *chaste*:

> I did not bid thee talke of chastitie,
> To ransack so the treasure of her minde, . . .
> Out with the moone line, I wil none of it;
> And let me have hir likened to the sun.

Lodowick continues:

> More bould in constancie . . . then Iudith was.

The King naturally objects to this line, as he remembers the fate of Holofernes.

It can hardly be doubted that Lodowick's lines were written deliberately to remind the King that he is proposing to commit a sin. Swinburne's word for Lodowick is quite undeserved. If Lodowick was Shakespeare's creation he is the only one of his poets who emerges with much credit.

Several characters in the plays written between 1595 and 1599 laugh at the fashionable absurdities of the sonneteers of the period. Mercutio, whose speech on Queen Mab shows that he has the instincts of a poet, quizzes Romeo about his conventional and sentimental love for Rosaline, though, unknown to him, Romeo is fully recovered:

> Now is he for the numbers that Petrarch flow'd in;
> Laura, to his lady, was a kitchen-wench – marry, she
> has a better love to berhyme her; Dido, a dowdy;
> Cleopatra, a gipsy; Helen and Hero, hildings and harlots;
> Thisbe, a gray eye or so, but not to the purpose.
>   (*Rom. & Jul.*, II. iv. 38–42)

Benedick, before he acknowledges his love for Beatrice, scoffs similarly at Claudio, whose words are 'a very fantastical banquet, just so many dishes'; and, later in the play, he confesses that he cannot write verse to Beatrice:

> Marry, I cannot show it in rhyme; I have tried: I
> can find no rhyme to a 'lady' but 'baby' – an
> innocent rhyme; for 'scorn', 'Horn' – a hard rhyme;
> for 'school', 'fool' – a babbling rhyme; very
> ominous endings. No, I was not born under a rhyming
> planet, nor I cannot woo in festival terms.
>   (*Much Ado*, V. ii. 30–7)

Both Benedick and Beatrice are in reaction against the conventions of romantic love; and, in terms of the comedy, Benedick's inability to rhyme is a proof of his sincerity.

Hotspur, irritated by Glendower, expresses his dislike of ballad-mongers:

> I had rather hear a brazen canstick turn'd,
> Or a dry wheel grate on the axle-tree;
> And that would set my teeth nothing on edge,
> Nothing so much as mincing poetry;
> 'Tis like the forc'd gait of a shuffling nag.
>
> (*1 Hen. IV*. III. i. 131–5)

His similes prove Hotspur to be a poet in spite of himself; and though much of *1 Henry IV* is in prose, Hotspur speaks mainly in verse, appropriately enough for his 'huffing part'.

Yet Shakespeare seems to have become dissatisfied with verse in the last five years of the sixteenth century. He felt temporarily that it tended to blur the distinction between one character and another, and that it interfered with the greater realism he wished to introduce, both in the dialogue of his plays and in its delivery on the stage. So we have his major characters of this period – Shylock, Falstaff, Benedick, Beatrice and Rosalind – speaking mainly in prose. When Orlando inadvertently speaks in verse –

> Good day, and happiness, dear Rosalind –
>
> (*A.Y.L.I.*, IV. i. 27)

Jacques immediately takes his leave with the words:

> Nay, then, God buy you, an you talk in blank verse.

Yet Jaques, the satirist, has spoken many lines of verse earlier in the play.

There are two poets in *Julius Caesar*, both of them mentioned by Plutarch. One of them, Cinna, appears in a short scene at the end of Act III. He is lynched by the mob because he shares his name with one of the conspirators. When he explains that he is not the conspirator, they decide to tear him for his bad verses. It is an effective little scene and it has an important dramatic function. In the previous scene Antony had whipped up the passions of the mob by appeals to pity and cupidity – by his increasingly sarcastic references to the honourable men, by his account of the assassination, by his reference to one of Caesar's victories, by the display of the blood-stained mantle and the mangled body, and, finally, by reading the will. The citizens rush off to burn the houses of the conspirators; Antony cries:

> Mischief, thou art afoot,
> Take thou what course thou wilt;
> (III. ii. 261–2)

and we hear that Brutus and Cassius have ridden 'like madmen through the gates of Rome'. What we need at this point is a scene to show the mob in action, in all its fury and irrationality: and the Cinna scene supplies this need to perfection.[2]

The second poet is introduced into Act IV, scene iii, for comic relief. The scene begins with a violent quarrel between Brutus and Cassius, a quarrel which ends with a reconciliation. After the scene with the Poet, Brutus reveals that Portia is dead. Although the intrusion of the poet is comic, his intentions are apparently serious and sensible. He has heard of the dispute between Brutus and Cassius and wishes to reconcile them. He is determined and he is brave. He tells Lucilius: 'Nothing but death shall stay me'. He addresses the generals as equals and annoys Brutus by his presumption. 'Saucy fellow, hence'. Cassius, on the other hand, is tolerantly amused by the Poet's – possibly unintentional – rhyming couplet:

> POET. Love, and be friends, as two such men should be.
> For I have seen more years, I'm sure, than ye.
> CASSIUS. Ha, ha! How vilely doth this cynic rhyme! . . .
> Bear with him, Brutus; 'tis his fashion.

To which Brutus replies:

> What should the wars do with these jigging fools?

Cassius is not sportive and never goes to a play, and Brutus is fond of music, so that the differing reactions of the two men are interesting. But Brutus, as we learn soon afterwards, has just heard of Portia's suicide.

The dialogue does not make clear, though it could be

made clear in performance, that the Poet is a fool. Plutarch's account explains why Cassius calls him a cynic:

Their friends, that were without the chamber, hearing them loud within and angry between themselves, they were both amazed and afraid also, lest it would grow to further matter: but yet they were commanded, that no man should come to them. Notwithstanding, one Marcus Phaonius, that had been a friend and follower of Cato while he lived, and took upon him to counterfeit a Philosopher not with wisdom and discretion, but with a certain bedlam and frantic motion: he would needs come into the chamber, though the men offered to keep him out. But it was no boot to let Phaonius, when a mad mood or toy took him in the head: for he was a hot hasty man, and sudden in all his doings, and cared for never a Senator of them all. Now, though he used this bold manner of speech after the profession of the Cynick Philosophers, (as who would say, Dogs,) yet his boldness did no hurt many times, because they did but laugh at him to see him so mad. This Phaonius at that time, in despite of the door-keeper, came into the chamber, and with a certain scoffing and mocking gesture, which he counterfeited of purpose, he rehearsed the verses which old Nestor said in Homer:

> My Lords, I pray you hearken both to me,
> For I have seen moe years than suchie three.

Cassius fell a laughing at him: but Brutus thrust him out of the chamber, and called him Dog and counterfeit cynic. Howbeit his coming in brake their strife at that time.

It will be observed that Shakespeare ends the quarrel before the appearance of the Poet, and that he makes the intruder a poet rather than a philosopher, despite Cassius' term 'cynic'. His rhymed couplet is not of his own composition but a quotation from Homer, and ought, perhaps, to be put in inverted commas.[3]

Why Shakespeare turned the philosopher into a poet is impossible to determine with any certainty; but he may have wished to provide a scene to reinforce the one in which Cinna the poet appears and so comment ironically on the position of the poet in his own society. Shakespeare knew that art was made 'tongue-tied by authority'. He could not in his plays deal directly with great public issues. This was not due, as Orwell thought, to cowardice, making him express subversive views only through the mouths of fools and madmen, but to the conditions under which the dramatists wrote. Even the harmless and orthodox treatment of the anti-alien riots in *Sir Thomas More* prevented the play from being staged. If Shakespeare had presumed to advise Southampton or Essex he would have been treated as unceremoniously as the Poet is treated by Brutus. It is therefore difficult to accept the theory that the unflattering portrait of Achilles in *Troilus and Cressida* was intended as a warning to Essex before his rebellion – even though Chapman compared Essex to Achilles in his dedication of an instalment of his translation of the *Iliad*. Although Coleridge said that Members of Parliament in his day would do well to read Samuel Daniel for the lessons he gave on public affairs in his poems, there is no evidence that Daniel ever had any political influence in his own day; and *Philotas*, which was thought to refer to the Essex conspiracy, brought him into trouble.

Hamlet is an amateur poet who composed some lines to be inserted in *The Murder of Gonzago*. Which the lines were no one has settled beyond all controversy; and they may indeed belong to the part of the play we do not hear, where the murderer gets the love of the victim's wife. But we have a taste of Hamlet's quality as a poet in the verses he sends to Ophelia:

> Doubt that the stars are fire;
> Doubt that the sun doth move,
> Doubt truth to be a liar;
> But never doubt I love.

> (II. ii. 115–18)

We may deduce, perhaps, that Hamlet is not a Copernican; but we must agree with his own verdict that he is 'ill at these numbers'.

The letter containing these verses is something of a mystery. Was it written before Ophelia broke off their relations or afterwards? If it was written afterwards, was it designed to lend colour to Polonius' view that Hamlet had been driven mad by her rejection of him? If so, it is curious that there is no mention of this rejection. If it was written before, why is it written in such an affected style? We cannot assume that Hamlet was merely playing at love in view of his avowal at her grave. Perhaps the most probable explanation is this. Shakespeare had to write a letter which could be used by Polonius as a proof of madness; and he left the audience in doubt about the date of the letter. If they imagined it was written before Ophelia's rejection of him and before his visit to her closet, the letter could be taken as the effusion of a fashionable young man in love. One is tempted to say that the writer of the letter could scarcely afford to criticize Osric's style.

The next Shakespearian poet is the satirist, honest Iago. He is called on to show his skill in impromptu composition to entertain Desdemona while she is anxiously awaiting news of Othello. Iago professes to find the task difficult:

> my invention
> Comes from my pate as birdlime does from frieze –
> It plucks out brains and all. But my Muse labours
> And thus she is deliver'd.   (*Oth.*, II. i. 125–8)

The verses that follow consist of four epigrammatic couplets, each couplet devoted to a different character – the fair and wise, the black and witty, the fair and foolish, the foul and foolish – followed by a twelve-line epigram 'on a deserving woman indeed'. Compared with the couplets used by Elizabethan satirists – Lodge, Hall, Marston and Donne – Iago's are much smoother, much more polished and much wittier. In some ways they are closer to those of the Augustan satirists, with the smart antitheses strengthened by alliteration. They reflect admirably the persona Iago wishes to impose on the world, the wordly wise debunker who is 'nothing if not critical', whose very cynicism is taken to be a proof of his honesty even though it is assumed to be something of a pose. He makes his acquaintances believe that he is pretending to be worse than he is in order to conceal the fact that he is worse than he pretends.

The fullest treatment of a poet is in *Timon of Athens*. He is given prominence in the first scene of the play as one of Timon's suitors; the poem he outlines to the Painter is clearly a mirror-image of the play; and he reappears in the last act because of the rumour that Timon has discovered gold. He and the Painter are both depicted as time-servers. The Poet's fourth speech is an aside, presumably part of a poem that has come into his head:

> When we for recompense have praised the vile,
> It stains the glory in that happy verse
> Which aptly sings the good.   (I. i. 16–18)

As Timon could not be regarded as vile, the lines may suggest that the Poet has in the past praised unworthy patrons in the hope of reward. In an age when poets depended largely on patronage it could hardly be expected that poets would dedicate their poems only to the virtuous. One wonders, for example, if all the people who received dedicatory sonnets to *The Faerie Queene* were worthy of Spenser's praises.[4]

The Painter asks the Poet if he is rapt 'in some dedication / To the great lord'. To which he replies:

> A thing slipp'd idly from me.
> Our poesy is as a gum, which oozes
> From whence 'tis nourish'd. The fire i' th' flint
> Shows not till it be struck; our gentle flame
> Provokes itself, and like the current flies
> Each bound it chafes.   (I. i. 23–8)

This account of the creation of poetry as the spontaneous overflow of powerful feelings suggests that Shakespeare, for once, is speaking through his character. The oozing gum – which, however, depends on two emendations in the Folio text – looks forward to Keats's aphorism that 'if poetry come not as naturally as the leaves to a tree, it had better not come at all'.

The ensuing dialogue brings out the Poet's genuine interest in the Painter's work and the latter's oscillation between self-praise and mock-modesty, and, later on, his perfunctory interest in the Poet's allegory:

> PAINTER: 'Tis a good piece.
> POET: So 'tis: this comes off well and excellent.
> PAINTER: Indifferent.
> POET: Admirable. How this grace
>   Speaks his own standing! What a mental power
>   This eye shoots forth! How big imagination
>   Moves in this lip! To th'dumbness of gesture
>   One might interpret.
> PAINTER: It is a pretty mocking of the life.
>   Here is a touch; is't good?
> POET: I will say of it
>   It tutors nature. Artificial strife
>   Lives in these touches livelier than life.
>
>   (I. i. 31–41)

The allegory of Fortune, the dramatic function of which is to prepare the audience for Timon's fall, is introduced by an obscure passage in which the Poet disclaims malice or particular reference to Timon's case, although he admits that his subject was suggested by this:

>   My free drift
> Halts not particularly, but moves itself
> In a wide sea of wax. No levell'd malice
> Infects one comma in the course I hold,
> But flies an eagle flight, bold and forth on,
> Leaving no tract behind.   (I. i. 48–53)

It is not surprising that the Painter asks 'How shall I understand you?' The general drift of the speech, however, is plain enough. It is similar to Jaques' speech in *As You Like It* (II. vii. 70–8):

>   Why, who cries out on pride,
> That can therein tax any private party?

> Doth it not flow as hugely as the sea,
> Till that the wearer's very means do ebb? . . .
> There then; how then? what then? Let me see wherein
> My tongue hath wrong'd him. If it do him right,
> Then he hath wrong'd himself. If he be free,
> Why then my taxing like a wild-goose flies,
> Unclaim'd of any man.[5]

Whatever we may think of the Poet's lack of integrity as revealed later in the play, his proposed poem is certainly neither venal nor flattering. It is a clear warning to Timon that when Fortune changes her mood he will be deserted by his friends. Later in the scene Apemantus tells the poet that he lies because he has feigned Timon to be a worthy fellow. The Poet retorts: 'That's not feign'd — he is so'; and there is no reason to doubt his sincerity. Apemantus may have been thinking of the common accusation, to which Sidney replied in his *Apology*, that poets were liars; and Apemantus receives the dubious support of Touchstone who contrasts 'poetical' with 'truthful', the truest poetry being the most feigning.[6]

The Poet and the Painter come to visit Timon when they hear that he is wealthy after all. The text of the play seems to be corrupt at this point, for Apemantus refers to the approach of the Poet and the Painter some 190 lines before they actually appear. In between there are scenes between Timon and the Banditti and between him and Flavius.[7] The Poet and the Painter in Act V, scene i, are seen through the eyes of Timon. They pretend that they are unaware of his discovery of gold; they are concerned not with the integrity of their respective arts, but only how they may be used for profit:

> Then do we sin against our own estate,
> When we may profit meet and come too late.
>
> (lines 39–40)

The Poet proposes to write 'a satire against the softness of prosperity, with a discovery of the infinite flatteries that follow youth and opulency'; and Timon, who overhears,

asks: 'Wilt thou whip thine own faults in other men?'
Once again we are reminded of Jaques, who is accused by
the Duke:

> Most mischievous foul sin in chiding sin!
> For thou thyself hast been a libertine
> As sensual as the brutish sting itself;
> And all th' embossed sores and headed evils
> That thou with licence of free foot hast caught
> Wouldst thou disgorge into the general world.
>
> (*A.Y.L.I.*, II. vii. 64–9)

Shakespeare appears to have been suspicious of the moral
stance of such satirists as Marston.

Something may be said in extenuation of the Poet. From
his own point of view, he can make a living only by patronage; a bankrupt patron is no use to him; and it was natural
that he should unblushingly turn again to the generous
Timon on hearing of the revival of his fortunes. He could at
least say that he had warned Timon in the days of his
prosperity that he would lose his friends if the wheel of
Fortune were to turn. The point is, however, not that the
Poet and Painter are exceptionally vile, but that in the
Athenian society depicted by Shakespeare, poetry and art
are mere commodities, just as the wares of the Jeweller and
the Merchant in the opening scene of the play. This fact is
brought out by the great speeches of Timon after his discovery of gold. Gold, he tells us, inverts the moral order of
society, making

> black white, foul fair,
> Wrong right, base noble, old young, coward valiant.
>
> (*Timon*, IV. iii. 28–9)

It destroys religion, promotes thieves into senators, gives a
second husband to the wappened widow, and thaws

> the consecrated snow
> That lies on Dian's lap!

It is the world of *Volpone* and *The Alchemist*, but painted in darker colours. Timon is brought to this understanding only after his downfall. In the days of his greatness he did not realize — perhaps he never realizes — that he himself was using his gold to buy love, and that he was therefore deeply involved in the perversion of values. The only characters in the play who emerge uncorrupted by the acquisitive society are Flavius and his fellow-servants.

Shakespeare's poets, whether amateur or professional, are never held up for our admiration; and his characters' remarks about poetry are uniformly disparaging. In his private sonnets he could proclaim that his powerful rhyme would outlast the monuments of princes, but he makes his characters speak each according to his kind, not according to the view of the author. In this, surely, he was wise. We are spared the embarrassment that Jonson sometimes gives us when he crowns his own head with laurel. Shakespeare's last word was to ask the indulgence of the audience to set him free.

Philip Edwards, in a brilliant chapter in *Shakespeare and the Confines of Art*, after discussing uncomplimentary remarks in the plays about poetry, argued that Shakespeare 'engaged in a continuous battle, a quarter of a century long, against his own scepticism about the value of his art as a model of human experience'. He 'sabotages his own affirmations and gives to every ringing cry an implausible echo'. It may well be that this view of Shakespeare's recurrent dissatisfaction with his art may explain his portraits of poets; or, as I have suggested, it may be rather a pervasive irony to protect a heart he would not wear upon his sleeve.[8]

3 Shaw and Shakespeare

It is commonly supposed that George Bernard Shaw believed that his own plays were superior to Shakespeare's and that he spent much of his time as a dramatic critic in belittling his great predecessor.[1] This is not wholly true. An examination of his attitude to Shakespeare throws light on the art of both dramatists. Most of Shaw's comments have been collected in Edwin Wilson's *Shaw on Shakespeare* (1961) and, where possible, references will be given to this book.

Shaw had loved Shakespeare from his youth. 'When I was twenty', he tells us, 'I knew everybody in Shakespeare, from Hamlet to Abhorson, much more intimately than I knew my living contemporaries.'[2] He wrote on his facsimile of the First Folio 'One of the Great Books of the World'.[3] Yet it is generally believed that he devoted much of his dramatic criticism to attacks on the poet and that he discussed whether he was greater than Shakespeare.

The motives of his iconoclastic attacks are quite straight-forward. In the first place, he wanted to propagand for the new drama of Ibsen, whose plays, despite violent hostility from most critics, were beginning to be performed in England. *The Quintessence of Ibsenism* had been published before Shaw became a dramatic critic. In 1931, when a new edition of his dramatic criticism appeared, he admitted this motive.[4]

Let me add now what I should have added then: that a certain correction should be made, especially in reading my onslaught on

Shakespear . . . for the devastating effect produced in the nineties by the impact of Ibsen on the European theatre. Until then Shakespear had been conventionally ranked as a giant among psychologists and philosophers. Ibsen dwarfed him so absurdly in those aspects that it became impossible for the moment to take him seriously as an intellectual force.

Secondly, Shaw wished to counteract bardolatry – the superstitious and hypocritical reverence for the plays exhibited by managers, actors, critics and the general public. It was hypocritical because by their savage cuts and barbarous alterations the actor-managers, such as Irving, showed that their real opinion of the poet was that he was an incompetent dramatist. For this opinion they were not wholly to blame: they were trying to adapt plays for the Victorian stage which had been written for the Elizabethan theatre, an enterprise that was doomed to failure. By their deeds they showed that they really believed that *as playwrights*, Scribe and Sardou were greatly superior to the bard they professed to worship.

Shaw had another motive. When he became dramatic critic of *The Saturday Review* in January 1895, he had written five and a half unsuccessful novels, but his career as a dramatist had hardly begun. The plays he wrote in the 'nineties were performed before coterie audiences; and he realized that the battle for Ibsen was also a battle for his own survival in the theatre.

In many ways Shaw's campaign was justifiable and salutary. English drama at the end of the nineteenth century – the drama of Pinero, Jones and Sutro – was concerned with trivial problems and, with the exception of *The Importance of Being Earnest*, it was lacking in style. Shaw was right in thinking that the English theatre could be saved only if it absorbed Ibsen; and he was also right in believing that the biggest obstacle to the understanding of Shakespeare was bardolatry.

In his campaign against the bardolaters Shaw made use of shock tactics – paradox, ridicule and hyperbole. He headed one notorious section of a preface with the question[5] :

'Greater than Shakespeare?' In his review of Ellen Terry's performance as Imogen he remarked[6] :

> With the single exception of Homer, there is no eminent writer, not even Sir Walter Scott, whom I despise so entirely as I despise Shakespear, when I measure my mind against his. The intensity of my impatience with him occasionally reaches such a pitch, that it would positively be a relief to me to dig him up and throw stones at him, knowing as I do how incapable he and his worshippers are of understanding any less obvious form of indignity.

But in the next paragraph he admits:

> I pity the man who cannot enjoy Shakespear. He has outlasted thousands of abler thinkers, and will outlast a thousand more.

Shakespeare's weakness, Shaw tells us elsewhere[7],

> lies in his complete deficiency in that highest sphere of thought, in which poetry embraces religion, philosophy, morality, and the bearing of these on communities, which is sociology. That his characters have no religion, no politics, no conscience, no hope, no convictions of any sort.

Shakespeare 'understood nothing and believed nothing'.[8] His 'morality is mere reach-me-down'.[9] He was unable to depict a hero.[10] Indeed,

> Bunyan's coward stirs your blood more than Shakespear's hero (Henry V) who actually leaves you cold and secretly hostile.[11]

Shaw's greatest mistake was to assume that the views expressed by Shakespeare's characters were his own. Again and again he quotes lines which are appropriate to a character in a particular situation, but which cannot properly be regarded as the expression of Shakespeare's own views on life. He declares that Shakespeare applies 'the vulgar hedonic test' to the worth of life and that therefore he 'comes out of his reflective period a vulgar pessimist, oppressed with a logical demonstration that life is not worth living'. The evidence for this is Macbeth's 'Out, out, brief candle', Gloucester's 'As flies to wanton boys are we to the gods',

Lear's 'blasphemous despair', and Hamlet's suicidal thoughts. But, of course, Macbeth has made life meaningless for himself by his own crimes; Gloucester's exclamation expresses the immediate reaction of one who has been brutally deceived and savagely blinded; and Hamlet's death-wish is an inevitable result of the dreadful situation in which he is placed.

In his comments on *Shakespeare and his Love*, Shaw questions many of Frank Harris's conclusions, without denying the possibility of using the plays for information about Shakespeare the man; but many Victorian critics, including some of the best, fell into the same error, and critics of our own day as diverse as A. L. Rowse and Ivor Brown are also guilty. Shaw's own attempts to portray Shakespeare in *The Dark Lady of the Sonnets* and 'A Dressing Room Secret' are farcical and not meant to be taken seriously.

Shaw believed, at least in his early years, that Shakespeare's philosophy of life was shallow, that he did not have a passion for reforming the world, and that he was a pessimist, 'quarrelling with God for not making men better'.[12] In other words, Shakespeare was a writer of tragedies, and these and his other plays were not didactic. Shaw himself was essentially a comic dramatist and he believed in his early years that he wrote plays to convert the public to his own views on life and society. But it is important to realize that his attitude changed after he had ceased to be a dramatic critic. In the preface to *Man and Superman* he admitted that 'Man will return to his idols and cupidities, in spite of all "movements" and all revolutions, until his nature is changed'[13]; and this belief was the basis of *Back to Methuselah*. Moreover, in his later years, he was less anxious to be regarded as a propagandist. As early as 1895 he declared that great writers[14]

> swallowed all the discussions, all the social questions, all the topics, all the fads, all the enthusiasms, all the fashions of their day in their nonage; but their theme finally was not this social question or that social question, this reform or that reform, but

humanity as a whole . . . Social questions are too sectional, too
topical, too temporal to move a man to the mighty effort which is
needed to produce great poetry.

He became anxious to point out his affinities with Shakespeare, comparing Falstaff's discourse on honour to Doo-
little's disquisition on middle-class morality[15], and claiming
that he played 'the old game in the old way, on the old
chessboard, with the old pieces, just as Shakespeare did'[16].
He wanted to be judged as an artist:[17]

> If you want to flatter me you must not tell me that I have saved
> your soul by philosophy. Tell me that, like Shakespear, Moliere
> . . . and Dickens, I have provided a gallery of characters which
> are realer to you than your own relations, and which successive
> generations of actors and actresses will keep alive for centuries.

Replying in his old age to Allardyce Nicoll, who had
treated him as a disciple of Robertson, Pinero and Ibsen,
Shaw declared that he had gone back[18]

> to Shakespear, to the Bible, to Bunyan, Walter Scott, Dickens
> and Dumas *père*, Mozart, and Verdi, in whom I had been
> soaked from my childhood.

He made a similar point in one of his last pronouncements.[19]

> I was going back atavistically to Aristotle, to the tribune stage,
> to the circus, to the didactic Mysteries, to the word music of
> Shakespear, to the forms of my idol Mozart, and to the stage
> business of the great players whom I had actually seen acting.

In his views on Shakespearian characterization, Shaw was
ahead of his time. Nineteenth-century critics from Hazlitt to
Bradley had extolled the poet for creating 'real' characters,
and the poorer critics wrote about them as though they had
actually lived. This was a mistake which was encouraged by
the fact that between 1700 and 1900 the novel was the
dominant literary form. Shaw rightly stressed the fact that
art and life are not the same and that the inconsistencies in
Shakespeare's characters are caused by a tension between his

plots and his creations. Shakespeare, he said,[20]

> survives because he coolly treated the sensational horrors of his
> borrowed plots as inorganic theatrical accessories, using them
> simply as pretexts for dramatizing human character as it exists in
> the normal world.

He followed Frank Harris in supposing that [21]

> the ferocious murders and treacheries and brutalities of the
> legendary Thane of Fife [were incompatible with] the humane
> and reflective temperament of the nervous literary gentleman
> whom Shakespear thrust into his galligaskins.

He argued that there was plenty of other bogus characterization in Shakespeare's plays, instancing Mercutio and Enobarbus. Mercutio in his first scene is 'a wit and fantasist of the most delicate order'. In his next scene 'he is a detestable and intolerable cad'.[22] It was clearly Shaw's Victorian dislike of bawdy which made him feel that the character who speaks about Queen Mab could not be guilty of the obscenities of the later scene. But, as Shaw was compelled to admit, the Elizabethans would not have found any incongruity since in the sixteenth century poetry and obscenity were often co-existent.

When Mrs Patrick Campbell was playing the part of Lady Macbeth, he told her:[23]

> If you want to know the truth about Lady Macbeth's character,
> she hasn't one. There never was such a person. She says things
> that will set people's imagination to work if she says them in the
> right way: that is all.
> *I* know: I do it myself.

Elsewhere Shaw makes Shakespeare say that Lady Macbeth was partly a portrait of his wife:[24]

> Apart from that, I defy (anyone) to find any sort of sense in Lady
> Macbeth. I couldn't conceive anybody murdering a man like that.
> All I could do when it came to the point was just to brazen it out
> that she did it, and then give her a touch of nature or two – from
> Ann – to make people believe she was real.

Shaw argued that Othello and Iago were equally unrealistic. Othello's jealousy is 'purely melodramatic', unlike that of Leontes which is drawn from life.[25] As for Iago, Shakespeare confesses:[26]

> A fellow who goes in for being frank and genial, unpretentious and second rate, content to be a satellite of men with more style, but who is loathsomely coarse, and has that stupid sort of selfishness that makes a man incapable of understanding the mischief his dirty tricks may do, or refraining from them if there is the most wretched trifle to be gained by them. But my contempt and loathing for the creature – what was worse, the intense boredom of him – beat me before I got into the second act. The really true and natural things he said were so sickeningly coarse that I couldn't go on fouling my play with them. He began to be clever and witty in spite of me.

In advising Ellen Terry on how to play Imogen, Shaw told her:[27]

> All I can extract from the artificialities of the play is a double image – a real woman divined by Shakespear without his knowing it clearly, a natural aristocrat, with a high temper and perfect courage, with two moods – a childlike affection and wounded rage; and an idiotic paragon of virtue produced by Shakespear's *views* of what a woman ought to be, a person who sews and cooks, and reads improving books until midnight . . . and is in a chronic state of suspicion of improper behaviour on the part of other people (especially her husband) with abandoned females.

It would not be difficult to defend the integrity of nearly all these characters. Macbeth is humanized, not dehumanized, by his fears; Enobarbus' choric function interacts with his individuality; Lady Macbeth, if considered in the light of Elizabethan theories of demonology, is – in the world of the play – entirely convincing; Shaw's account of Iago's transformation after Act I seems to have little to do with Shakespeare's character who is as coarse in the first scene as in Act II; and, as for Imogen, Elizabethan aristocrats knew how to sew, Ovid's *Metamorphoses* is not exactly an improving book, and Imogen suspects her husband of adultery only when he has ordered Pisanio to murder her. On Othello, however, Shaw forestalled such critics as Bridges and Stoll.

He was, indeed, right to stress the difference between a dramatic character and a person in real life, especially when one remembers the mode of Shakespeare criticism prevailing then. A character from a play of Ibsen's middle period is drawn more realistically and consistently than most Elizabethan characters, even when one makes allowances for the differing psychological theories. Although more can be said about the character of Rosalind, there is a good deal of truth in Shaw's remarks that [28]

> Rosalind is not a complete human being: she is simply an extension into five acts of the most affectionate, fortunate, delightful five minutes in the life of a charming woman.

But it would be wrong to imagine that Shaw regarded all Shakespeare's characters as inconsistent and unreal. He described Helena as an Ibsenite heroine; he approved of Isabella; he thought the Countess in *All's Well That Ends Well* was 'the most beautiful old woman's part ever written'; and, more surprisingly, he told the New Shakespeare Society that Cressida was most enchanting and Shakespeare's first real woman.[29] Indeed, he showed a particular fondness for the very plays which most Victorian critics regarded as dark, problematical and unsatisfactory.

Shaw realized that Shakespeare's powers of characterization depended on his mastery of style. In a review of a production of *All's Well That Ends Well*, he declared:[30]

> Even the individualization which produces that old-established British speciality, the Shakespearean 'delineation of character', owes all its magic to the turn of the line, which lets you into the secret of its utterer's mood and temperament, not by its commonplace meaning, but by some subtle exaltation, or stultification, or slyness, or delicacy, or what not in the sound of it. In short, it is the score and not the libretto that keeps the work alive and fresh.

This realization of the supreme importance of the Shake-spearean *score* was the central theme of Shaw's dramatic criticism. Each performance was weighed in the balances — and generally found wanting — by this test. Again and again he complains that actors were insensitive to the music of Shakespeare's lines. He made the point negatively in *The Daily News*:[31]

> Shakespear's power lies in his enormous command of word music, which gives fascination to his most blackguardly repartees and sublimity to his hollowest platitudes.

The elocutionist at the end of the nineteenth century devoted 'his life to the art of breaking up verse into prose'.[32] Much later, indeed, I knew of a producer who had the whole of *Antony and Cleopatra* typed out as prose, so that his actors should not be tempted to speak the lines as verse. Yet, as Shaw points out, when 'you have experienced emotion deep enough to crave for poetic expression . . . verse will seem an absolutely natural and real form of speech to you'.[33]

As a former music critic, Shaw often resorted to analogies from opera. He compared Da Ponte's libretto of *Don Giovanni* with *Much Ado About Nothing*.[34] If you wreck the beauty of Shakespeare's lines 'by a harsh, jarring utterance . . . you will make your audience wince as if you were singing Mozart out of tune'.[35] On Dorothea Baird's Rosalind, he said that her 'dainty, pleading little torrent of gabble will not do for Shakespear'. Her 'tiny ladylike patter' resembles 'a canary trying to sing Handel'.[36] Of Janet Achurch's Cleo-patra—he admired her in modern roles—he said: 'The lacerating discord of her wailings is in my tormented ears as I write, reconciling me to the grave.'[37] Wilson Barrett lacked the special musical and vocal gift[38]

> necessary for playing the part of Othello. The play remains magnificent by the volume of its passion and the splendor of its word-music, which sweep the scenes up to a plane on which sense is drowned in sound. The words do not convey ideas: they are

streaming ensigns and tossing branches to make the tempest of passion visible.

In advising Mrs Patrick Campbell on her playing Lady Macbeth, he told her:[39]

When you play Shakespear, don't worry about the character, but go for the music. It was by word music that he expressed what he wanted to express; and if you get the music right, the whole thing will come right. And neither he nor any other musician ever wrote music without *fortissimi* and thundering ones too. It is only your second rate people who write whole movements for muted strings and never let the trombones and the big drum go. It is not by tootling to him *con sordino* that Lady Macbeth makes Macbeth say 'Bring forth men children only'. She lashes him into murder.

And you must modulate. Unless you can produce in speaking exactly the same effect that Mozart produces when he stops in C and then begins again in A flat, you can't play Shakespear.

It was to players who appreciated these points that Shaw responded. He praised Miss Rehan as Helena in *A Mid-summer-Night's Dream* for giving [40]

beauty of tone, grace of measure, delicacy of articulation: in short, all the technical qualities of verse music, along with the rich feeling and fine intelligence without which those technical qualities would soon become monotonous. When she is at her best, the music melts in the caress of the emotion it expresses.

What he liked about Lillah McCarthy was that she[41]

was saturated with declamatory poetry and rhetoric from her cradle, and had learnt her business out of London by doing work in which you were either heroic or nothing ... The art of acting rhetorical and poetical drama, vulgarized and ridiculous, very soon became a lost art in the fashionable London theatres. Rhetoric and poetry vanished with it. But when I dragged rhetoric and poetry back its executive technique became again indispensable.

Shaw likewise praised Courtenay Thorpe's playing of the Ghost in *Hamlet* and said he could well understand why Shakespeare insisted on playing the part himself:[42]

The weird music of that long speech which should be the
spectral wail of a soul's bitter wrong crying from one world to
another in the extremity of its torment

should not be given to 'the most squaretoed member of the
company'.

It is significant that Shaw was critical of Granville-
Barker's Shakespearian productions.[43]

Barker's production of his own plays and Galsworthy's were
exquisite . . . whereas his style and taste were as different from
mine as Debussy's from Verdi's. With Shakespear and with me
he was not always at his happiest best.

But some of the qualities of those productions may well have
been due to the fact that Shaw attended rehearsals.

There is no doubt that Shaw's insistence on Shakespeare's
word-music was salutary in the 'nineties; and, unfortunately
during the past twenty years, a style of production has
developed, which makes his remarks necessary. That
brilliant young actor, David Warner, ruined the effectiveness
of his Henry VI by his treatment of the verse. He did not
follow Shaw's advice to Ellen Terry – 'play *to* the lines,
through the lines, *on* the lines, but never between the lines'[44]
– and he went out of his way to conceal the rhetorical artifice
and word-music of the great Towton speech.

On the subject of cutting the text of Shakespeare's plays
Shaw modified his position. In writing to Ellen Terry, he
suggested a number of cuts in *Cymbeline*, although he
objected to those which Irving had made.[45] He seems at this
time to have assumed that, under the conditions of the
Victorian stage, some cutting was necessary, but he objected
to the cutting of 'poetical' passages which were often the
first to suffer. He lamented that he had never seen a performance of *Hamlet* in which Fortinbras appeared. He
remarked that 'The magic of scenery put Shakespear on a
Procrustean bed'[46]; and he pointed out:[47]

For the terrible cutting involved by modern hours of performance; the foredoomed futility of the attempt to take a work

originally conceived mainly as a long story told on the stage, with
plenty of casual adventures and unlimited changes of scene, and
to tight-lace it into something like a modern play consisting of a
single situation in three acts . . . stood inexorably between the stage
and the real Shakespear.

A few years later, in 1919, he said that 'cutting must be
dogmatically ruled out'.[48]

The simple thing to do with a Shakespear play is to perform it.
The alternative is to let it alone. If Shakespear made a mess of it,
it is not likely that Smith or Robinson will succeed where he
failed.

He noted that the full, though not complete, version of
Hamlet given by Forbes Robertson was much less tedious
than the cut versions performed by his rivals, as William
Poel once explained why a performance of *Cymbeline* seemed
too long with the words 'That is because they've cut so
much'. In 1925 Shaw complained to John Barrymore of his
acting version:[49]

Shakespear, with all his shortcomings, was a very great playwright; and the actor who undertakes to improve his plays undertakes thereby to excel to an extraordinary degree in two pro-
fessions in both of which the highest success is extremely rare.

He compared a cut in another play to cutting two bars out of
a Mozart symphony.[50]

In spite of *Cymbeline Refinished*, Shaw had come to realize
that Shakespeare knew his business as a playwright. Poel's
productions, on a bare stage, may have contributed to this
realization. Poel's theories about the staging of Shakespeare's
plays were unsound; he cut the plays to suit his often eccentric interpretations; he sometimes cast women for masculine
roles, thereby reversing Elizabethan practice: but he did
succeed in demonstrating that the proscenium arch and
scene-changes were both unnecessary and undesirable.

Shaw was the best of all critics of Shakespearian acting,
partly because he was steeped in the plays, partly because he

was a dramatist and producer himself, and partly because he was also a first-rate music critic. It may also be claimed that, despite his iconoclasm and buffoonery, he was often stimulating as a critic of Shakespeare. At the period when he was writing, his very irreverence was a service. 'When I began to write', he declared truly, 'William was a divinity and a bore. Now he is a fellow-creature.'[51]

There are few of Shakespeare's plays on which Shaw has not made some revealing comment. Sometimes he is perverse, as in his remarks on *As You Like It* or *Antony and Cleopatra*; but it is obvious even in these cases that he appreciated both Rosalind and Shakespeare's 'huge command of rhetoric and stage-pathos'.[52] He enjoyed Shakespeare more than the bardolators did, and set him beside his favourite Mozart. He told his official biographer, Henderson:[53]

To Shaw the wonderful storm trio in which the King, the Fool and the sham madman have their parts 'concerted', as musicians say, like the statue, the hero, and the comic valet in Shaw's favourite *Don Giovanni*, is the summit of Shakespeare's achievement as poet and playwright.

The rediscovery of Shakespeare as a living force in the theatre was due to the efforts of scholars who never saw his plays performed properly, of an eccentric producer who cut many of Shakespeare's finest passages, of a stage-designer, Craig, whose Shakespearian designs were never used in England, and of a dramatic critic whose avowed aim was to topple Shakespeare from his pedestal. As Hamlet reminds us,

> There's a divinity that shapes our ends.
> Rough-hew them how we will.

4 Shakespeare's Imagery and the Critics

My object, in this chapter, is to consider the attitude, during the last three centuries, to Shakespeare's use of imagery. There is no evidence that any of his contemporaries were aware of what Caroline Spurgeon was to call 'iterative imagery'; and, although Beaumont, Fletcher and Massinger sometimes echoed Shakespeare's plays, they made no attempt to imitate his characteristic use of metaphor. Ben Jonson is reported by Dryden[1] to have said, in reference to some obscure speeches in *Macbeth*, that 'it was horror'. We do not know to which speeches he was referring, but there are many in which one metaphor evolves from another in a way which would offend a purist:

> And Pity, like a naked, new-born babe
> Striding the blast, or heaven's cherubins, horsed
> Upon the sightless couriers of the air,
> Shall blow the horrid deed in every eye,
> That tears shall drown the wind.

The image of the new-born babe bestriding the storm, and of the cherubim riding upon the wings of the wind, leads on to that of the wind itself followed by rain which is compared with tears, tears which are also caused by the wind. Although modern readers regard the lines as superbly characteristic of Shakespeare, one can imagine that Jonson would not approve of them.

The next generation of poets regarded Shakespeare with

the same kind of suspicion accorded by the poets of the 'Movement' to Dylan Thomas's very different style. Dryden himself, in spite of his recognition of Shakespeare's greatness, complained[2] that his

> whole style is so pestered with figurative expressions that it is affected as it is obscure . . . 'Tis not that I would explode[3] the use of metaphors from passions, for Longinus thinks 'em necessary to raise it: but to use 'em at every word, to say nothing without a metaphor, a simile, an image, or description, is I doubt to smell a little too strongly of the buskin.

Dryden's feeling against what he regarded as an excessive use of imagery is revealed even more plainly in his adaptations of Shakespeare's plays. The long speech of Ulysses on the power of time, which is not so much a logical argument as a series of brilliant images, was omitted altogether; and Troilus' farewell to Cressida, which contains twelve images in sixteen lines, is reduced by Dryden to a single weak image:[4]

> Our envious fates
> Jostle betwixt, and part the dear adieus
> Of meeting lips, clasped hands, and locked embraces.

Even when Dryden and other adapters preserved one of Shakespeare's images, they deliberately simplified the expression of it. In Davenant's version of *Macbeth*, for example, the famous lines

> Will all great Neptune's ocean wash this blood
> Clean from my hand? Nay, this my hand will rather
> The multitudinous seas incarnadine,
> Making the green one red

become deplorably tame and metrically wooden:[5]

> Can the Sea afford
> Water enough to wash away the stains?
> No, they would sooner add a tincture to
> The Sea, and turn the green into a red.

Davenant cuts out Neptune, mangles the great third line, and apparently misunderstands the fourth, thereby justifying his claim to be Shakespeare's illegitimate son.

Little was said in the eighteenth century about Shakespeare's imagery. Pope does remark[6] in his preface that all his metaphors are 'appropriated, and remarkably drawn from the true nature and inherent qualities of each subject'; Joseph Warton complained[7] that some passages in *King Lear* 'are too turgid and full of strained metaphors'; and Lord Kames briefly commended[8] him for the way in which his images were formed of particular objects rather than of generalities. Dr Johnson deplored[9] Shakespeare's quibbles but made only incidental comment on his images.

The only eighteenth-century critic who devoted himself to the study of Shakespeare's imagery was the Rev. Walter Whiter, a learned Cambridge scholar, who published *A Specimen of a Commentary on Shakespeare* in 1794. The first sixty pages consist of an intelligent, but unremarkable, commentary on *As You Like It*. The remaining two hundred pages are given a separate title: 'An Attempt to Explain and Illustrate various passages of Shakespeare on a new principle of criticism derived from Mr Locke's Doctrine of the Association of Ideas'. Whiter tells us in his preface:

> I have endeavoured to unfold the secret and subtle operations of genius from the most indubitable doctrine in the theory of metaphysics. As these powers of the imagination have never, I believe, been adequately conceived, or systematically discussed; I may perhaps be permitted, on this occasion, to adopt the language of science and to assume the merit of DISCOVERY.

Whiter's boast was justifiable. Locke had pointed out [10] that

> Ideas, that in themselves are not at all of kin, come to be so united in some men's minds, that it is very hard to separate them; they always *keep in company*, and the one no sooner at any time comes into the understanding, but its *associate* appears with it; and if they are more than two which are thus united, *the whole gang* always inseparable shew themselves together.

Whiter emphasizes that Locke's theory relates not to ideas which are naturally connected, but to 'those ideas, which have *no* natural alliance or relation to each other, but which have been united only by chance or by custom'.[11] He declares that commentators had displayed great learning in annotating Shakespeare's intentional allusions to the customs of his own age and to the objects of his satire, but they had neglected to mark[12]

> those *indirect* and *tacit* references, which are produced by the writer with *no* intentional allusion; or rather they have not unfolded those trains of thought, alike pregnant with the materials, *peculiar* to his age, which often prompt the combinations of the poet in the wildest exertions of his fancy, and which conduct him, unconscious of the effect, to the various peculiarities of his imagery or his language . . . In the fictions, the thoughts, and the language of the poet, you may ever mark the deep and unequivocal traces of the age in which he lived, of the employments in which he was engaged, and of the various objects which excited his passions or arrested his attention.[12]

Whiter proceeds to show[13] that 'a certain word, expression, sentiment, circumstance, or metaphor' leads Shakespeare to 'the use of that appropriate language, by which they are each of them distinguished', even where the metaphor is no longer continued; that 'Certain terms containing an equivocal meaning, or sounds suggesting such a meaning, will often serve to introduce other words and expressions of a similar nature' – in other words, Shakespeare's images are sometimes linked by unconscious puns; that the recollection 'of a similar phraseology, of a known metaphor, or of a circumstance, *not* apparent in the text' will lead Shakespeare to use language or imagery derived from these sources; and that an impression on the mind of the poet, 'arising from something which is frequently presented to his senses, or which passes within the sphere of his ordinary observation' will suggest to him 'the union of words and sentiments, which are not necessarily connected with each other'.

The rest of Whiter's treatise, apart from an unfortunate

c

digression on the Rowley poems, is devoted to the presentation of evidence in support of his four propositions. He argues,[14] for example, that in Apemantus' lines in *Timon of Athens*

> What, think'st
> That the bleak air, thy boisterous chamberlain,
> Will put thy shirt on warm? Will these moist trees,
> That have outlived the eagle, page thy heels,
> And skip when thou point'st out?

the word *moist* should not be emended to *mossed*, since a moist shirt was an unaired one, and the epithet was suggested by the previous mention of shirt.

Whiter might, however, have taken this to be an example of the linking of images by unconscious quibbles: *mossed* could be the correct word, suggested to Shakespeare through the intermediary of *moist*. For he himself gives many examples[15] of such links, some of them based on the alternative meanings of weed and suit:

> That we should *dress* us fairly to our end.
> Thus we may gather honey from the *weed*.
>
> (*Henry V*, IV. i. 11)

> Besides, forget not
> With what contempt he wore the humble *weed*;
> How in his *suit* he scorn'd you.
>
> (*Coriolanus*, II. iii. 229)

> JACQUES: I am ambitious for a motley *coat*.
> DUKES: Thou shalt have one.
> JACQUES: It is my only *suit*;
> Provided that you *weed* your better judgments.
>
> (*As You Like It*, II. vii. 45)

One interesting example is to be found in one of Whiter's notebooks.[16] The Sergeant describes how Macbeth

> *carved* out his passage,
> Till he *faced* the slave;
> Which ne'er shook hands, nor bade farewell to him,
> Till he *unseam'd* him from the nave to th'chaps.

The link between *carved, faced* and *unseam'd* is that all three words are associated with tailoring.

Whiter was the first to point out the presence of image-clusters, including the famous one of flatterers-dogs-sweets, rediscovered in the present century.[17] He shows [18] that the imagery of Romeo's speech in Act I, before he meets Juliet, is repeated in his last speech in the tomb, where he uses the same sequence of stars-seal-dateless-bargain-bitter-bark. Elsewhere[19] he shows that in *Troilus and Cressida*, *The Merry Wives of Windsor* and *Romeo and Juliet*: 'a Wanton Female – a Punk – and the attendant on such a personage, a Pandar, is connected with a Vessel – sailing upon the seas'. He has many examples of the influence of the stage on Shakespeare's imagery, and he shows how the poet's language is sometimes suggested by words in his source, though used with a totally different meaning. He points out,[20] for example, that when the Duke in *Measure for Measure* discourses on the text 'Let your light so shine before men', the language he employs is influenced by the story, on the adjacent page of St Mark's Gospel, of the woman who had an issue of blood:

> And there was a certain woman, which was diseased
> with an issue of blood twelve years . . . When she
> heard of Jesus, she came in the press behind, and
> touched his garment . . . And immediately when Jesus
> did know in himself the vertue that went out of him,
> he turned him about in the press and said . . . who did
> touch me?

> Heaven doth with us, as we with torches do,
> Not light them for themselves; for if our *virtues*
> Did not *go forth of us*, 'twere all alike
> As if we had them not. Spirits are not finely *touch'd*
> But to fine *issues*.

Whiter even hints at the use of iterative imagery when he remarks[21] that there is scarcely a play of Shakespeare 'where we do not find some favourite vein of metaphor or allusion by which it is distinguished'. Although Whiter's book was sometimes cited in the notes to the *New Variorum Shakespeare*, it seems not to have been known to E. E. Kellett who discussed image-clusters and unconscious puns,[22] or to Caroline Spurgeon who rediscovered the use of iterative imagery.

One final example may be given of Whiter's perceptive comments. In one of his notebooks[23] he discusses the line in *Romeo and Juliet* (II, iii, 3):

> And flecked darkness, like a drunkard reels.

He shows how

> this strange imagery has been produced, in which the Dawn is connected with the Drunkard. The darkness of Night, we see, which at the Dawn become flecked with streaks of Light, is associated with the Drunkard, because the poet is impressed with one application of the term *flecked*, which is used to express the spots (or blotches) in the face of a drunken man. But what is more curious, another property is introduced belonging to the drunken man, which is that of reeling; and we shall acknowledge that this circumstance has nothing to do with the imagery of Night, flecked by the streaks of light, which it is only the business of the poet to illustrate. Darkness or night, as connected with the dawn, possesses in our mind no property, from which we should have associated its departure with the reeling of a drunkard. But here again the poet was spellbound; and this imagery was forced upon his mind by another influence of the associating principle. Night is described in this very play, according to the opinion of some, as a runaway, although the passage is obscure . . . and Warburton compares a line in *The Merchant of Venice:*
>
> For the close night doth play the runaway.
>
> Thus we see, that because Night or Darkness is flecked with spots, as a drunkard is, she is compared to a drunkard, and because night is described sometimes as running away, she is here depicted as reeling away.

Most reviewers of Whiter's book seem to have regarded it as eccentric and there is no evidence that the critics of the Romantic period were acquainted with it. Coleridge in his lectures seems not to have said anything directly on Shakespeare's imagery, but in *Biographia Literaria*, in his discussion of the 'specific symptoms of poetic power' as revealed in *Venus and Adonis*, he remarked:[24]

> It has been before observed that images, however beautiful, though faithfully copied from nature, and as accurately represented in words, do not of themselves characterize the poet. They become proofs of original genius only as far as they are modified by a predominant passion; or by associated thoughts or images awakened by that passion; or when they have the effect of reducing multitude to unity, or succession to an instant; or lastly, when a human and intellectual life is transferred to them from the poet's own spirit.

The modification of imagery by a predominant passion is the cause of iterative imagery.

Most Victorian critics focused their attention on the characters, as Coleridge and Hazlitt had done, but there were one or two who showed some interest in Shakespeare's imagery. H. Elwin, who edited *Macbeth* in 1853 under the misleading title of *Shakespeare Restored*, calls attention to the deliberate ambiguity of some of his expressions, and in his preface, oddly entitled 'A Lamp for the Reader', he has some general remarks on Shakespeare's style, its 'significant peculiarities':[25]

> These facts of phraseology, and achievements of expression, may appropriately be denominated *the illustrative mechanism* of his composition. Profusely employed throughout his wondrously-contrived dialogues, they are often treated as obscurities, because unappreciated; although, the principle of their application being recognized, they cast a brilliant and certain light upon his treasure-stored page.

Elwin proceeds to comment on Shakespeare's 'practice of continuing a metaphor to an unprecedented extent'. He illustrates this from the lines in *Macbeth* (I, vii):

> But here, upon this *bank* and *school* of time,
> We'd jump the life to come. But in these cases

> We still have judgment here; that we but *teach*
> Bloody *instructions*.

He then comments on the imagery of the passage:

Bank is used for *bench*, and *time*, for *mortal life*; which, qualified as *a bench and school of instruction*, is placed in antithesis to *the life to come*. Here the idea of calling this life *the school of eternity*, as preparing man for the part he is to perform there, is not only thoroughly in accordance with the truthful genius of Shakespeare, but it is beautifully sustained in the expressions that follow it, 'that we but *teach* bloody instructions'. The turn of Macbeth's thought is toward a comparison of the measured time in which, during childhood, we are fitted to fill well the indeterminate period of manhood; and the finite life of this world, in which we purchase for ourselves success or failure in an unlimited futurity. The feeling expressed is this: If here only upon this bench of instruction, in this school of eternity, I could do this without bringing these, my pupil days, under suffering, I would hazard its effect on the endless life to come . . . The term *bank*, was, possibly, anciently employed for the raised benches of a school; but the judicious selection of it here is, at all events, rendered evident, since it was used to indicate a bench occupied by many persons, placed one above another; as '*a bank* of rowers'. And the world, with its occupants of various orders, is the *bank* here typified.

Not many critics would agree that *schoole* of the Folio should be interpreted as *school* rather than *shoal*; and Elwin's interpretation of *bank* is likewise questionable. But the passage illustrates his recognition of Shakespeare's use of continued metaphor.

In the last quarter of the nineteenth century, the New Shakespeare Society occasionally turned its attention to the question of imagery. On 10 January 1879, the Rev. J. Kirkman read a paper[26] entitled 'Animal Nature *Versus* Human Nature in *King Lear*', in which he not merely tabulated 133 separate mentions by twelve different persons of 64 different animals, but argued that 'Darwin would state on biological grounds precisely the same fact in nature as Shakespeare worked out on moral or psychological principles'. Kirkman ends by asserting that if man forgets his nobler qualities he falls back to his animal origins, the moral being (in Tennyson's words) that he should 'let the ape and tiger die'.

Three months later, on 25 April, Emma Phipson, writing on 'The Natural History Similes in Henry VI', maintained that there was no other 'dramatist to whom such constant use of animal metaphors can be ascribed as a special characteristic'.[27] Here, perhaps, we have the first example of imagery being used as a test of Shakespeare's authorship, though Whiter had tried to prove that the Rowley poems were genuine. On 22 April 1887 Furnivall read a paper[28] on 'Shakespeare's Metaphors' by Otto Schlapp, who pointed out the scarcity of mixed metaphor in the early plays and its frequency later. On 8 April 1892 Grace Latham examined 'Some of Shakespeare's Metaphors and his Use of them in the Comedies'.[29] Although her account is pedestrian, she does make a number of valid points about the dramatic function of imagery. She suggests that in *A Midsummer-Night's Dream* Shakespeare for the first time 'employs metaphor to supply the imagination of the audience with the scenery the Elizabethan stage did not possess'; that in the mature comedies the 'form of the metaphors is now employed more frequently to show character'; that the metaphor within metaphor is caused by Shakespeare's wish 'to display character, feeling, ideas'; that in *Measure for Measure* 'the metaphors are still further subordinated to the characters that speak them, and the situations to which they belong'; and that in *The Winter's Tale*

> we get fragmentary metaphorical speech, instead of a succession of metaphorical pictures, as in the middle and early period, Shakespeare having realized that if we require something more than plain, unvarnished speech to express feeling, it also needs a special kind of mind . . . to produce highly-finished metaphor, complete in all its parts.

In this paper we have the germ of later studies of imagery by Spurgeon, Clemen and Morozov.

F. C. Kolbe, not long afterwards, wrote a series of articles in a South African journal, *Southern Cross*, which he revised and collected many years[30] later in a volume entitled *Shakespeare's Way* (1930). His thesis was that Shakespeare repeated throughout each play 'at least one set of words or ideas in harmony with the plot. It is like the effect of the dominant note in a melody'. Kolbe showed, for example, that the idea of false-seeming occurs 120 times in *Much Ado About Nothing*, that *love* and *folly* are mentioned 140 times each in *Twelfth Night*, that words of mercantile import occur nearly 300 times in *The Merchant of Venice*, that the key words of *Macbeth* are *blood*, *sleep*, *darkness*, and that the play deals with 'one episode in the universal war between *Sin* and *Grace*'. Kolbe is not consistent in his explanation of this characteristic of Shakespeare's plays: at one point he speaks of it as deliberate artifice, but in general he seems to assume that it rather reveals the unconscious workings of Shakespeare's mind.[31] Kolbe's method has been adopted by several later critics as an adjunct to the study of imagery.[32]

E. E. Kellett, in his 'Notes on a Feature of Shakespeare's Style',[33] rediscovered, apparently without knowledge of Whiter, the association of ideas linking many of Shakespeare's images, and he provided a number of examples of the way in which consecutive ideas and images are linked by hidden puns. In *The Tempest*,[34] for example, the word *cast*, in the sense of 'thrown' suggested to Shakespeare the casting of a play and, in the following lines, a number of theatrical terms:

> though some *cast* again,
> And by that destiny, to perform an *act*,
> Whereof what's past is *prologue*, what to come
> In yours and my *discharge*

where *discharge* means 'performance'. It is but a step from Kellett to William Empson's *Seven Types of Ambiguity* and M. M. Mahood's *Shakespeare's Word-Play*.[35]

The concentration on imagery between the two wars may

have been influenced by the rediscovery of the Meta-
physicals and by the Imagist movement. In the twenties
there was a whole series of books and articles which touched
on the subject: Henry W. Wells' *Poetic Imagery* (1924),
Stephen J. Brown's *The World of Imagery* (1927), George
Rylands' *Words and Poetry* (1928), Elizabeth Holmes'
Aspects of Elizabethan Imagery (1929) and essays by J.
Middleton Murry and others. At the same time Caroline
Spurgeon began to publish the results of her study of
Shakespeare's imagery,[36] and the first of her projected books
on the subject, *Shakespeare's Imagery and What it Tells us*,
appeared in 1935. It must be confessed that the first part
of the book, in which we are informed of the revelation of
Shakespeare the man through the imagery, is not very
revealing. That Shakespeare was sensitive, that he had
remarkable powers of observation, and that he was intimately
acquainted with nature, merely confirms what we knew
before; that he 'is absolutely clear-eyed, but rarely bitter'
can hardly be proved by a study of imagery; and we cannot
legitimately deduce that he was a good carpenter because he
admired good carpentry, or that he blushed easily because
he noticed that people do blush.[37]

The second part of the book is more valuable. Miss
Spurgeon proves her contention that many of the plays have
what she calls 'iterative imagery', a group of images drawn
from one special field. The limitations of her method have
become apparent during the thirty years which have elapsed
since her book was published. It has been shown, for
example, that the iterative imagery can often be interpreted
in more than one way; that her card index leads to the
ascription of equal significance to a conventional derived
image and to a highly charged imaginative image; that at
times the imagery may reflect the poet's personal feelings
which may run counter to the theme of the play; that many
plays have several strands of iterative imagery; that we ought
not to consider imagery in isolation from character, plot and
structure; and that, as Rosemond Tuve has pointed out,[38]

'the basis upon which images are now most frequently differentiated and classified, i.e. the area from whence comparisons are drawn because of personal predilections of the author' is 'an unfirm basis, if not indeed an aesthetically irrelevant consideration'. These are all serious criticisms but they do not, I think, render Miss Spurgeon's book entirely worthless. It is difficult to believe that the sickness imagery in *Hamlet*, the cooking imagery in *Troilus and Cressida*, and the clothing imagery in *Macbeth* are quite without significance, even if we disagree with Miss Spurgeon's interpretation of them.

Meanwhile G. Wilson Knight had begun his series of interpretations with a modest booklet entitled *Myth and Miracle* (1929), soon followed by *The Wheel of Fire* (1930) and many others. Although these books have been influential, I do not propose to discuss them here, partly because I have written of them elsewhere,[39] and partly because they are concerned with many other things besides imagery.

The next important book on imagery was W. H. Clemen's *Shakespeares Bilder* (1936), revised after the war as *The Development of Shakespeare's Imagery* (1951). He concentrated on the dramatic function of imagery, showing how Shakespeare used it as decoration in his early plays, and organically in his mature ones, both to reveal character and to create atmosphere. He also showed that the plays from *Richard II* onwards had interwoven patterns of imagery which contributed to their dramatic effect.[40]

Meanwhile, before the publication of Clemen's English edition, Edward A. Armstrong had analysed in *Shakespeare's Imagination* (1946) a number of image-clusters in Shakespeare's plays associated with various birds and insects (e.g. kite, goose, beetle) and he suggested – though this was incidental to his main purpose – that the presence of these clusters could be used to establish Shakespeare's authorship of disputed scenes. The evidence is striking; but it needs to be supplemented by a study of Shakespeare's contemporaries to make certain that the associations are peculiar to Shakespeare. An American correspondent has recently called my attention to one of the 'Shakespearian' clusters in Webster. As Armstrong himself points out,[41] the wider the net has to be cast in seeking the constituent parts of a cluster, the greater is the element of chance. The kite-cluster in *The Two Noble Kinsmen*, for example, which I have myself used as a test of authorship, is spread over 31 lines.[42] It would need a mathematician to work out the odds against this being fortuitous.

Donald Stauffer's excellent book, *Shakespeare's World of Images* (1949) despite its title, was not primarily concerned with imagery. Brents Stirling's *Unity in Shakespearian Tragedy* (1956) argued that the unity in six of the plays was provided, or at least reinforced, by the imagery. Meanwhile Robert B. Heilman in *This Great Stage* (1948) and *Magic in the Web* (1956) had analysed the patterns of imagery in *King Lear* and *Othello* and related them to the characters and the structure of the plays. He carried the study of the dramatic use of imagery to the limit and sometimes, as in his analysis of sight-imagery in *King Lear*, he went, perhaps, beyond the limit. But the interpretation of the two plays, and especially of *King Lear*, still seems to me of considerable value. The big guns of the Chicago school were called up to demolish *This Great Stage*.[43] W. R. Keast declared that it was 'in almost all respects a bad book'; that *King Lear* is 'strictly unintelligible on Heilman's assumptions'; that 'the effect of the play suggested by his interpretation is one which no one has ever attributed to *King Lear*, which is, moreover, inappropriate to tragedy, and which, finally, Shakespeare's text does not support'.[44] It seems to me, on the contrary, that the interpretation of the play which emerges from Heilman's book is perfectly intelligible, largely traditional, and supported throughout by continual reference to the text. It is a pity that Keast set out to make a speech for the prosecution, since the tone of his article makes one distrust even the valid criticisms he offers of Heilman's method.

One other book may be mentioned – Maurice Charney's

Shakespeare's Roman Plays (1961) – which is a model of its kind.[45] He does not make the mistake of discussing imagery apart from its dramatic context and he is fully aware that the plays were written to be performed. The book shows that in the hands of a sensitive critic the study of imagery can be illuminating.

Nevertheless, it must be confessed that in recent years the study of imagery has fallen into disfavour. It was not to be supposed that Stoll or Charlton would approve of the school of Knight; but their criticisms have been reinforced by those of Rosemond Tuve, Helen Gardner and Roland M. Frye.[46] Even L. C. Knights, who began his career with an attack on Bradley and the proclamation that *Macbeth* was 'a statment of evil',[47] has come round, if reluctantly, to the admission that character is important.

It is not my business to estimate the value of the New Criticism and its contributions to the interpretation of Shakespeare, but perhaps I may, in conclusion, outline some of the ways in which the study of Shakespeare's imagery could be profitably pursued in the future. In the first place, a lot more needs to be done on the sources of Shakespeare's images: what little has been done suggests that many of them have a literary origin.[48] But although, for example, the cluster of flatterers-dogs-sweets may have a literary origin,[49] Shakespeare's continued use of it, especially in *Timon of Athens*, may have a personal significance. Secondly, it is desirable to have a comprehensive study of the use of imagery by Shakespeare's contemporaries, particularly the dramatists. It may be found that some of the image-clusters which are thought to be peculiar to Shakespeare may rather be due to some association shared by his contemporaries. At the same time, as many of the image-clusters discovered by Armstrong, who is an ornithologist, were connected with birds, it may well be that many others remain to be discovered. Thirdly, it is important to distinguish between kinds of imagery and not to lump together the prosaic, the conventional, the casual and the imaginative, as Caroline

Spurgeon did, believing she was following an objective, scientific method. Fourthly, every image must be considered in its context, in relation to the speaker and to the situation. The images can, indeed, be studied scene by scene, rather than by the spatial method favoured by Wilson Knight. Several critics have noted how imagery is used to differentiate character and how Othello, after he is infected with Iago's jealousy, uses the same kind of imagery as his enemy.[50] Lastly, as Clemen has emphasized,[51] the study of imagery cannot be isolated from other branches of criticism. We need 'to correlate the separate methods of investigation and to show the interdependence of style, diction, imagery, plot, technique of characterization and all the other constituent elements of drama'. It will often be found that the study of imagery reinforces, rather than supersedes, other methods. I found, for example, when I came to make a detailed study of the imagery of *Macbeth*, twelve years after I had edited the play, that the resulting interpretation was identical to the one I had reached before; and this was not, I think, because I was already incubating the disease in 1948.

5 Image and Symbol
in Shakespeare's Histories

Ever since the publication of Caroline Spurgeon's book in 1935, the study of Shakespeare's imagery has attracted a great deal of critical attention. Her theories have been questioned and modified in various ways. It has been doubted whether the field from which images happen to be drawn is as significant as the kind of images the poet employed. More stress has been laid on the dramatic function of the imagery; it has been shown that imagery ought not to be considered in isolation; and several critics have demonstrated that to concentrate on the iterative image that is numerically predominant is bound to over-simplify and miss the richness and complexity of the plays. But it is noticeable that nearly all the imagistic criticism of the last thirty years has been concerned with the tragedies, and that hardly anything has been written about the imagery of the Histories. The main exceptions have been Richard Altick's well-known essay on the symphonic imagery of *Richard II*,[1] chapters on the same play by Wolfgang Clemen and Brents Stirling, and an essay by E. C. Pettet on *King John*,

There are three reasons for this comparative neglect. It was not until the middle of the 'nineties that Shakespeare fully realized the dramatic function of imagery, and the three plays in which iterative imagery was first employed – *Romeo and Juliet*, *A Midsummer-Night's Dream* and *Richard II* – were all written about the same time. Four of the

Histories belong to an earlier period. Then, secondly, it may have been assumed that most of the Histories were less poetically organized than the tragedies; but in this connection it should be remembered that when they were first published both *Richard III* and *Richard II* were classed as tragedies. Thirdly, many critics believe that *Henry VIII* and *1 Henry VI* were not wholly Shakespeare's, and a few critics still believe that he had a collaborator in the Second and Third Parts of *Henry VI*.

1 Henry VI is a special case. Although there is nothing unlikely in the assumption that Shakespeare as a young man wrote in the manner of Marlowe, Greene or Peele, as Auden sometimes wrote in the manner of Eliot, there are some scenes in the play which appear to have been written in ignorance of others. One example may be given. In the very first scene we hear that Lord Talbot would have defeated a French army

> If Sir John Fastolfe had not played the coward.
> He, being in the vaward, placed behind
> With purpose to relieve and follow them
> Cowardly fled, not having struck one stroke.

In Act III, the same incident is repeated:

> CAP.: Whither way, Sir John Fastolfe in such haste?
> FAST.: Whither away! To save myself by flight:
>   We are like to have the overthrow again.
> CAP.: What! will you fly, and leave Lord Talbot?
> FAST.:   Ay.

In Act IV, Fastolfe is deprived of his knighthood and banished. If the same dramatist wrote all three passages he must have intended to delete the first: but as it is an integral part of the scene, it seems much more likely that two writers were responsible.

The dual, or multiple, authorship of the play is supported by the incidence of imagery. In Act II, Scene v, for example, the scene in which Mortimer dies, there are eighteen images in 125 lines. In Act V, Scene iv, the scene in which Joan is exposed as a licentious witch, there is no imagery in 175 lines. The difference might be explained by the fact that one is a serious death-scene and the other is intended to be comic. But the former appears to be characteristically Shakespearian, and the latter contains no indisputably Shakespearian touches.

The characteristic images in the play are similes rather than metaphors. Most of them are unoriginal and only a few seem to be the result of direct observation:

> My thoughts are whirled like a potter's wheel . . .
> Glory is like a circle in the water . . .
> As a child's bearing-cloth.

More characteristic and colourless are these examples from the first act: 'like captives bound to a triumphant car'; 'like pale ghosts'; 'like drowned mice'; 'like lions wanting food'. The commonest biblical and classical names are dragged in for comparisons: Samson, Deborah, Cain, Goliath, Hector, Nestor, Paris, Hercules, Hannibal, Nero. Only one is at all unusual:

> Thy promises are like Adonis' gardens,
> Which one day bloom and fruitful are the next.

This, indeed, was thought to be such a recondite allusion that it was used as a proof that the plays could not have been written by the poacher from Stratford. But one suspects that the author could have derived the information from the third book of *The Faerie Queene*, or from some lost source.

With *2 Henry VI* we are on surer ground. It is significant that five of the image-clusters discovered by Caroline Spurgeon and Edward Armstrong are present in the play, though without some of the associations which they afterwards collected.[2] The cluster linking the drone with *eagle*, *creeping* and *sucking* does not in IV. i mention the *weasel*, *cat* and *music*, as in Shakespeare's later plays. This is what we should expect, for the clusters gradually attract to themselves additional associations.

But although there is no doubt that Shakespeare was responsible for the whole play, and although the verse is generally more competent than in Part I, there is no attempt to vary the verse to suit the different characters. The immaturity is particularly apparent in the imagery. It is shown in the commonplace, and often proverbial, nature of his similes (e.g. 'Smooth runs the water where the brook is deep'); in the numerous allusions to classical figures – Dido, Ajax, Medea, Althaea; in the over-elaborate working out of comparisons, sometimes shared by two characters; and, above all, in his decorative, rather than dramatic use of imagery. In the scene of Suffolk's murder, for example, the Captain, who has apparently been Suffolk's servant, describes nightfall in these terms:

> The gaudy, blabbing, and remorseful day
> Is crept into the bosom of the sea;
> And now loud-howling wolves arouse the jades
> That drag the tragic melancholy night;
> Who, with their drowsy, slow and flagging wings,
> Clip dead men's graves, and from their misty jaws
> Breathe foul contagious darkness in the air.
> Therefore bring forth the soldiers of our prize.

The objection to these lines is not that they are out of character, for Shakespeare often uses minor characters as a chorus, and the pirate captain is afterwards used to give an eloquent denunciation of Suffolk's vices, complete with an appropriate Latin tag: it is rather that they paint the scene in an uneconomical and entirely conventional way, with twelve tired epithets in seven lines.

In the scene in which Suffolk parts from the Queen, there is a much more dramatic use of imagery. Suffolk says:

> If I depart from thee, I cannot live,
> And in thy sight to die, what were it else
> But like a pleasant slumber in thy lap?
> Here could I breathe my soul into the air,
> As mild and gentle as the cradle-babe
> Dying with mother's dug between its lips.

This is still comparatively clumsy and verbose, but the imagery is called forth by the situation: it is organic, not decorative.

There are two examples of a long epic simile. In one of them of nine lines, York compares the loss of the territories in France to piracy: in the other, the King compares the arrest of Gloucester to a calf being taken to the slaughter-house. Both are admirable in their way, but Shakespeare in his later work wisely limited the use of such similes to passages of epic narration, as in the sergeant's account of the battle in *Macbeth*, or in the Dido episode in *Hamlet*.

The difference between Shakespeare's mature imagery and that of *2 Henry VI* is apparent — so apparent, indeed, that it is impossible to believe that two passages in Act V were written at the same time as the rest of the play. One of them is Young Clifford's discovery of his father's body during the battle of St. Albans:

> Shame and confusion! All is on the rout;
> Fear frames disorder, and disorder wounds
> Where it should guard. O War, thou son of hell,
> Whom angry heavens do make their minister,
> Throw in the frozen bosoms of our part
> Hot coals of vengeance! Let no soldier fly.
> He that is truly dedicate to war
> Hath no self-love; nor he that loves himself
> Hath not essentially, but by circumstances,
> The name of valour. O, let the vile world end,
> And the premised flames of the last day
> Knit earth and heaven together!
> Now let the general trumpet blow his blast,
> Particularities and petty sounds
> To cease! Wast thou ordained, dear father,
> To lose thy youth in peace and to achieve
> The silver livery of advised age,
> And in thy reverence and thy chair-days thus
> To die in ruffian battle? Even at this sight
> My heart is turned to stone; and while 'tis mine
> It shall be stony. York not our old men spares;

> No more will I their babes. Tears virginal
> Shall be to me even as the dew to fire;
> And beauty, that the tyrant oft reclaims,
> Shall to my flaming wrath be oil and flax.

If this speech is compared with that of the Captain in Act IV, the difference of style is apparent. Instead of the regular end-stopped lines of the earlier speech, with conventional epithets and images, we have a freer and more colloquial rhythm, frequent enjambement, and original epithets; and the imagery of disorder and of the Last Judgment is characteristic of a much more mature Shakespeare.

There is no trace of these lines in the bad quarto which has instead:

> O! dismall sight, see where he breathlesse lies,
> All smeard and weltred in his luke-warme blood,
> Ah, aged pillar of all Comberlands true house,
> Sweete father, to thy murthred ghoast I sweare,
> Immortal hate vnto the house of Yorke,
> Nor neuer shall I sleepe secure one night,
> Till I haue furiously reuengde thy death,
> And left not one of them to breath on earth.

Young Clifford's speech continues in the Folio in a more conventional and earlier style:

> Henceforth I will not have to do with pity:
> Meet I an infant of the house of York,
> Into as many gobbets will I cut it
> As wild Medea young Absyrtus did;
> In cruelty will I seek out my fame.
> Come, thou new ruin of old Clifford's house;
> As did Æneas old Anchises bear,
> So bear I thee upon my manly shoulders;
> But then Æneas bare a living load,
> Nothing so heavy as these woes of mine.

The bad quarto omits the lines about Medea, but retains the gist of the Anchises simile:

> And thus as old Ankysses sonne did beare
> His aged father on his manly backe,

> And fought with him against the bloodie Greeks
> Euen so will I.

The conclusion is inescapable that Shakespeare made alterations to the play some years after its first performance,
probably for a revival after the success of *Henry IV* and
Henry V.

The other passage which clearly belongs to a later
stratum of the play is in the last scene:

> Of Salisbury, who can report of him,
> That winter lion, who in rage forgets
> Aged contusions and all brush of time
> And, like a gallant in the brow of youth,
> Repairs him with occasion?

The corresponding words in the quarto are simply 'But did
you see old Salisbury?' But the next speech, which reverts to
a more primitive style, is reproduced, if inaccurately, in the
quarto.

If one compares *3 Henry VI* with *The True Tragedie*, it is
clear that the actors endeavoured to preserve the substance
of each scene, but they cut the more 'poetical' speeches
which were inessential to the plot. Gloucester's tremendous
speech in III. 3 is cut from 62 lines to 30, and among the
passages sacrificed is one of the most effective of Shakespeare's similes:

> And I – like one lost in a thorny wood
> That rents the thorns and is rent with the thorns,
> Seeking a way and straying from the way;
> Not knowing how to find the open air,
> But toiling desperately to find it out –
> Torment myself to catch the English crown;
> And from that torment I will free myself
> Or hew my way out with a bloody axe.

Gloucester's later soliloquy, after the murder of Henry VI,
apart from a few vulgarizations, is reproduced entire; but the
King's more poetical soliloquy on the Towton molehill is cut
from 54 lines to 13. The cuts include the two similes at the

beginning of the speech and Henry's praise of the shepherd's life. In the last 40 lines there is only one image: melodious, vivid and charming as the passage is, Shakespeare obtains his effect by skilful rhetorical repetitions and by an extraordinary purity of diction:

> the shepherd's homely curds,
> His cold thin drink out of his leather bottle,
> His wonted sleep under a fresh tree's shade,
> All which secure and sweetly he enjoys,
> Is far beyond a prince's delicates –
> His viands sparkling in a golden cup,
> His body couched in a curious bed,
> When care, mistrust, and treason waits on him.

The very absence of imagery in one of the most memorable passages in the play is an indication of the mainly decorative function of imagery in Shakespeare's early work.

Caroline Spurgeon, indeed, showed that these early Histories contain a large number of garden images and she pointed out that in *3 Henry VI* there were an unusually large number of images taken from sea-faring.[3] The garden images become more functional in *Richard II*; but the sea-faring images do not, as iterative images were later to do, throw much light on the theme of the play.

In *Richard III* the imagery becomes for the first time functional and organic. Several critics have called attention to the animal imagery in the play, used mainly to characterize the villain-hero. He is compared to a dog, a hell-hound, a toad, a spider, a hedgehog, a hog and a boar – the last being suggested by his crest.

Neither Caroline Spurgeon nor Professor Clemen referred to another group of images which is quantitatively important and qualitatively significant: these are the images drawn from the stage. The Duchess of York asks Queen Elizabeth:

> What means this *scene* of rude impatience?

She replies:

> To make an *act* of tragic violence.

Margaret compares Elizabeth to a stage queen:

> I called thee then poor shadow, painted queen,
> The presentation of but what I was,
> The flattering index of a direful pageant . . .
> A queen in jest, only to fill the scene.

Earlier in the same scene, Margaret says she is a witness to a 'dire induction',

> hoping the consequence
> Will prove as bitter, black, and tragical.

These images are used to present the fall of princes as a tragic pageant and they reinforce the element of ritual in the play to which A. P. Rossiter called attention.[4] But much of the stage imagery is used by Richard himself or in reference to him by others. In the third scene he speaks of himself as seeming 'a saint when most I play the devil'. In Act III he compares himself to 'the formal vice, Iniquity', who moralizes 'two meanings in one word'. His mother complains that beneath 'a virtuous vizor' he conceals 'deep vice'. This stage imagery throws light on Richard's role and character. His hypocrisy may be regarded as the application of the actor's art to real life. Sir Edmund Chambers, indeed, argued that in *Richard III* Shakespeare the actor was pursuing the psychological secrets of his craft, the play being 'a professional notebook full of the nicest and most penetrating observation'.[5] It would, perhaps, be more accurate to say that Shakespeare presents his Machiavellian villain as one who perverts the art of acting to obtain his own ends in real life. This is made clear by several passages, notably by the dialogue between Richard and Buckingham in III. v:

> GLOU.: Come, cousin, canst thou quake and change thy colour,
> Murder thy breath in middle of a word,
> And then again begin, and stop again,
> As if thou wert distraught and mad with terror?
> BUCK.: Tut, I can counterfeit the deep tragedian;
> Speak and look back, and pry on every side,

> Tremble and start at wagging of a straw,
> Intending deep suspicion. Ghastly looks
> Are at my service, like enforced smiles;
> And both are ready in their offices
> At any time to grace my stratagems.

Here the stage-imagery has been turned into direct description; and when, two scenes later, Richard enters between two bishops we observe the stratagems being put into operation. The imagery of *Richard III* is no longer decorative, but an integral part of the design.

Richard II exhibits a further state in the development of Shakespeare's use of imagery. Pater remarked that in this play 'dramatic form approaches to something like the unity of a . . . single strain of music'; and Altick wrote of its 'symphonic imagery' and of the numerous groups of inter-related images. But one of the main characteristics of the play, one of the chief means by which Shakespeare achieves its particular tone, is the frequent use of religious imagery and allusion. This characteristic is oddly ignored in Altick's otherwise comprehensive account. Richard compares his false friends to Judas, and those who show 'an outward pity' to Pilate. Bolingbroke, because he has broken his oath of allegiance, is 'damned in the book of heaven'; and Bolingbroke, in his turn, compares Exton to Cain. The Bishop of Carlisle compares England to Golgotha and warns Bolingbroke not to set house against house. Richard declares that he has been delivered to his 'sour cross' and in his last soliloquy quotes twice from the Sermon on the Mount.

These religious associations have links with the comparison of Richard with the sun — 'the searching eye of heaven', 'the blushing discontented sun' — and with Richard's belief that God is mustering 'Armies of pestilence' to strike the yet unborn children of the rebels. The theme of the divine right of kings is counterpointed with that of the king's own mortality:

> Within the hollow crown
> That rounds the mortal temples of a king

> Keeps Death his court; and there the antic sits
> Scoffing his state and grinning at his pomp;
> Allowing him a breath, a little scene,
> To monarchize, be fear'd, and kill with looks,
> Infusing him with self and vain conceit,
> As if this flesh which walls about our life
> Were brass impregnable.

The date of *King John* is still under dispute; but if as some believe, it was written before *The Troublesome Raigne*, it must have been considerably revised, for most of the verse is more mature than that of the three parts of *Henry VI*. The imagery of the play is often striking and it is certainly not merely decorative; but it is also puzzling. The personifications and the imagery connected with bodily movement, regarded by Caroline Spurgeon as characteristic of the play, seem to have no special dramatic significance; and though E. C. Pettet is right to call attention to the imagery drawn from the fire and fever and to suggest that it may have proliferated from the scene of Arthur's attempted blinding and of John's death, here again the dramatic function is obscure.

In most respects *1 Henry IV* exhibits a considerable advance on the earlier Histories. Structure, characterization, and verse are all masterly. There are no weak scenes and no unrealized characters. But in one respect the play is something of a retrogression: the images used by Shakespeare seem less organic than those in *Richard II* or even in *Richard III*. Many of them are effective in themselves and some of them are a vivid means of characterization, as when the King says that Hotspur is

> Amongst a grove, the very straightest plant;

and Westmoreland replies that Worcester's teaching makes Hotspur

> prune himself, and bristle up
> The crest of youth against your dignity.

Even more revealing are Hotspur's own lines:

By heaven, methinks, it were an easy leap
To pluck bright honour from the pale-faced moon;
Or dive into the bottom of the deep,
Where fathom-line could never touch the ground,
And pluck up drowned honour by the locks;
So he that doth redeem her thence might wear,
Without corrival, all her dignities.

Hal, at the end of the first scene in which he appears, defines his role by a comparison with the sun:

Herein will I imitate the sun
Who doth permit the base contagious clouds
To smother up his beauty from the world,
That when he please again to be himself,
Being wanted, he may be more wondered at,
By breaking through the foul and ugly mists
Of vapours that did seem to strangle him.

The King, in a later scene, comparing his son with Richard II, says that they both had made themselves too common,

seen, but with such eyes,
As, sick and blunted with community,
Afford no extraordinary gaze,
Such as is bent on sun-like majesty
When it shines seldom in admiring eyes.

The King, by using the sun-image, reminds us of Hal's earlier words, which unfortunately give to a modern audience the impression of cold-blooded calculation, like his father's, but which Shakespeare can hardly have intended.

The second part of *Henry IV* is much more interesting from the point of view of our subject because Shakespeare reverts to the use of iterative imagery. To use Elizabeth Barrett Browning's phrase about Horne, Shakespeare malleted the metaphors into the groundwork of his play. All through the play our attention is called to disease and senility. The King is dying, and like Charles II he takes an unconscionable time about it. Northumberland is crafty-sick. Shallow is senile, and he talks a lot about the friends of his youth who are dead. Falstaff, in spite of his vitality, is suffering from various diseases, and he implies that the Chief Justice is senile and that Doll Tearsheet has the pox. The iterative image reinforces the atmosphere of disease, so that we are made to realize that the country itself is sick. There are more than thirty images drawn from sickness and physic.[6]

In the first scene Northumberland, hearing the news of Hotspur's death, compares himself to

> the wretch, whose fever-weakened joints
> Like strengthless hinges, buckle under life,
> Impatient of his fit, breaks like a fire
> Out of his keeper's arms.

Morton, in the same scene, calls England

> a bleeding Land,
> Gasping for life.

In the long scene between Falstaff and the Lord Chief Justice most of the conversation is about disease and bodily infirmity — 'deafness', 'sick', 'apoplexy', 'lethargy', 'a kind of sleeping in the blood, a whoreson tingling', 'the disease of not listening', 'physician', 'gout', 'pox', and several of the images are taken from the same field. Falstaff, for example, says:

> Your Lordship may minister the potion of imprisonment
> to me in respect of poverty; but how I should be your
> patient to follow your prescriptions, the wise may
> make some dram of a scruple, or indeed a scruple itself.

The Chief Justice says he is 'loath to gall a new-healed wound'; and Falstaff complains:

> I can get no remedy against this consumption of the
> purse: borrowing only lingers and lingers it out,
> but the disease is incurable.

In the last words of the scene he declares that he 'will turn diseases to commodity'.

In scene 3, there is one image from mental illness; two from surfeiting and vomit; there is one burning image suggested by fever, and the Archbishop declares 'The commonwealth is sick', the barest and simplest use of this particular image.

There are fewer sickness images in Act II, three scenes of which are in prose. But Hal speaks of the discolouring of 'the complexion of his greatness' and of his heart bleeding inwardly. Poins says that Falstaff's 'immortal part needs a physician'; and Mistress Quickly says that Falstaff, and Doll are 'as rheumatic as two dry toasts'.

In Act II, the King, suffering from insomnia, speaks of sleep as Nature's nurse, and again refers to the sick commonwealth:

> Then you perceive the body of our kingdom
> How foul it is; what rank diseases grow,
> And with what danger near the heart of it.

To which Warwick replies:

> It is but as a body yet distempered,
> Which to his former strength may be restored,
> With good advice and little medicine.

The King recalls Richard II's words to Northumberland:

> The time will come, that foul sin, gathering head,
> Shall break into corruption.

In the Gloucestershire scene there is little imagery, but the theme of sickness is presented directly by the portrait of Justice Shallow and by the group of conscripts, Mouldy, Wart and Feeble. Even Bullcalf pretends he is diseased.

In Act IV the Archbishop, in defending the rebellion to Westmoreland, bases his whole argument on analogies of disease:

> We are all *diseased*;
> And with our surfeiting and wanton hours
> Have brought ourselves into a burning *fever*,

> And we must *bleed* for it: of which *disease*
> Our late king, Richard, being *infected*, died.

He disclaims being a physician of the commonwealth, but declares that he wishes

> To diet rank minds sick of happiness,
> And purge the obstructions, which begin to stop
> Our very veins of life.

He promises that if their grievances are remedied the rebels will knit their 'powers to the arm of peace', and claims that

> Our peace will, like a broken limb united,
> Grow stronger for the breaking.

The madness of rebellion would thus be cured.

In the last scene of this act the dying King again speaks of his sick kingdom; Hal contrasts the golden crown with the gold that is 'medicine potable' and denies that his blood was infected with joy when he thought his father dead.

In the last act there is hardly any disease imagery, for we are to suppose that with the accession of Henry V the sickness of the commonwealth, caused largely by the sins of usurpation and rebellion, has been cured.

A little-known nineteenth-century critic, Elwin, has an interesting comment on Henry's soliloquy on sleep:[7]

> Nothing, perhaps, displays more largely how he [Shakespeare] luxuriated in plenitude of power, than his constantly-repeated practice of constructing his sentences in a fanciful allusion, altogether differing from their express purport. As when, in the upbraidings addressed by King Henry IV to that sleep that has become a fugitive from his couch, in order to indicate an involuntary association of ideas in the mind of the royal soliloquizer, whose repose is interrupted by the rebellion of his subjects, the phraseology is fashioned to the notion of a *visitation* of justice, on a scene of tumult; *seizing* and *hanging* on high the *ruffians* of the riot:
>
> > 'And in the *visitation* of the winds,
> > Who *take* the *ruffian* billows by the top,

Curling their monstrous heads, and *hanging* them
With deaf'ning clamours in the *slippery* clouds.'

The epithet, *slippery*, glances at doubtful agents of authority, who permit offenders to escape; whilst its direct reference is to the effect produced by the distant billows of a stormy sea; each one in succession seeming to be suspended for a moment in the clouds, from which it presently glides again into the deep.

Henry V is less interesting from the point of view of imagery; the Chorus wishes for

a Muse of fire that would ascend
The brightest heaven of invention

and laments the inadequacies of the Elizabethan stage – this wooden O' – to portray the heroic deeds of Henry V. But the weaknesses of the play are not theatrical, but poetical. Some of the best scenes are in prose – the account of Falstaff's death and the conversation on the eve of Agincourt between Williams and the King – and some of the verse is deplorably prosaic. The Archbishop of Canterbury's 60-line speech about the salique law is flatter than anything in Shakespeare's early histories. The King's speeches before Harfleur, on the other hand, are painfully inflated. One of his best speeches – his reply to Westmoreland before the battle of Agincourt – obtains its effect, without a single image, by the simplicity of its rhetorical appeal:

If we are marked to die, we are enow
To do our country loss; and if to live,
The fewer men the greater share of honour . . .
We few, we happy few, we band of brothers;
For he to-day that sheds his blood with me
Shall be my brother.

His address to the three conspirators has as many as fifteen images but none of them is particularly striking:

As dogs upon their masters, worrying you . . .
Thou that did'st bear the key of all my counsels . . .
                    the truth of it stands off as gross

As black and white . . .
Glistering semblances of piety . . .
For this revolt of thine, methinks, is like
Another fall of man.

Much more impressive is the speech on the cares of kingship, based, we are told on passages by Sir Thomas Elyot, Priscian, Erasmus and Horace. Here, apart from references to Phoebus, Hyperion and 'Night, the child of hell', there is hardly any imagery. There is, it is true, one splendid image –

the tide of pomp
That beats upon the high shore of this world –

but it comes in the middle of a complex sentence which stretches over 24 lines.

No, thou proud dream,
That play'st so subtly with a king's respose;
I am a king that find thee; and I know
'Tis not the balm, the sceptre and the ball,
The sword, the mace, the crown imperial,
The intertissued robe of gold and pearl,
The farced title running 'fore the king,
The throne he sits on, nor the tide of pomp
That beats upon the high shore of this world,
No, not all these, thrice gorgeous ceremony,
Not all these, laid in bed majestical,
Can sleep so soundly as the wretched slave,
Who with a body fill'd, and vacant mind
Gets him to rest, crammed with distressful bread;
Never sees horrid night, the child of hell,
But, like a lackey, from the rise to set
Sweats in the eye of Phoebus, and all night
Sleeps in Elysium . . .

The diction, the structure and the control displayed in these lines are beyond the range of the early Shakespeare. But the play is, nevertheless, poetically something of a disappointment after the two parts of *Henry IV*.

Caroline Spurgeon argued that 'the keynote to the

dominating atmosphere of the earlier and best part of the play' was 'swift and soaring movement'. But it may well be objected that the number of flight images is too small to be significant; that only one of the images quoted by Miss Spurgeon comes from the earlier part of the play; that these images do not help in the interpretation of the play; and that few readers would agree that the earlier part of the play is the best. The best is surely Act IV; and almost the only first-rate passage in Act I is the comparison of the state to the kingdom of the bees. It is not, of course, original. It is found in the *Georgics*, in Elyot and Lyly; and T. W. Baldwin[8] has argued convincingly that Shakespeare made use of Willichius' commentary on Virgil, since he 'used the same classifications and the same order as Willichius'. But the comparison is worked out with great gusto and it contains, as Edward Armstrong showed, one of Shakespeare's characteristic image-clusters. The word *hum*, as usual, is associated with death (*executors*), sleep (*yawning*), food (*honey*), music (*singing*) and wealth (*gold*).

After writing *Henry V*, Shakespeare turned to Plutarch's *Lives* for historical stories. Then, at the very end of his career, he was able to write a play about Queen Elizabeth's father. Since Spedding's study of *Henry VIII*, published in 1850, most critics have assumed that the play was written in collaboration with Fletcher, a theory which receives some confirmation from the knowledge that Shakespeare and Fletcher did collaborate in two other plays. Although Peter Alexander and G. Wilson Knight have argued for Shakespeare's sole authorship, it is not denied that some scenes are very much in Fletcher's style.

Attempts have been made to determine the authorship of the play by a study of its imagery. There appear to be none of the image-clusters which have hitherto been isolated in Shakespeare's works. But some of the other plays in the First Folio are equally barren of clusters. A more profitable line to follow was the detection of iterative imagery. Miss Spurgeon demonstrated that the iterative image of the play

was that of bodily movement, especially of a body being
weighed down. Buckingham in the first scene says that many

> Have broke their backs with laying manors on 'em
> For this great journey.

In the second scene, Katherine says that the people, com-
plaining of Wolsey's exactions, use language which 'breaks
the sides of loyalty', exactions which 'to bear'em The back is
sacrifice to the load'. Buckingham in II. i protests:

> And if I have conscience, let it sink me,
> Even as the axe falls, if I be not faithful.

In II. ii there are several images of bodily movement –
crept, dives, gripped – but none of bearing a heavy burden. In
II. iii the Old Lady asks Anne if she has limbs 'to bear that
load of title' and tells her:

> if your back
> Cannot vouchsafe this burthen, 'tis too weak
> Ever to get a boy.

In the trial scene the King, speaking of his troubled conscience, tells the Bishop of Lincoln:

> You remember
> How under my oppression I did reek –

that is, he sweated under the burden. In III. ii – the scene
of Wolsey's disgrace – he confesses that the King has
heaped graces on him. The Lord Chamberlain urges Surrey
not to press 'a falling man too far'. Wolsey tells Cromwell
that the King

> from these shoulders,
> These ruin'd pillars, out of pity, taken
> A load would sink a navy, too much honour.
> O' 'tis a burden, Cromwell, 'tis a burden
> Too heavy for a man that hopes for heaven!

and he says that Anne 'was the weight that pulled' him down.
In the last act Cranmer tells Gardiner

> Lay all the weight ye can upon my patience

and Cromwell declares it is cruel 'To load a falling man'.

The interesting thing about the distribution of these images is that it cuts right across the usual allocation of the scenes to Shakespeare and Fletcher. There are none of these images in V. i, a scene usually ascribed to Shakespeare[9] – and there are several in V. iii, which is usually ascribed to Fletcher. Moreover, in the scene of Wolsey's disgrace, which is thought to be Shakespeare's up to the exit of the King and Fletcher's thereafter, the iterative image is to be found in the second half of the scene. Miss Spurgeon duly observed this and she concluded that Shakespeare, and not Fletcher, was responsible for Wolsey's famous farewell. She did not realize, however, the full implications of her conclusion. The speech has all the metrical characteristics which have made critics ascribe it to Fletcher; and if Shakespeare wrote it, the elaborate metrical arguments to prove that Fletcher had a hand in the play fall to the ground.

Another group of images, relating to shipwreck and storm, is present in many scenes including some which have been ascribed to Shakespeare and others which have been ascribed to Fletcher. Buckingham in the first scene refers to a metaphorical tempest. A Gentleman in II. i says that the Commons wish Wolsey 'ten fathom deep'. The King in II. iv speaks of his guilty feelings about his marriage to his brother's widow:

> Thus hulling in
> The wild sea of my conscience, I did steer
> Toward this remedy.

Katherine in III. i speaks of herself as 'Shipwreck'd upon a kingdom' and Wolsey warns her that kings 'grow as terrible as storms' to disobedient subjects. In the next scene the Lord Chamberlain says that the King 'coasts' (like a vessel following the windings of the coast); Wolsey describes himself as swimming beyond his depth and left 'to the mercy of a rude stream'; and tells Cromwell that he had

> Sounded all the depths and shoals of honour,

D

and found Cromwell a way, 'out of his wreck', to rise. The
Third Gentleman in IV. i compares the noise of the people
to that made by shrouds 'in a stiff tempest'. Wolsey is
described in IV. ii as

> An old man, broken with the storms of state.

A study of the imagery of the play lends no support to the
theory of dual authorship. But the recent work of A. C
Partridge and Cyrus Hoy show that 'certain grammatical
peculiarities . . . seem to establish the presence of two
hands, and they substantiate broadly the divisions of the play
made upon other grounds, by Spedding and Hickson'.[10]
A study of the handwriting as well as of the imagery has
proved beyond question that Shakespeare contributed to the
censored play on Sir Thomas More: and I have tried elsewhere to show, from a study of the imagery alone, that he
was part-author of *Edward III*.[11] In both these cases there
is no evidence which conflicts with that of the imagery. The
problem of the authorship of *Henry VIII*, where the evidence
is conflicting, remains unsolved.

I have tried to show that there is no iterative imagery in
the earliest Histories; that there are traces of it in *Richard II*,
and a whole complex of patterns of imagery in *Richard II*
that there is iterative imagery in *King John* though it
throws little light on the theme of the play; that there is no
such imagery in *1 Henry IV*; that the sickness imagery of
2 Henry IV contributes a great deal to the atmosphere; and
that the weighing down and shipwreck imagery of *Henry*
VIII would seem to indicate that if there really were two
authors they must have worked in close harmony.

In other respects the sequence of Histories written in the
sixteenth century shows a gradual progression in the use of
imagery. In the three parts of *Henry VI* the usual form of
image is the simile; in the later Histories, it is the metaphor
Shakespeare hardly ever uses in his later Histories the long
epic simile which is prevalent in *Henry VI*. In *1 Henry IV*
there is one long comparison between building a house and

planning a war (IV. iii. 41–62) which is so unusual in so late a play that critics have argued that it reflects the poet's experience in repairing New Place, the house he had bought in 1597.

The other development in the use of imagery which may be noted is that in the later plays more is derived from life and less from books. Shakespeare continued, as we have seen, to draw some of his images from Ovid; but there are fewer of them, they came as naturally as the leaves to a tree, and they are no longer decorative. Some of the bookish similes in *Henry VI* give one the impression that the upstart crow, who had only a grammar school education, was anxiously determined to show that he could beat the University wits at their own game. After the success of *Venus and Adonis* he lost this anxiety.

This survey of the imagery of the Histories goes some way to explain why they have attracted less attention from imagistic critics than the tragedies have done. But it may nevertheless be claimed that in *Richard II* Shakespeare first realized the truth of Coleridge's words[12] on imagery as proof of original genius; and that in *2 Henry IV* he first exploited this discovery to the full. The way was open to the achievement of the great tragedies where image and structure, plot and character, are perfectly integrated.

6 The Imagery of *Romeo and Juliet*

It has long been recognized that in the three plays written about the year 1595 – or, as some scholars think, some years earlier – Shakespeare's imagery became more functional than it had been in the previous comedies and histories. As Caroline Spurgeon demonstrated, imagery is used in *A Midsummer-Night's Dream* to create the atmosphere of the enchanted wood near Athens; and in *Richard II*, as Richard D. Altick showed, the various imagistic themes are interwoven with great subtlety.[1] In these plays, as in *Romeo and Juliet*, the percentage of rhymed verse is higher than in earlier plays; and this is probably due, not to the fact that Shakespeare was revising his juvenilia, but rather because he came to these plays fresh from the composition of *Venus and Adonis*, *Lucrece* and some of the sonnets. It will be recalled that Coleridge in his *Biographia Literaria* quoted some lines from *Venus and Adonis* as an example of the kind of imagery which was a proof of original genius; and it may be that in the more leisurely composition of his two narrative poems Shakespeare learnt things which he could afterwards use in his plays.

As in *A Midsummer-Night's Dream*, one of the dramatic functions of the imagery is to enable the audience to visualize the setting. On the Elizabethan stage, Capulet's orchard would have a wall for Romeo to climb and Juliet would have a balcony; but the orchard and the moonlight could be created only by the poetry. When Romeo sees a light at

Juliet's window he compares it to the east, and Juliet to the sun.

> Arise, fair sun, and kill the envious moon.

Juliet, being a maid, is said to be wearing the vestal livery of the maiden goddess, Diana, and Romeo urges her to cast it off. Then he compares her eyes to twinkling stars, and suggests that

> her eyes in heaven
> Would through the airy region stream so bright
> That birds would sing and think it were not night.

A few lines later Romeo speaks of Juliet as a bright angel, 'a winged messenger of heaven'. When he addresses her directly, Juliet says he is 'bescreened in night' and asks him how he climbed the orchard walls. He replies that he has 'night's cloak' to hide him from the eyes of Juliet's kinsmen. Juliet says that she would blush, were it not for 'the mask of night' on her face, at the way her love has been revealed to him by 'the dark night'. Romeo begins to swear by the moon,

> That tips with silver all those fruit-tree tops;

but Juliet urges him not to swear by the inconstant moon which changes day by day. When she says good-night, Romeo says:

> A thousand times the worse, to want thy light.

And when she calls him again, Romeo exclaims:

> How silver-sweet sound lovers' tongues by night,
> Like softest music to attending ears!

In this scene the night is mentioned eighteen times, and the moon and the stars thirteen times. Shakespeare turns the limitations of the Elizabethan stage to his own advantage since he makes the audience create the scene through the eyes of the lovers.

A second example of atmospheric painting is in the scene where Romeo and Juliet part at dawn. It belongs, as Professor Spencer has shown, to a long tradition of aubades in many different languages. The debate on whether it was the song of the nightingale or of the lark is lent an added force in Shakespeare's play because, as both the lovers know, it is not merely a matter of regret that the dawn has come so soon to interrupt the rites of love, but Romeo's life depends on his getting away from Verona before daylight. The Friar had first enjoined him not to stay till the watch was set, but later he provides an alternative.

> Either be gone before the watch be set,
> Or by the break of day disguis'd from hence.[2]

Juliet mentions the pomegranate tree in the orchard and Romeo calls her attention to the signs that dawn is breaking.

> Look, love, what envious streaks
> Do lace the severing clouds in yonder east.
> Night's candles are burnt out, and jocund day
> Stands tiptoe on the misty mountain tops.

and, later on, he agrees with her that the grey is not 'the morning's eye' but the reflection 'of Cynthia's brow'.

A third example of the creation of atmosphere is the final scene in the vault of the Capulets. It is prepared for in IV. 3 by the speech in which Juliet, just before she drinks the Friar's potion, is afraid of being stifled in the vault, or else, affected by

> The horrible conceit of death and night

and the thought of Tybalt 'festering in his shroud', of ghosts, loathsome smells and 'shrieks like mandrakes' torn out of the earth', that she will be driven mad and dash out her brains with one of the bones. In V. 3 Paris' page is half afraid to stand alone in the churchyard. When Romeo arrives, he compares the vault to Death, with a 'detestable maw' and 'rotten jaws'; but on seeing Juliet, dressed in white, he says that

> her beauty makes
> This vault a feasting presence full of light.

He sees the corpse of Tybalt in his 'bloody sheet'; he calls the vault 'this palace of dim night'; he speaks of worms as Juliet's chambermaids; and Friar Laurence asks, on his arrival, what torch

> vainly lends his light
> To grubs and eyeless skulls?

After Juliet awakens, the Friar urges her to

> come from that nest
> Of death, contagion, and unnatural sleep.

But the most impressive images are those that personify Death as a lover of Juliet:

> Death, that hath suck'd the honey of thy breath,
> Hath had no power yet upon thy beauty.
> Thou art not conquer'd: Beauty's ensign yet
> Is crimson in thy lips and in thy cheeks
> And Death's pale flag is not advanced there . . .
> Shall I believe
> That unsubstantial Death is amorous,
> And that the lean abhored monster keeps
> Thee here in dark to be his paramour?

These lines are the culmination of a whole series of similar images. The Chorus speaks of the death-marked love of the protagonists. Romeo, just before the marriage, talks of love-devouring Death (II. 6). Hearing of Romeo's banishment, Juliet says (III. 2):

> I'll to my wedding-bed;
> And death not Romeo, take my maidenhead.

In the next scene the Friar tells Romeo:

> Affliction is enamour'd of thy parts,
> And thou art wedded to calamity.

When she is told that she must marry Paris, Juliet says that if the marriage is not delayed they must

> make the bridal bed
> In that dim monument where Tybalt lies.   (III. 5)

The Friar, telling her of his scheme for her to avoid the marriage, says that it 'cop'st with Death himself to scape from it' (IV. 1). After her supposed death, Capulet tells Paris:

> O son! the night before thy wedding-day
> Hath Death lain with thy wife. There she lies,
> Flower as she was, deflowered by him.
> Death is my son-in-law, Death is my heir;
> My daughter he hath wedded.

Paris says he has been beguiled by death.

In all these passages Death is looked on as a lover, and sometimes in the form of a monster. J. E. Hankins[3] cites a passage from *The French Academie*:

> The Prophet propoundeth heere the grave as a great and horrible monster, that hath a throate, with a stomach and belly, as it were a deepe gulfe and bottomlesse pitte to swallowe up and consume all.

It will be remembered that Caroline Spurgeon, in one of her first contributions to the study of imagery, afterwards incorporated in *Shakespeare's Imagery* (1935), declared that

> in *Romeo and Juliet* the beauty and ardour of young love is seen by Shakespeare as the irradiating glory of sunlight and starlight in a dark world. The dominating image is light, every form and manifestation of it; the sun, moon, stars, fire, lightning, the flash of gunpowder . . . while by contrast we have night, darkness, clouds, rain, mist and smoke.

She goes on to point out that each of the lovers thinks of the other as light; that Juliet speaks of cutting up her lover into little stars; that Romeo imagines Juliet's eyes in heaven; that Juliet complains that their bethrothal is

> Too like the lightning, which doth cease to be
> Ere one can say 'It lightens';

and that both Romeo and the Friar use the image of the explosion of gunpowder. In II. 6, the Friar warns Romeo that

> These violent delights have violent ends,
> And in their triumph die, like fire and powder,
> Which as they kiss consume:

and, a few scenes later (III. 3), he says that Romeo's wit

> Like powder in a skilless soldier's flask
> Is set afire by thine own ignorance.

When he hears of Juliet's supposed death, Romeo asks the apothecary for a poison that will be as rapid in its effect

> As violently as hasty powder fir'd
> Doth hurry from the fatal cannon's mouth.

One would not wish to question the insight displayed by Miss Spurgeon in her demonstration of the importance of these images; but it may nevertheless be suggested that the significance of the light images is different from that of the gunpowder ones. She tries to link them by saying that Shakespeare 'saw the story in its swift and tragic beauty, as an almost blinding flash of light, suddenly ignited and as swiftly quenched'. This, indeed, is suggested by the few lightning images; but the gunpowder images, as used by the Friar, rather indicate the destructive effects of passion.[4]

The point is not without substance, not merely because of the attempts of historical critics (such as Franklin B. Dickey in *Not Wisely But Too Well*) and of moralists (such as John Masefield) to put the blame for the tragedy on the lovers rather than on the haters, but because the Friar, who is in some sense a *raisonneur*, is continually preaching on the conflict between grace and rude will, on the dangers of precipitancy, and on the error of allowing passion to usurp the place of reason. These are commonplaces but, especially

as they tend to be long-drawn-out, they are put in the play,
partly to qualify, but not of course to annul, the whole-
hearted sympathy the lovers are bound to receive.

Two other points are worth making. Many of the fire
images – in contrast to those concerned with light – are
related to the anger and rage of the warring factions; and
this again underlines the danger of considering all these
images under one heading. Sometimes they symbolize love,
and sometimes hate.

The other point is this. Although in much of the star
imagery Shakespeare is concerned with their brightness, in
others he is concerned with their astrological significance –
and these link up with the straightforward statements about
fate. The lovers are described in the Prologue as star-crossed[5]
and, just before Romeo's first meeting with Juliet he
expresses his premonition of untimely death:

> My mind misgives
> Some consequence yet hanging in the stars
> Shall bitterly begin his fearful date
> With this night's revels, and expire the term
> Of a despised life closed in my breast
> By some vile forfeit of untimely death,
> But he that hath the steerage of my course
> Direct my sail![6]

Walter Whiter called attention to the fact that Romeo
in the last scene repeats the same imagery when he proposes
to

> shake the yoke of inauspicious stars
> From this world-wearied flesh

and enjoins his lips to

> seal with a righteous kiss
> A dateless bargain to engrossing Death!
> Come, bitter conduct, come, unsavoury guide!
> Thou desperate pilot, now at last run on
> The dashing rocks thy sea-sick weary bark.[7]

In between these passages, which mark the beginning and end of his relations with Juliet, Romeo refers more than once to the influence of the stars. When Mercutio dies, he speaks of 'This day's black fate'; when he slays his bride's cousin, he cries 'O, I am Fortune's fool!'; and when he hears of Juliet's death he exclaims: 'Then I defy you, stars!' Even the Friar admits to Juliet that fate, or providence, has brought about the catastrophe:

> A greater power than we can contradict
> Hath thwarted our intents.

Shakespeare would not have inserted these references to fate and the influence of the stars at all the key moments of the play — just before the lovers meet, just after the deed that leads to Romeo's banishment, when he hears of Juliet's death, just before he takes poison, and just before Juliet's suicide — if he had not intended the play to be, in some sense, a tragedy of fate. They reinforce the clear statement of the Prologue.[8]

Another important pointer to the meaning of the play is the frequent use of religious terminology. A foretaste of this is given early in the play when Romeo claims that he will never fall into the heresy of believing any woman more beautiful than Rosaline:

> When the devout religion of mine eye
> Maintains such falsehood, then turn tears to fires;
> And these, who, often drown'd, could never die,
> Transparent heretics, be burnt for liars!

Already, in spite of the conventional nature of his love for Rosaline, he has substituted the love of woman for the love of God; and, in the sonnet which he shares with Juliet when they first meet, the religious imagery is again apparent. Juliet is a saint, and Romeo a pilgrim:

> ROM.: If I profane with my unworthiest hand
> This holy shrine, the gentle fine is this:
> My lips, two blushing pilgrims, ready stand
> To smooth that rough touch with a tender kiss.

JUL.: Good pilgrim, you do wrong your hand too much,
Which mannerly devotion shows in this;
For saints have hands that pilgrims' hands do touch,
And palm to palm is holy palmers' kiss.

ROM.: Have not saints lips, and holy palmers too?

JUL.: Ay, pilgrim, lips that they must use in prayer.

ROM.: O, then, dear saint, let lips do what hands do;
They pray, grant thou, lest faith turn to despair.

JUL.: Saints do not move, though grant for prayers' sake.

ROM.: Then move not, while my prayer's effect I take.

He kisses her at this point, not as most editions indicate, after the next line:

Thus from my lips by thine my sin is purg'd.

JUL.: Then have my lips the sin that they have took.

ROM.: Sin from my lips? O trespass sweetly urged.
Give me my sin again.

JUL.:   You kiss by th' book.

The religious terminology is continued in the Balcony scene. Juliet is compared to a 'bright angel', 'a winged messenger of heaven' as she stands above Romeo, and he again calls her a saint. He offers to be new-baptized – nor merely to lose the name of Montague but in his new religion, and Juliet confesses that he is the god of her idolatry, and he calls her his soul. Even when Juliet hears that he has slain Tybalt, she cannot in her oxymorons forget her religious terminology – 'fiend angelical . . . damned saint . . . the spirit of a fiend In mortal paradise'. In the next scene Romeo tells the Friar that banishment, like the deprivation of the light of God's countenance, is 'purgatory, torture, hell itself'. The carrion flies that kiss Juliet's hand are guilty of the sin of sacrilege and the damned use the word 'banished' in hell. When the Nurse advises Juliet to marry Paris, she is called a fiend. It is clear that the lovers have replaced the worship of God by the worship of each other. A similar idea is expressed twice by Brooke:

For each of them to other is as to the world the sun (1726)

and

Love is thy Lord (1432)

The last important group of images relate to sea-voyages, and I have suggested elsewhere that here too Shakespeare was influenced by Brooke's poem, who uses five similes of storms at sea, some of them of considerable length.[9] In the third of these, Juliet's bed is compared to the long desired port, at which Romeus' 'steerless ship', his 'sea-beaten bark' at last arrives. This resembles the lines quoted above from Romeo's last speech. Another voyage image, as we have seen, is used just before he first meets Juliet. In the Balcony Scene, he tells Juliet:

> I am no pilot, yet wert thou as far
> As that vast shore wash'd with the farthest sea,
> I should adventure for such merchandize.[10]

The Nurse is compared to a sail — the association of bawd and ship occurs several times in Shakespeare's plays, as Whiter noticed — and Romeo's rope-ladder is

> a tackled stair,
> Which to the high topgallant of my joy
> Must be my convoy in the secret night.

In III. 5 Capulet tells his daughter that

> in one little body
> Thou counterfeit'st a bark, a sea, a wind:
> For still thy eyes, which I may call the sea,
> Do ebb and flow with tears; the bark thy body is,
> Sailing in this salt flood; the winds thy sighs,
> Who raging with thy tears and they with them,
> Without a sudden calm will overset
> Thy tempest-tossed body.

Shakespeare in other plays compares the love quest to a voyage, and there are some striking examples in *Troilus and Cressida*:

> Her bed is India; there she lies, a pearl;
> Between our Illim and where she resides

> Let it be called the wild and wand'ring flood;
> Ourself the merchant, and this sailing Pandar,
> Our doubtful hope, our convoy, and our bark.

Just before Cressida finally capitulates, Troilus compares himself to

> a strange soul upon the Stygian banks
> Staying for waftage.

But in *Romeo and Juliet* the tempest-tossed bark is an appropriate symbol for the lovers who (to use Greville's phrase) are weather-beaten in the sea of this world and brought to their deaths by the opposition of the stars as well as by the hatred of their respective families.

7 Image and Symbol in *Hamlet*

[1]

Caroline Spurgeon demonstrated long ago the importance of the sickness imagery in *Hamlet*. Although there is a considerable amount of disease imagery in two plays written about the same time as *Hamlet*, *2 Henry IV* and *Troilus and Cressida*, there is comparatively little in *Twelfth Night* and *Othello*, so that we can hardly explain it by the prevalence of the plague in London, especially as only one of the images in *Hamlet* is concerned with that particular disease. Nor is it likely that the disease imagery is a reflection of Shakespeare's own state of health: the illnesses referred to range from cancer to pleurisy, and from the dislocation of a limb to the pox, and it is unlikely that Shakespeare was unfortunate enough to suffer from them all, or if he did that he would have survived to write *The Tempest*.

To Caroline Spurgeon herself the disease images reflect 'not only the outward condition which causes Hamlet's spiritual illness, but also his own state.' She argues that 'when the play opens Hamlet has already begun to die . . . because all the springs of life are being gradually infected by the disease of the spirit which is . . . killing him.' She concludes, therefore, that to Shakespeare's imagination[1]

> The problem in Hamlet is not predominantly that of will and reason, of a mind too philosophic or a nature temperamentally unfitted to act quickly; he sees it . . . not as the problem of an

individual at all, but as something greater and even more mysterious, as a condition for which the individual himself is apparently not responsible.

Professor W. H. Clemen, however, has given a very different interpretation of the disease imagery. He suggests[2] that it originates from the Ghost's description of the effects of Claudius's poison:

> And in the porches of my ears did pour
> The leperous distilment; whose effect
> Holds such an enmity with blood of man
> That swift as quicksilver it courses through
> The natural gates and alleys of the body,
> And with a sudden vigour it doth posset
> And curd, like eager droppings into milk,
> The thin and wholesome blood: so did it mine;
> And a most instant tetter bark'd about,
> Most lazar-like, with vile and loathsome crust,
> All my smooth body.

Professor Clemen argued that 'a real event described at the beginning of the drama' exercises 'a profound influence upon the whole imagery of the play'. 'The picture of the leprous skin disease' buries itself 'deep in Hamlet's imagination and continues to lead its subterranean existence, as it were, until it reappears in metaphorical form.' Professor Clemen continues:

As Miss Spurgeon has shown, the idea of an ulcer dominates the imagery, infecting and fatally eating away the whole body; on every occasion repulsive images of sickness make their appearance. It is certain that this imagery is derived from that one real event. Hamlet's father describes in that passage how the poison invades the body during sleep and how the healthy organism is destroyed from within, not having a chance to defend itself against attack. But this now becomes the *leitmotif* of the imagery: the individual occurrence is expanded into a symbol for the central problem of the play. The corruption of land and people throughout Denmark is understood as an imperceptible and irresistible process of poisoning. And, furthermore, this poisoning reappears as a *leit-*

motif in the action as well – as a poisoning in the 'dumb-show', and finally, as the poisoning of all the major characters in the last act. Thus imagery and action continually play into each other's hands and we see how the term 'dramatic imagery' gains a new significance.

Although Professor Clemen's suggestion is an attractive one, it is impossible to accept it without considerable modification. Eleven of the disease images occur before the Ghost's description of the poisoning. Clemen, indeed, quotes one of these with the comment that it 'is a faint warning, preparing the way . . . for the future'. We do not know, of course, in what order the scenes were written; and it is conceivable that these earlier images were suggested to Shakespeare by his knowledge of what was to come. But Clemen seems to blur the distinction between the effects of poisoning and those of an organic disease; and it is important to observe that it is not merely in Hamlet's imagination that the disease imagery persists: it is used by other characters as well.

It has been suggested[3] that Shakespeare's use of sickness imagery may have been influenced by Sidney's account of the function of 'high and excellent *Tragedie*, that openeth the greatest woundes, and sheweth forth the *Ulcers* that are covered with *Tissue*'. Sidney had just described the effect of a performance of a tragedy on a tyrant, and this may have prompted Hamlet's remarks about 'guilty creatures sitting at a play.' It is not impossible that, before beginning his series of great tragedies, Shakespeare turned to Sidney's essay to refresh his memory on his conception of the function of tragedy.

Whatever the origins of the disease imagery, its interpretation must obviously depend on the dramatic context of each individual image – by whom it is used, and to what it refers. Not all writers on imagery have taken this precaution. Many of the images throw little light on the interpretation of character: they seem designed merely to provide atmosphere. Francisco, for example, remarks that he is 'sick at heart'; Hamlet tells Polonius that old men's eyes are 'purging thick amber and plum-tree gum'; he describes the witching time of night when

> hell itself breathes out
> Contagion to this world;

Claudius tells how England's

> cicatrice looks raw and red
> After the Danish sword;

and he speaks of his love for Gertrude as his 'plague'; Hamlet refers to the way the peasant's kibe is galled by the courtier's heel; and the Gravedigger talks of the 'many pocky corses now-a-days that will scarce hold the laying in'. Collectively such passages contribute to the tone of the play, but individually they cannot be used to support any particular interpretation.

A number of the disease images, as we have seen, are related to the poisoning of Hamlet's father, and one is used in the corresponding incident in 'The Murder of Gonzago', where Lucianus describes his poison:

> With Hecate's ban thrice blasted, thrice infected . . .
> On wholesome life usurp immediately.

Several of the images refer to the sickness of the state, which is supposed at first to be due to the threat of war, but which the audience soon realizes is the result of Claudius's crime. Horatio in the first scene surmises that the appearance of the Ghost 'bodes some strange eruption to our state', just as, at the time of the murder of Caesar,

> the moist star
> Was sick almost to doomsday with eclipse.

Claudius supposes that Fortinbras mistakenly believes that, as a result of the elder Hamlet's death, Denmark is 'disjoint and out of frame'; and, although this image is taken from building, it seems to link up with Hamlet's cry:

—

> The time is out of joint. O cursed spite
> That ever I was born to set it right!

Marcellus interprets the appearance of the Ghost to mean that

> Something is rotten in the state of Denmark.

Hamlet again and again uses disease imagery in reference to the King's guilt. He thinks of himself as a surgeon probing a wound:

> I'll tent him to the quick. If he but blench,
> I know my course.

In the play-scene, he compares Claudius, by implication, to a 'galled jade'; and he tells Guildenstern that he should have sent for the doctor rather than for himself, because 'for me to put him to his purgation would perhaps plunge him into more choler'. When he spares the praying King, he concludes his explanation with the remark:

> This physic but prolongs thy sickly days.

In the scene with his mother, he compares Claudius to a 'mildewed ear Blasting his wholesome brother'; and, in the last scene of the play, he asks Horatio:

> Is't not to be damn'd
> To let this canker of our nature come
> In further evil?

It is true that Claudius reciprocates by using disease images about his nephew. He compares his leniency with Hamlet to the behaviour of 'the owner of a foul disease' who

> To keep it from divulging, let it feed
> Even on the pith of life.

He supports his stratagem of sending Hamlet to England with the proverbial maxim:

> Diseases desperate grown
> By desperate appliance are reliev'd,
> Or not at all.

Later in the same act, when he is hatching his plot with Laertes, Claudius comes to what he calls 'the quick of th'ulcer':

> Hamlet comes back; what would you undertake
> To show yourself in deed your father's son,
> More than in words?

It is surely obvious that these images should not be used to prove that Hamlet is diseased or neurotic: they exhibit rather Claudius's guilty fear of his nephew.

Other images of disease are used by Hamlet to refer to the Queen's adultery. 'Heaven's face', he tells her, 'Is thought-sick at the act' and even 'a sickly part of one true sense Could not so mope' as to allow her to fall in love with Claudius. He urges her not to try and excuse herself by thinking he is mad:

> Lay not that flattering unction to your soul . . .
> It will but skin and film the ulcerous place,
> Whiles rank corruption, mining all within,
> Infects unseen.

And in a later scene Gertrude herself refers to her 'sick soul'.

Laertes uses three disease images, two of them in his warning to Ophelia not to allow herself to be seduced by the Prince:

> The canker galls the infants of the spring
> Too oft before their buttons be disclos'd,
> And in the morn and liquid dew of youth
> Contagious blastments are most imminent.

After the death of his father, he tells the King that the prospect of revenge on Hamlet 'warms the very sickness' in his heart.

One of the disease images is used by Hamlet in reference to the futile war between Norway and Poland:

> This is the imposthume of much wealth and peace,
> That inward breaks, and shows no cause without
> Why the man dies.

We have already examined most of the disease imagery without finding any evidence to support the view that it is a reflection of Hamlet's disease; but a few significant examples remain to be considered. In attempting to stiffen Laertes' resolution to kill Hamlet, Claudius has a long speech in which he uses three disease images; one has been quoted above, the other two being in the following passage:

> Not that I think you did not love your father,
> But that I know love is begun by time,
> And that I see, in passages of proof,
> Time qualifies the spark and fire of it.
> There lives within the very flame of love
> A kind of wick or snuff that will abate it;
> And nothing is at a like goodness still,
> For goodness, growing to a pleurisy,
> Dies in his own too much: that we would do
> We should do when we would; for this 'would' changes
> And hath abatements and delays as many
> As there are tongues, are hands, are accidents,
> And then this 'should' is like a spendthrift's sigh,
> That hurts by easing.

The speech is intended to persuade Laertes to murder Hamlet; but as Laertes and Hamlet are placed in a similar position, and as Hamlet's vengeance has at this point in the play already suffered 'abatements and delays', it has been thought that Claudius is making an unwitting comment on his nephew. But neither the 'goodness, growing to a pleurisy', nor the sigh, 'that hurts by easing' could be applied to Hamlet, unless we had reason to believe, on other grounds, that the words were applicable. It seems possible, moreover, that the beginning of the speech, on the waning of love, may have been suggested by the fact that Gertrude has been obeying Hamlet's injunction not to go to his uncle's bed.

Another speech containing disease imagery has likewise been applied to Hamlet. While he is waiting for his encounter with the Ghost, he comments on the drunkenness of the Danish court, a fault which gives his countrymen a bad reputation abroad. He then proceeds to generalize on the way a single defect may spoil a man's reputation:

> So oft it changes in particular men
> That, for some vicious mole of nature in them,
> As in their birth, wherein they are not guilty,
> Since nature cannot choose his origin:
> By the o'ergrowth of some complexion,
> Oft breaking down the pales and forts of reason;
> Or by some habit that too much o'erleavens
> The form of plausive manners – that these men,
> Carrying, I say, the stamp of one defect,
> Being nature's livery or fortune's star,
> His virtues else, be they as pure as grace,
> As infinite as man may undergo,
> Shall in the general censure take corruption
> From that particular fault: the dram of eale
> Doth all the noble substance of a doubt
> To his own scandal.

Hamlet is speaking of how an inherited defect or some bad habit leads people to overlook a man's infinite virtues. The apparent irrelevance of the speech has led some critics to suppose that Hamlet, consciously or unconsciously, was thinking of himself and of the tragic flaw in his own character. But apart from the necessity of distracting the attention of the audience by a complex speech so that they will again be startled by the appearance of the Ghost, the drunkenness of the court is a very relevant theme. Professor Peter Alexander has, moreover, rightly protested about the application of these words to the speaker.[4] He does not suffer from 'some vicious mole of nature'. In the general censure (or opinion) he is still 'The expectancy and rose of the fair state'; and he is concerned not with the question of whether a single defect outweighs infinite virtues, but with the effect of that defect (as Polonius would put it) on his reputation.

Hamlet does tell Guildenstern unmetaphorically that his wit is diseased; but this, of course, is part of his pretence of

madness. He uses one disease image which is more significant. In his soliloquy in III. 1, he shows that people refrain
from committing suicide because of their dread of something
after death, fear that they will be punished either for their
sins in general or for committing suicide. Hamlet continues:

> Thus conscience does make cowards of us all,
> And thus the native hue of resolution
> Is sickled o'er with the pale cast of thought,
> And enterprises of great pitch and moment
> With this regard their currents turn awry
> And lose the name of action.

Most critics would agree that these lines are an important
clue to the interpretation of the play; but, as Professor
Clemen points out,

> The customary interpretation of this passage, "reflection
> hinders action", does it an injustice. For Hamlet does not say
> "reflection hinders action", he simply utters this image. The
> fact that he does not utter that general maxim, but this image,
> makes all the difference. For this image is the unique and
> specific form of expression of the thought underlying it, it can-
> not be separated from it. If we say "reflection hinders action",
> we make a false generalization; we replace a specific formulation
> by an apothegm. And thereby we eradicate in this passage that
> quality which is peculiarly Shakespeare's or, what is more,
> peculiarly Hamlet's. Here the image does not serve the purpose
> of merely casting a decorative cloak about the thought; it is
> much rather an intrinsic part of the thought . . . "Native hue of
> resolution" suggests that Shakespeare viewed resolution as an
> innate human quality, not as a moral virtue to be consciously
> striven after.

It should be noted also, as G. R. Elliott and A. Sewell have
pointed out, that in the unmetaphorical statement which
precedes this image Hamlet refers not to himself in particular
but to all men:

> Thus conscience does make cowards *of us all*.

It is therefore plain from this examination that there is not a single disease image in the play which can be unequivocally applied to Hamlet. It cannot be doubted that the main function of this imagery is to underline the sin and corruption at the court of Denmark, the Queen's sin, Claudius's crime and his fear of retribution.

On the other hand, there are enough verbal echoes of Timothy Bright's *Treatise of Melancholy*[5] to make it reasonably certain that Shakespeare was consciously depicting Hamlet as suffering from melancholia; but one could not deduce this from the imagery alone.

[2]

The Elizabethans and Jacobeans lived under the shadow of death, not merely because of the frequent visitations of the plague. Marston and Tourneur, as well as Webster, were 'much possessed by death'. But *Hamlet* is the only one of Shakespeare's tragedies in which he considers what happens after death, both to the soul and the body. It is not merely that the Ghost comes from the grave to hint horrifically at the secrets of his prison-house, and that Hamlet himself wonders

> what dreams may come
> When we have shuffled off this moral coil:

but we are reminded continually of what Professor R. D. Altick has called 'the odour of mortality'.[6]

Hamlet speaks of the corpse of Polonius as 'the guts', and tells Claudius that Polonius is at supper, at the Diet of Worms:

> Not where he eats, but where he is eaten. A certain convocation of politic worms are e'en at him. Your worm is your only emperor for diet: we fat all creatures else to fat us, and we fat ourselves for maggots.

Hamlet proceeds to show how a king may go a progress through the guts of a beggar, and he tells Claudius that if he does not find Polonius's corpse within a month he will *nose* it.

The graveyard scene is designed not merely to provide a last expression of Hamlet's love for Ophelia, a transition between the self-reproaches of 'How all occasions' and the calm of 'The readiness is all', and an opportunity for screwing up Laertes's hatred of Hamlet to the sticking point, but also to underline the death imagery. Hamlet's meditation on the various skulls serves as a *memento mori:* he himself is about to die. He speaks of the way the gravedigger jowls a skull to the ground, 'as if 'twere Cain's jawbone, that did the first murder', of 'the pate of a politician', such as Polonius, of a courtier, such as Osric, 'chapless, and knock'd about the mazard with a sexton's spade', of the skull of a lawyer, and finally of Yorick's skull. Hamlet asks the gravedigger how long a man will lie in the earth ere he rot, and is told eight or nine years, although Yorick's skull, buried twenty-three years, still stinks. Then Hamlet traces the noble dust of Alexander till he finds it stopping a bung-hole:

> Alexander was buried, Alexander returneth to dust; the dust is earth; of earth we make loam; and why of that loam whereto he was converted might they not stop a beer-barrel?
> Imperious Caesar, dead and turned to clay,
> Might stop a hole to keep the wind away.
> O, that that earth which kept the world in awe
> Should patch a wall t'expel the winter's flaw!

All through the play there are words and images which reinforce the idea of corruption. Hamlet in his first soliloquy, feeling himself contaminated by the frailty of his mother, wishes that his sullied (or solid) flesh would melt – the image being suggested, probably, by dirty snow. He complains that 'things rank and gross in nature' possess the garden of the world. When he hears of the appearance of the Ghost, he suspects 'foul play' and 'foul deeds', and the Ghost re-iterates the word 'foul' and speaks of 'the fat weed That *rots* itself in ease on Lethe wharf'. He urges Hamlet not to *taint* his mind; and the Prince, in the previous scene, has remarked that foreigners *soil* the addition of the Danes with *swinish* phrase because of their vice of drunkenness. The Ghost again says that Denmark's ear is 'rankly abused' by the story of his death, and that Lust

> Will sate itself in a celestial bed
> And prey on garbage.

Laertes tells Ophelia that 'no soil not cautel doth besmirch The virtues of' Hamlet's will. Polonius speaks of his son's youthful vices as 'the taints of liberty', and he suggests that Reynaldo should lay 'slight sullies' on Laertes, 'As 'twere a thing a little soil'd i' the working'. In the next scene, Hamlet tells Polonius not to let Ophelia walk in the sun since 'the sun breeds maggots in a dead dog, being a good kissing carrion'. Later in the same scene he confesses to Rosencrantz and Guildenstern that the air seems to him but 'a foul and pestilent congregation of vapours', and that man seems to be a 'quintessence of dust'. Before the play-scene Hamlet tells Horatio that if his uncle's guilt is not revealed by his reactions to one speech in 'The Murder of Gonzago', his

> imaginations are as foul
> As Vulcan's stithy.

Claudius confesses that his offence is *rank*; Hamlet speaks of 'the rank sweat of an enseamed bed', and accuses his mother of 'making love Over the nasty sty'. He urges her not to 'spread the compost on the weeds To make them ranker'; he talks of 'rank corruption, mining all within'; and he describes the kisses of Claudius as 'reechy'. The smell of sin thus blends with the odour of corruption.

Contrasted with the stench of death and evil, as more than one critic has recognized, is the perfume of flowers continually associated with Ophelia. Hamlet's love for her is compared by Laertes to a sweet-smelling violet,

> The perfume and suppliance of a minute.

Ophelia retorts to Laertes's warnings by urging him not to tread 'the primrose path of dalliance'. She speaks of Hamlet, as he once was, as the 'rose of the fair state',

> That unmatch'd form and feature of blown youth;

Hamlet tells his mother that her adultery has taken off

> the rose
> From the fair forehead of an innocent love;

and Laertes, seeing Ophelia mad, addresses her as 'rose of May', Ophelia distributes flowers on her last appearance on the stage, and the last picture we have of her alive is weaving 'fantastic garlands'. Laertes, replying to the churlish priest, tells the bearers to lay Ophelia's body in the earth:

> And from her fair and unpolluted flesh
> May violets spring.

Finally, the Queen scatters flowers in the grave, giving 'sweets to the sweet'. The flower imagery might almost be designed to disprove the harsh views of Ophelia's character expressed by Madariaga and Rebecca West.

Wilson Knight calls his essay on the life-themes in *Hamlet*[7] 'Rose of May'; but as Ophelia is driven to madness and death, the flowers and perfumes associated with her do not seriously counterbalance the odour of corruption: they are merely like flowers on a grave.

[3]

The painted cheek of the harlot is an image of hypocrisy, of the contrast between appearance and reality, of the 'seeming' which Hamlet attacks on his first appearance. Polonius, instructing Ophelia to read a prayer-book to account for her solitude while she lies in wait for Hamlet, remarks

> that with devotion's visage
> And pious action we do sugar o'er
> The devil himself.

The King comments in words that are the first proof the audience is given of the truth of the Ghost's story:

> How smart a lash that speech doth give my conscience!
> The harlot's cheek, beautied with plastering art
> Is not more ugly to the thing that helps it
> Than is my deed to my most painted word.

In the same scene Hamlet takes up the theme. In the strange letter which Polonius had obtained from his daughter, Hamlet had spoken of 'the most beautified Ophelia', and now in his interview with her he implies illogically that since harlots paint, women who paint are harlots:

> I have heard of your paintings too, well enough; God hath given you one face, and you make yourselves another. You jig, you amble, and you lisp . . . and make your wantonness your ignorance.

Just before this he had told Ophelia that

> the power of beauty will sooner transform honesty from what it is to a bawd, than the force of honesty can translate beauty into his likeness.

Beauty is not truth, truth not beauty: beauty arouses sexual desire and so corrupts chastity. In the play-scene Hamlet accuses Ophelia of unchastity and in the closet-scene he explains why. There he tells his mother that since hell can mutiny in a matron's bones, the young can be expected to be licentious:

> To flaming youth let virtue be as wax
> And melt in her own fire; proclaim no shame
> When the compulsive ardour gives the charge,
> Since frost itself as actively doth burn,
> And reason pandars will.

In the same scene Hamlet tells Gertrude that her act of adultery

> takes off the rose
> From the fair forehead of an innocent love,
> And sets a blister there –

branded like a harlot.

Hamlet confesses at the end of Act II that 'like a whore' he has unpacked his heart with words and started cursing 'like a very drab'. In the graveyard scene, he instructs Yorick's skull:

> Now get you to my Lady's chamber, and tell her, let her paint
> an inch thick, to this favour she must come.

All through the play Hamlet is troubled by the contrast between appearance and reality, between his mother's apparent grief and her subsequent behaviour, and between the apparently innocent Ophelia and what he imagines her to be. The King too uses painting – in this case oil-painting, not cosmetics – as an image of falsity, when he asks Laertes:

> Are you like the painting of a sorrow,
> A face without a heart?

Both Laertes and Polonius warn Ophelia about the contrast between Hamlet's words of love and his dishonourable intentions. Polonius speaks of Hamlet's vows as

> Mere implorators of unholy suits,
> Breathing like sanctified and pious bonds[8]
> The better to beguile.

He means that Hamlet, under promise of marriage, intends to seduce Ophelia. Hamlet himself treats Polonius as 'a fishmonger' – a pandar – and Polonius speaks of 'loosing' his daughter to Hamlet.

This harlot imagery is linked with references to Fortune. The curious dialogue between Hamlet and his schoolfellows seems almost to have been inserted for the express purpose of making this connection:

GUILD.: On Fortune's cap we are not the very button.
HAM.: Nor the soles of her shoe?

ROS.: Neither, my lord.

HAM.: Then you live about her waist, or in the middle of her favours?

GUILD.: Faith, her privates we.

HAM.: In the secret parts of Fortune? O, most true, she is a strumpet.

Later in the same scene, in the extract from the Dido play, the First Player has two references to Fortune. After the murder of Priam, Aeneas cries:

> Out, out, thou strumpet, Fortune! All you gods,
> In general synod, take away her power;
> Break all the spokes and fellies from her wheel,
> And bowl the round nave down the hill of heaven,
> As low as to the fiends.

In his next speech, the Player says that whoever had seen Hecuba, the mobled queen,

> With tongue in venom steep'd,
> 'Gainst Fortune's state would treason have pronounc'd.

Hamlet tells Horatio that he admires him as one who is not passion's slave, an instrument on which the strumpet Fortune can play any tune she likes:

> A man that Fortune's buffets and rewards
> Hast ta'en with equal thanks; and blest are those
> Whose blood and judgment are so well comeddl'd
> That they are not a pipe for Fortune's finger
> To sound what stop she please.

Later in the same scene he again uses the image of the pipe as a means of showing Guildenstern that he cannot be so easily played upon:

> Why, look you now, how unworthy a thing you make of me! You would play upon me; you would seem to know my stops; you would pluck out the heart of my mystery; you would sound me from my lowest note to the top of my compass; and there is much music, excellent voice, in this little organ, yet cannot you make it speak. 'Sblood, do you think I am easier to be play'd on than a pipe?

There are other significant Fortune images in 'The Murder of Gonzago'. The Player King meditates on the changes and chances of this mortal life:

> This world is not for aye; nor 'tis not strange
> That even our loves should with our fortunes change;
> For 'tis a question left us yet to prove,
> Whether love lead fortune or else fortune love.

He goes on to give examples – of the desertion of a fallen great man by his favourites, of the upstart who makes friends of his former enemies. Hamlet similarly comments on the way the adult actors have lost their popularity because the child actors are all the rage, on the way courtiers like Rosencrantz and Guildenstern, who used to make fun of Claudius, now buy his portrait to wear round their necks, on the hope that a great man's memory may outlive his life half a year. The Player King, again, declares that

> Our wills and fates do so contrary run
> That our devices still are overthrown;
> Our thoughts are ours, their ends none of our own.

This links up with the words of Hamlet in the last scene of the play where, instead of the strumpet fortune or a blind fate, we have the idea of a providence which, unknown to us, directs our lives:

> There's a divinity that shapes our ends
> Rough-hew them how we will.

This conviction enables Hamlet to face what he thinks may be his death with the knowledge that an opportunity will be provided by God for him to execute justice on his father's murderer:

> We defy augury: there is a special providence in the fall of a
> sparrow. If it be now, 'tis not to come; if it be not to come, it
> will be now; if it be not now, yet it will come – the readiness is all.

There is one other Fortune image that remains to be mentioned. Rosencrantz, after the play-scene and the threat

to the life of Claudius, tells him how the lives of all his subjects depends on him. Majesty, he implies, is like the wheel
of the strumpet, Fortune:

> It is a massy wheel,
> Fix'd on the summit of the highest mount,
> To whose hugh spokes ten thousand lesser things
> Are mortis'd and adjoin'd; which when it falls,
> Each small annexment, petty consequence,
> Attends the boisterous ruin.

The performance of 'The Murder of Gonzago' gave
Shakespeare the opportunity of discussing a number of
things connected with the stage – the popularity of the child-
actors, the value of the Dido play, the moral effect of drama,
the besetting faults of actors, and the need to avoid exaggeration and unnaturalness.[9] At first sight some of the
dialogue may seem to have little relevance to the theme of
Hamlet, except in so far as it fills out the outlines of the
Prince's character and tastes. But Shakespeare never indulges
in topical allusions for their own sake,[10] and the passages
connected with acting link up with several themes in the
remainder of the play. The child actors 'cry out on the top of
question, and are most tyrannically clapp'd for't'. They
illustrate the fickleness of public taste, and Hamlet compares
it with the fickleness of the court with regard to Claudius.
They also illustrate the vice of over-acting, the lack of
temperance, to be discerned also in the actor who out-
herods Herod, the 'robustious, periwig-pated fellow' who
tears 'a passion to tatters, to very rags, to split the ears of the
groundlings'. Hamlet's ideal actor, like his ideal friend, is
not passion's slave, but passion's master.

> For in the very torrent, tempest, and, as I may say, whirlwind of
> passion, you must acquire and beget a temperance, that may give
> it smoothness.

Hamlet himself, after he had listened to Aeneas's speech,
works himself into an hysterical passion which is the very

opposite of what he recommends, as he soon recognizes and
confesses:

> Why, what an ass am I! This is most brave,
> That I, the son of a dear father murder'd,
> Prompted to my revenge by heaven and hell,
> Must, like a whore, unpack my heart with words,
> And fall a-cursing like a very drab,
> A stallion!

Hamlet praises the Dido play because it was 'well digested
in the scenes, set down with as much modesty as cunning'.
These qualities are not apparent in the extract we have of it,
and we must assume either that Hamlet was not an infallible
critic, or that Shakespeare was adopting an inflated epic style
in order to distinguish it from the very language of men used
in the rest of the play. 'Modesty' is a word Hamlet uses
again in his advice to the Players, who are urged not to overstep
the modesty of nature'. 'The purpose of playing', Hamlet
declares, 'is to hold, as 'twere, the mirror up to nature'. This
is true, not merely in the primary sense that the actor should
give an accurate and natural representation of human behaviour, but in the sense that the play itself should be a
faithful representation of life. In the previous scene Ophelia
had described Hamlet as 'the glass of fashion and the mould
of form', a courtier who served as a model for others. In the
closet-scene, Hamlet proposes to set up a glass in which the
Queen can see herself and her sin reflected, the glass taking
the form of a verbal description. Hamlet's portraits of his
father and of his uncle perform a similar function After his
struggle with Laertes at Ophelia's grave, Hamlet tells Horatio
that he is sorry he forgot himself:

> For by the image of my cause I see
> The portraiture of his.

Later in the same scene, parodying Osric's affected style,
Hamlet again uses a mirror image with regard to Laertes:

> But, in the verity of extolment, I take him to be a soul of great
> article, and his infusion of such dearth and rareness as, to make

true diction of him, his semblable is his mirror, and who else would trace him, his umbrage, nothing more.

Hamlet means that only in a mirror can Laertes find his equal.

There are many images in the play derived from the theatre. The portents in the first scene are described as 'prologue to the omen coming on'. Hamlet in the next scene speaks of the various outward signs of grief as 'actions that a man might play'; and, when he is discussing the way drunkenness detracts from his countrymen's achievement, 'though perform'd at height', a stage metaphor may be at the back of his mind. At the end of Act II, he speaks of himself as having received 'the cue for passion' and as being 'prompted' to his revenge. He tells Ophelia: 'I could interpret between you and your love, if I could see the puppets dallying'. He asks Horatio, after he has intervened in the play before the King, and recited some nonsense verses:

> Would not this, sir, and a forest of feathers . . . with two Provincial roses on my raz'd shoes, get me a fellowship in a cry of players, sir?

He calls Claudius 'a vice of kings' and 'a king of shreds and patches'. Gertrude, on hearing of Ophelia's madness, says that

> Each toy seems prologue to some great amiss.

The King tells Laertes that if the plot of the poisoned rapier fails,

> And that our drift look through our bad performance

they can fall back on the poisoned goblet. Hamlet, finding his death-warrant, and wondering how to extricate himself from the net, tells Horatio that

> Ere I could make a prologue to my brains,
> They had begun the play.

When Horatio warns him that news of the death of Rosencrantz and Guildenstern will shortly arrive from England, Hamlet replies:

> It will be short: the interim is mine.

Finally, when he is dying, Hamlet speaks to the courtiers standing by:

> You that look pale and tremble at this chance,
> That are but mutes or audience to this act.

No doubt this imagery drawn from the stage may partly be explained by Shakespeare's professional interests — 'the dyer's hand subdued to what it works in' — and partly by the performance of 'The Murder of Gonzago' in the central scene of the play. But the imagery also serves to illustrate the function of drama. Just as Claudius's conscience is caught by 'The Murder of Gonzago', so *Hamlet* itself may hold a mirror up to its audience; and just as Hamlet holds up a glass in which Gertrude may see herself, so Shakespeare holds up a glass in which we may see ourselves. The stage imagery, like that concerned with cosmetics, also brings out the contrast between appearance and reality, between seeming grief and heartfelt sorrow, between the fiction and the dream of passion and the essential passions of the heart. Above all, perhaps, the imagery raises one of the central problems of the play — why is it that Hamlet can put on an antic disposition, and take part, as dramatist and actor, in the play performed before the King, yet apparently be unable to avenge his father's death? Why is it he can 'act' and not *act*?

[4]

The largest group of images, however, and one of the most important, is that concerned with war and violence. These images were doubtless suggested, at least in part, by the

warlike activities of the elder Hamlet and of Fortinbras, and
partly too by the martial qualities, sometimes not sufficiently
recognized, of Prince Hamlet, which are underlined by the
rites of war ordered by Fortinbras for his obsequies. But the
dramatic function of the imagery is to emphasize that Claudius
and Hamlet are engaged in a duel to the death, a duel which
does in fact lead to both of their deaths.

Hamlet speaks of himself and his uncle as 'mighty opposites' between whose 'pass and fell incensed points' Rosencrantz and Guildenstern had come. All through the play the
war imagery reminds us of the struggle. Bernardo proposes
to 'assail' Horatio's ears which are 'fortified against' his
story. Claudius in his first speech tells of discretion fighting
with nature, and of the 'defeated joy' of his marriage. Later
in the scene he complains that Hamlet has a 'heart un-
fortified'. Laertes urges his sister to 'keep in the rear' of her
affection, 'Out of the shot and danger of desire'; and he
speaks of the 'calumnious strokes' sustained by virtue and
of the danger of youth's rebellion. Ophelia promises to take
Laertes's advice as a 'watchman' to her heart. Polonius in the
same scene carries on the martial imagery. He urges her to
set her 'entreatments at a higher rate Than a command to
parle'. In the next scene Hamlet speaks of the way 'the
o'ergrowth of some complexion' often breaks down 'the
pales and forts of reason'. The Ghost describes how the
poison used by Claudius

> Holds such an enmity with blood of man
> That swift as quicksilver it courses through
> The natural gates and alleys of the body.

The last line may have been suggested either by the assault
on a city or from sluices. The Ghost, below the stage, is
called a 'pioner'. Polonius compares the temptations of the
flesh to a 'general assault'. The noise of Ilium's fall 'takes
prisoner Pyrrhus' ear', and Pyrrhus's sword is 'rebellious
to his arm'. Hamlet thinks the actor would 'cleave the general
ear with horrid speech' and says that 'the clown shall make

hose laugh whose lungs are tickle a'th'sere' (i.e. easily set
off). He speaks of 'the slings and arrows of outrageous
ortune' and derides the King for being 'frighted with false
ire'. Rosencrantz talks of the 'armour of the mind', and
Claudius admits that his 'guilt defeats' his 'strong intent' of
repentance.

Hamlet fears that Gertrude's heart is so brazed by custom
hat it is 'proof and bulwark against sense', and he speaks of
he way 'the compulsive ardour' (sexual appetite) 'gives the
charge'. He tells his mother that he will outwit Rosencrantz
and Guildenstern:

> For 'tis the sport to have the engineer
> Hoist with his own petar; and't shall go hard
> But I will delve one yard below their mines
> And blow them at the moon.

The Ghost speaks of Gertrude's 'fighting soul' and Gertrude
ompares Hamlet's hairs to 'sleeping soldiers in the alarm'.

Claudius says that slander's whisper 'As level as the
annon to his blank Transports his pois'ned shot'; he tells
Gertrude that when sorrows come 'They come not single
pies But in battalions' and that Laertes's rebellion, 'Like to
murd'ring piece, in many places Gives me superfluous
eath'; and he is afraid that his plot against Hamlet will
blast in proof'.

Six of the images are taken from naval warfare. Polonius
ells Ophelia that he thought Hamlet meant to *wreck* her
II. i. 112) and he advises Laertes to *grapple* his friends to
is heart with hoops of steel' (I. iii. 63) and, in a later scene,
e proposes to *board* the Prince (II. ii. 169). Hamlet,
quibbling on 'crafts', tells his mother:

> O, 'tis most sweet
> When in one line two crafts directly meet.
> (III. iv. 290)

n the same scene, he speaks of the hell that *mutines* in a
natron's bones; and, in describing his voyage to England, he

tells Horatio that he 'lay Worse than the mutines in the bilboes'.

In addition to these war images there are two from archery[12] and a large number concerned with violent action – *sharked up*, *wrung*, *throw to earth*, *tear to tatters*, *break* and *lash* are a few examples. There are four images concerned with knives, as when the Ghost tells Hamlet that his visitation is to whet his 'almost blunted purpose'.

The images of war and violence should have the effect of counteracting some interpretations of the play, in which the psychology of the hero is regarded as the centre of interest. Equally important is the struggle between Hamlet and his uncle. Hamlet has to prove that the Ghost is not a devil in disguise, luring him to damnation, by obtaining objective evidence of Claudius' guilt. Claudius, for his part, is trying to pierce the secret of Hamlet's madness, using Rosencrantz and Guildenstern, Ophelia, and finally Gertrude as his instruments. Hamlet succeeds in his purpose, but in the very moment of success he enables Claudius to pierce the secret of his madness. Realizing that his own secret murder has come to light, Claudius is bound to arrange for Hamlet's murder; and Hamlet, knowing that the truth of his antic disposition is now revealed to his enemy, realizes that if he does not kill Claudius, Claudius will certainly kill him.

We have considered most of the patterns of imagery in the play – there are a few others which do not seem to throw much light on its meaning – and I think it will be agreed that just as Heilman's analysis of the imagery of *King Lear* showed that concentration on the iterative image of a tortured body gave a one-sided view of that play, so the various image-patterns we have traced in *Hamlet* show that to concentrate on the sickness imagery, especially if it is divorced from its context, unduly simplifies the play. I do not pretend that a study of all the imagery will necessarily provide us with one – and only one – interpretation; but it will at least prevent us from assuming that the play is wholly concerned with the psychology of the hero. It may also prevent us from adopting the view of several modern critics – Wilson Knight, Rebecca West, Madariaga, L. C. Knights – who all seem to debase Hamlet's character to the extent of depriving him of the status of a tragic hero. It may also prevent us from assuming that the complexities of the play are due to Shakespeares's failure to transform the melodrama he inherited, and to the survival of primitive traits in his otherwise sophisticated hero.

8 Image and Symbol in *Macbeth*

Una Ellis-Fermor, in her posthumous collection of essays, remarked that the peculiar feature of Shakespeare's art[1]

> and that I venture to consider the distinctive mode in dramatic writing, is to be found in his way of revealing the profound movements of character or the hidden logic of event. His readers receive so nearly direct an impression of these that the immediacy, which is one source of the theatre's compelling power, is undimmed in the transmitting. We remain continuously immersed in the character's experience; we never cease to be Macbeth; we are never invited to observe him.

There is a complementary passage in Maeterlinck's preface to his translation of *Macbeth*. He declared[2] that the mode of life in which the protagonists are

> steeped, penetrates and pervades their voices so clearly, animates and saturates their words to such a degree that we see it much better, more intimately, and more immediately than if they took the trouble to describe it to us. We, like themselves, living there with them, see from within the houses and the scenery in which they live; and we do not need to have those surroundings shown to us from without any more than they do. It is the countless presence, the uninterrupted swarm of all those images that form the profound life, the secret and almost unlimited first existence of the work. Upon its surface floats the dialogue necessary to the action. It seems to be the only one that our ears seize; but, in reality, it is to the other language that our instinct — our unconscious sensibility, our soul — listens; and if the spoken words

touch us more deeply than those of any other poet, it is because they are supported by a great host of hidden powers.

The 'hidden powers' are not supernatural but the images used, consciously or unconsciously, by the poet. In the present essay the outward action of the play will be taken for granted, and neither the dramatic effectiveness of individual scenes nor even the characters will be directly considered. We shall be concerned solely with the imagistic structure of the play and in the ways in which it deepens and subtilizes the purely dramatic structure. Although the patterns of imagery overlap, so that some lines will have to be considered more than once, it will be convenient to discuss the patterns under nine different headings.

[1]

The Powers of Light and Darkness

There is a contrast throughout the play between the powers of light and darkness. It has often been observed that many scenes are set in darkness. Duncan arrives at Inverness as night falls; he is murdered during the night; Banquo returns from his last ride as night is again falling; Lady Macbeth has light by her continually; and even the daylight scenes during the first part of the play are mostly gloomy in their setting – a blasted heath, wrapped in mist, a dark cavern. The murder of Duncan is followed by darkness at noon – 'dark night strangles the travelling lamp'. Before the murder Macbeth prays to the stars to hide their fires and Lady Macbeth invokes the night to conceal their crime:

> Come, thick night,
> And pall thee in the dunnest smoke of hell,
> That my keen knife see not the wound it makes,

> Nor heaven peep through the blanket of the dark
> To cry 'Hold, hold'.

Macbeth, as he goes towards the chamber of the sleeping Duncan, describes how

> o'er the one half-world
> Nature seems dead, and wicked dreams abuse
> The curtain'd sleep.

The word 'night' echoes through the first two scenes of the third act; and Macbeth invokes night to conceal the murder of Banquo:

> Come, seeling night,
> Scarf up the tender eye of pitiful day . . .
> Light thickens, and the crow
> Makes wing to th' rooky wood;
> Good things of day begin to droop and drowse,
> Whiles night's black agents to their preys do rouse.

In the scene in England and in the last act of the play – except for the sleep-walking scene – the darkness is replaced by light.

The symbolism is obvious. In many of these contexts night and darkness are associated with evil, and day and light are linked with good. The 'good things of day' are contrasted with 'night's black agents'; and, in the last act, day stands for the victory of the forces of liberation (V. iv. 1; V. vii. 27; V. viii. 37). The 'midnight hags' are 'the instruments of darkness'; and some editors believe that when Malcolm (at the end of Act IV) says that 'The Powers above / Put on their instruments' he is referring to their human instruments – Malcolm, Macduff and their soldiers.

Whether the Weird Sisters are witches, or norns (as Kittredge argued), or demons disguised as witches (as W.C. Curry thought) was left in doubt by the poet, and this doubt, to which each member of the audience can hazard an answer, adds to the sense of mysterious evil. As several critics have noticed,[3] this evil supernatural is balanced by the good supernatural of Edward the Confessor's powers of healing. Although the episode had a topical interest, since James I was reluctantly beginning to touch for the King's Evil, it was also thematically relevant. Edward, like the Weird Sisters, has the gift of prophecy; his 'healing benediction' and the blessings which 'hang about his throne' contrast with the curses of the ministers of darkness and of Macbeth himself.

The opposition between the good and evil supernatural is paralleled by similar contrasts between angel and devil, heaven and hell, truth and falsehood — and the opposites are frequently juxtaposed:

> This supernatural soliciting
> Cannot be ill; cannot be good.

> Merciful powers
> Restrain in me the cursed thoughts that nature
> Gives way to in repose!

> It is a knell
> That summons thee to heaven or to hell.

Several critics have pointed out the opposition in the play between night and day, life and death, grace and evil, a contrast which is reiterated more than four hundred times.[4]

The dominant figure in *Macbeth* is, as I have shown elsewhere,[5] antithesis; and this links up with the juxtaposition of opposites mentioned above. One kind of antithesis, moreover, is of particular importance: this is the opposition between desire and act mentioned by the Porter. Drink, he tells us, provokes the desire, but it takes away the performance. The gap between desire and performance is mentioned again and again by Macbeth and by his wife. Lady Macbeth, for example, urges, the evil spirits not to allow 'compunctious visitings of nature' to intervene between her purpose and its fulfilment. She asks her husband if he is afraid to be the same in 'act and valour' as he is in desire. Macbeth tells his wife that he has 'strange things' in his head 'that will to hand'.

The opposition takes the most striking form in the numerous passages contrasting eye and hand, culminating in Macbeth's cry –

> What hands are here? Ha! They pluck out mine eyes –

and in the scene before the murder of Banquo when the bloodstained hand is no longer Macbeth's, but Night's:

> Come, seeling night,
> Scarf up the tender eye of pitiful day,
> And with thy bloody and invisible hand
> Cancel and tear to pieces that great bond
> Which keeps me pale.

In the sleep-walking scene, Lady Macbeth's unavailing efforts to wash the smell of the blood from her hand symbolize the indelibility of guilt; and Angus in the next scene declares that Macbeth feels

> His secret murders sticking on his hands.

The soul is damned for the deeds committed by the hand.

It has recently been argued[6] that the opposition between the hand and eye provides the clearest explanation of that division in Macbeth between his clear 'perception of evil and rapt drift into evil'. Lawrence W. Hyman suggests that Macbeth is able to do the murder only because of the deep division between his head and his hand. The

> almost autonomous action of Macbeth's dagger, as if it had no connection with a human brain or a human heart, explains the peculiar mood that pervades the murder scene . . . As soon as he lays down the dagger, however, his 'eye' cannot help but see what the hand has done.

[2]

The Murder of Sleep

The Master of the *Tiger*, whose wife has offended the First
Witch, is threatened with the punishment of insomnia:[7]

> Sleep shall neither night nor day
> Hang upon his penthouse lid;
> He shall live a man forbid.

This is the first statement of a theme which acquires great
significance later in the play. After the murder of Duncan,
Macbeth complains of the way he and his wife

> sleep
> In the affliction of these terrible dreams
> That shake us nightly.

They lie 'on the torture of the mind . . . In restless ecstasy',
while Duncan in his grave 'After life's fitful fever . . . sleeps
well'. Lady Macbeth tells her husband after the banquet:

> You lack the season of all natures, sleep.

The anonymous Lord (III. vi) looks forward to the time
when, with the overthrow of the tyrant, they may give
'sleep to our nights'. Macbeth thinks that if he kills Macduff
he will 'sleep in spite of thunder'. Lady Macbeth, because of
'a great perturbation in nature' and 'slumbery agitation'
walks in her sleep and re-enacts the murders of Duncan,
Banquo and Lady Macduff.

> She is troubled with thick-coming fancies,
> That keep her from her rest.

The key passage in the theme of sleeplessness occurs just
after the murder of Duncan, and it was suggested to Shakespeare by a passage in Holinshed's *Chronicles* a few pages
before the account of Macbeth. After King Kenneth had

slain his nephew, he lived in continual fear, 'for so commeth it to passe, that such as are pricked in conscience for anie secret offense committed, have ever an unquiet mind'. A voice 'was heard as he was in bed in the night time to take this rest', telling him that his sin was known to God and that he and his issue would be punished for it.

> For even at this present are there in hand secret practises to dispatch both thee and thy issue out of the waie, that other maie injoy this kingdome which thou doost indevour to assure unto thine issue. The king, with this voice being stricken into great dread and terror, passed that night without anie sleep comming in his eies.

So Macbeth, after the murder, tells his wife:

> Methought I heard a voice cry, 'Sleep no more!
> Macbeth does murther Sleep', – the innocent Sleep;
> Sleep, that knits up the ravell'd sleave of care,
> The death of each day's life, sore labour's bath,
> Balm of hurt minds, great Nature's second course,
> Chief nourisher in life's feast . . .
> Still it cried, 'Sleep no more!' to all the house:
> 'Glamis hath murther'd Sleep, and therefore Cawdor
> Shall sleep no more, Macbeth shall sleep no more!'

The voice which Macbeth thinks comes from without is really the echo of his own conscience. As Bradley commented, the voice 'denounced on him, as if his three names gave him three personalities to suffer in, the doom of sleeplessness'; and, as Murry says'[8] 'we are straightway plunged into an abyss of metaphysical horror'. The murder of a sleeping guest, of a sleeping king, of a saintly old man, the murder, as it were, of sleep itself, carries with it the appropriate retribution of insomnia.

[3]

The Milk of Human Kindness

One group of images to which Cleanth Brooks called attention is an essay in *The Well-Wrought Urn* was that concerned with babes; and it has been suggested by Professor M. C. Bradbrook[9] that Shakespeare may have noticed in the general description of the manners of Scotland included in Holinshed's *Chronicles* that every Scotswoman 'would take intolerable pains to bring up and nourish her own children'; and H. N. Paul pointed out[10] that one of the topics selected for debate before James I, during his visit to Oxford in the summer of 1605, was whether a man's character was influenced by his nurse's milk. Whatever the origin of the images in *Macbeth* relating to breast-feeding, Shakespeare uses them for a very dramatic purpose. Their first appearance is in Lady Macbeth's invocation of the evil spirits to take possession of her:

> Come to my woman's breasts,
> And take my milk for gall, you murd'ring ministers,
> Wherever in your sightless substances
> You wait on nature's mischief.

They next appear in the scene where she incites Macbeth to the murder of Duncan:

> I have given suck, and know
> How tender 'tis to love the babe that milks me –
> I would, while it was smiling in my face,
> Have pluck'd my nipple from his boneless gums,
> And dash'd the brains out, had I so sworn as you
> Have done to this.

In between these two passages, Macbeth himself, debating whether to do the deed, admits that

> Pity, like a naked new-born babe
> Striding the blast,

would plead against it; and Lady Macbeth, when she first considers whether she can persuade her husband to kill Duncan, admits that she fears his nature:

> It is too full o' th' milk of human kindness
> To catch the nearest way.

Later in the play, Malcolm, when he is pretending to be worse even than Macbeth, says that he loves crime:

> Nay, had I pow'r, I should
> Pour the sweet milk of concord into hell,
> Uproar the universal peace, confound
> All unity on earth.

In these passages the babe symbolizes pity, and the necessity for pity, and milk symbolizes humanity, tenderness, sympathy, natural human feelings, the sense of kinship, all of which have been outraged by the murderers. Lady Macbeth can nerve herself to the deed only by denying her real nature; and she can overcome Macbeth's scruples only by making him ignore his feelings of human-kindness – his kinship with his fellowmen.

Cleanth Brooks suggests therefore that it is appropriate that one of the three apparitions should be a bloody child, since Macduff is converted into an avenger by the murder of his wife and babes. On one level, the bloody child stands for Macduff; on another level, it is the naked new-born babe whose pleadings Macbeth has ignored. Dame Helen Gardner took Cleanth Brooks to task for considering these images in relation to one another.[11] She argued that in his comments on 'Pity, like a naked new-born babe' he had sacrificed

> a Shakespearian depth of human feeling . . . by attempting to interpret an image by the aid of what associations it happens to arouse in him, and by being more interested in making symbols of babes fit each other than in listening to what Macbeth is saying. *Macbeth* is a tragedy and not a melodrama or a symbolic drama of retribution. The reappearance of 'the babe symbol' in the apparition scene and in Macduff's revelation of his birth has

distracted the critic's attention from what deeply moves the imagination and the conscience in this vision of a whole world weeping at the inhumanity of helplessness betrayed and innocence and beauty destroyed. It is the judgment of the human heart that Macbeth fears here, and the punishment which the speech foreshadows is not that he will be cut down by Macduff, but that having murdered his own humanity he will enter a world of appalling loneliness, of meaningless activity, unloved himself, and unable to love.

Although this is both eloquent and true, it does not quite dispose of Brooks's interpretation of the imagery. Dame Helen shows that, elsewhere in Shakespeare, 'a cherub is thought of as not only young, beautiful, and innocent, but as associated with the virtue of patience'; and that in the *Macbeth* passage the helpless babe and the innocent and beautiful cherub 'call out the pity and love by which Macbeth is judged. It is not terror of heaven's vengeance which makes him pause, but the terror of moral isolation.' Yet, earlier in the same speech Macbeth expresses fear of retribution in this life – fear that he himself will have to drink the ingredients of his own poisoned chalice – and his comparison of Duncan's virtues to 'angels, trumpet-tongued' implies a fear of judgment in the life to come, notwithstanding his boast that he would 'jump' it. We may assume, perhaps, that the discrepancy between the argument of the speech and the imagery employed is deliberate. On the surface Macbeth appears to be giving merely prudential reasons for not murdering Duncan; but Shakespeare makes him reveal by the imagery he employs that he, or his unconscious mind, is horrified by the thought of the deed to which he is being driven.

Dame Helen does not refer to the breast-feeding images – even Cleanth Brooks does not mention one of the most significant – yet all these images are impressive in their contexts and, taken together, they coalesce into a symbol of humanity, kinship and tenderness violated by Macbeth's crimes. Dame Helen is right in demanding that the precise meaning and context of each image should be considered, but wrong, I believe, in refusing to see any significance in the group as a whole. *Macbeth*, of course, is a tragedy; but I know of no valid definition of tragedy which would prevent the play from being at the same time a symbolic drama of retribution.

[4]

The Tailor and the Equivocator

The porter of Macbeth's castle pretends that he is acting as the Porter of Hell Gate, a character in some mystery plays,[12] and opening the gate to let in the damned souls – a farmer who had hanged himself in the expectation of plenty, an equivocator who committed treason, and a tailor who stole from his customers. All are damned like Macbeth, and they were all topical in 1606. Father Garnet, who had been hanged for complicity in the Gunpowder Plot, had defended equivocation, and he had gone under the name of Farmer.

Later in the play there is another passage about equivocation, which had a topical meaning for Shakespeare's original audience in the summer of 1606. Lady Macduff's son asks her what a traitor is.

LADY M.: Why, one that swears and lies.
SON: And be all traitors that do so?
LADY M.: Everyone that does so is a traitor, and must be hang'd.

But although Shakespeare was clearly alluding to topical events in these passages, and although they are anachronistic, it is important to realize that they have another dramatic function. In the last act of the play, when Birnam Wood appears to move to Dunsinane and one of the impossibilities comes to pass, Macbeth begins

> To doubt the equivocation of the fiend
> That lies like truth;

and when Macduff tells him how he was born, and he realizes that the promise that 'none of woman born' could harm him will not protect him after all, Macbeth speaks of the juggling, or equivocating, fiends,

> That keep the word of promise to our ear,
> And break it to our hope.

In attempting to destroy Macduff and his family, in accordance with the warning of the First Apparition, Macbeth had set in motion forces that eventually destroyed him.

The topical references therefore link up with the equivocation of the fiends; but there is a more subtle equivocation soon after the Porter scene when Macbeth expresses his feigned grief:

> Had I but died an hour before this chance
> I had liv'd a blessed time; for, from this instant,
> There's nothing serious in mortality.
> All is but toys: renown and grace is dead;
> The wine of life is drawn, and the mere less
> Is left this vault to brag of.

Macbeth's intention in this speech is to avert suspicion from himself by following his wife's advice to make their 'griefs and clamour roar upon' Duncan's death. But as he speaks the words, the audience knows that he has unwittingly spoken the truth. It is true that Macbeth would have been blessed if he had died before Duncan, that by the murder renown and grace are dead, and that for him life would be meaningless, a succession of empty tomorrows, a tale told by an idiot. It is only later that Macbeth realizes to the full the truth of his words, that instead of lying like truth, he has told the truth while intending to deceive.

The third of the imaginary knockers at the gate is an English tailor.[13] Ever since Caroline Spurgeon published her findings on Shakespeare's imagery, it has been known that the iterative image of *Macbeth* is of a man in ill-fitting garments. But there are two qualifications which must be made. In the first place, there are a number of tailoring images apart from those relating to ill-fitting garments. In the description of Macbeth's fight with Macdonwald, the Sergeant says that 'he unseam'd him from the nave to the chaps', like a tailor ripping a garment in two. Macbeth describes the daggers of the chamberlains as 'Unmannerly breech'd with gore' and urges his fellow-thanes to 'put on manly readiness', while Macduff in the last act says 'Put we on Industrious soldiership'. The second qualification which must be made of Caroline Spurgeon's interpretation is that there is no reason to think that Shakespeare thought of Macbeth as a little man in garments which were too big for him. The point about the image, as Cleanth Brooks demonstrated, is that the garments did not belong to him. When he is hailed as Thane of Cawdor, he asks 'Why do you dress me in borrow'd robes?' Shortly afterwards, Banquo tells Ross and Angus:

> New honours come upon him,
> Like our strange garments, cleave not to their mould
> But with the aid of use.

Macbeth argues that he should not murder Duncan so soon after gaining a great reputation in the wars:

> I have bought
> Golden opinions from all sorts of people,
> Which would be worn now in their newest gloss,
> Not cast aside so soon.

Lady Macbeth retorts with an adaptation of the same image

> Was the hope drunk
> Wherein you dress'd yourself?

In the last act of the play, both Caithness and Angus speak of Macbeth's ill-fitting garments:

> He cannot buckle his distemper'd cause
> Within the belt of rule.

> Now does he feel his title
> Hang loose about him, like a giant's robe
> Upon a dwarfish thief.

The contrast between the man and his clothes is a symbol
of the hypocrisy to which Macbeth is committed. He has to
'look like the innocent flower, But be the serpent under't'; he
has to 'mock the time with fairest show' and make his face
a vizard to his heart; and in the last act he complains of the
hypocritical loyalty – the mouth-honour – he receives from
his own subjects. Life itself, he declares, is a walking shadow,
a poor player,

> That struts and frets his hour upon the stage
> And then is heard no more. It is a tale
> Told by an idiot, full of sound and fury,
> Signifying nothing.

This is a bitterer version of Prospero's lines when he
interrupts the masque. 'We are such stuff as dreams are
made on'. Macbeth thinks of us acting – and not acting
well – in a blood and-thunder melodrama written by a crazy
poet, a sort of Nathaniel Lee. It is twice removed from reality
by the badness of the play and the badness of the acting.

There are intimations of damnation earlier in the play, as
in the Porter scene and in Macduff's words:

> Shake off this downy sleep, death's counterfeit,
> And look on death itself! Up, up, and see
> The great doom's image.

There is a valuable comment on these lines in a recent book
on T. S. Eliot's plays.[14] Mr Jones suggests that Macduff,
standing upon the upper stage, calls up the 'sleepers of the
house' to witness the 'great doom's image,' the Last Judgment. The characters, 'flocking on to the stage by every
entrance', and wearing night shirts, like shrouds, 'present a
visual resemblance to the spirits rising from their graves on
the Last Day'.

> As from your graves rise up and walk like sprites.

Lady Macbeth asks:

> What's the business
> That such a hideous trumpet calls to parley
> The sleepers of the house?

Shakespeare calls the alarm-bell, which Lady Macbeth has really heard, a trumpet, to remind us again of the Last Judgment.

[5]

Sickness and Medicine

Another important group of images is concerned with sickness and medicine, and it is significant that they all appear in the last three acts of the play after Macbeth has ascended the throne; for Scotland is suffering from the disease of tyranny, which can be cured, as fever was thought to be cured, only by bleeding or purgation. The tyrant, indeed, uses sickness imagery of himself. He tells the First Murderer that so long as Banquo is alive he wears his health but sickly; when he hears of Fleance's escape he exclaims 'Then comes my fit again'; and he envies Duncan in the grave, sleeping after life's fitful fever, since life itself is one long illness. In the last act of the play a doctor, called in to diagnose Lady Macbeth's illness, confesses that he cannot

> minister to a mind diseas'd,
> Pluck from the memory a rooted sorrow,
> Raze out the written troubles of the brain,
> And with some sweet oblivious antidote
> Cleanse the stuff'd bosom of that perilous stuff
> Which weights upon the heart.

Macbeth then professes to believe that what is amiss with Scotland is not his own evil tyranny but the English army of liberation:

> What rhubarb, cyme, or what purgative drug
> Would scour these English hence?

On the other side, the victims of tyranny look forward to wholesome days when Scotland will be freed. Malcolm says that Macbeth's very name blisters their tongues and he laments that 'each new day a gash' is added to Scotland's wounds. In the last act Caithness refers to Malcolm as 'the medicine of the sickly weal',

> And with him pour we in our country's purge
> Each drop of us.

Lennox adds:

> Or so much as it needs
> To dew the sovereign flower and drown the weeds.

Macbeth is the disease from which Scotland is suffering; Malcolm, the rightful king, is the *sovereign* flower, both royal and curative. Macbeth, is it said,

> Cannot buckle his distemper'd cause
> Within the belt of rule.

James I, in *A Counter-blast to Tobacco*, referred to himself as 'the proper Phisician of his Politicke-bodie', whose duty it was 'to purge it of all those diseases, by Medicines meet for the same'. It is possible that Shakespeare had read this pamphlet, although, of course, disease-imagery is to be found in most of the plays written about this time. In *Hamlet* and *Coriolanus* it is applied to the body politic, as indeed it was by many writers on political theory. Shakespeare may have introduced the reference to the King's Evil to suggest that the evil from which Scotland is suffering can be cured only by the touch of the rightful and religious king, Malcolm.

[6]

Man and Beast

There is less animal imagery in *Macbeth* than in *Othello* or *King Lear*, but the references to animals and birds do much to create the atmosphere of the play. The animals associated with the Weird Sisters, for example, are used to give a colouring of mystery and evil to the scenes in which they appear: the grey cat and toad in the first scene, the swine and the tailless rat in the third, and the gruesome ingredients of the cauldron in IV. 1 – toad, snake, newt, frog, bat, adder, blind-worm, lizard, owl, dragon, wolf, shark, goat, tiger, baboon and sow.

Macbeth and Banquo are compared to lions and eagles. The croaking raven Lady Macbeth imagines welcoming Duncan's arrival under her battlements is contrasted with the temple-haunting martlet described by Banquo. Lady Macbeth urges her husband to be like the proverbial serpent hidden under the innocent flower. The murder of Duncan is accompanied by the howling of a wolf, the scream of an owl, and the noise of crickets; and later we hear of portentous happenings – a falcon killed by an owl, Duncan's horses eating each other.

As several critics have noted, Macbeth's description of different kinds of dogs conveys to us a sense of order in diversity, an order which is overthrown by unnatural crimes. The passage was inserted not mainly because of James I's proclamation on the subject, but to stress the order existing in nature – *naturae benignitas* – 'the diverse functions and variety within a single species testifying to an overruling harmony and design'; but, ironically, the speech is used as an incitement to murder. In his fear of retribution Macbeth declares that they have 'scorch'd the snake, not kill'd it', and his mind is full of scorpions. Later he speaks of Banquo as the 'grown serpent'. The murder of Banquo is preceded by references to bat, beetle, and the crow making wing to the rooky wood, and Macbeth invokes night to 'seel up the tender eye of pitiful day', as the eyelids of a hawk were sewn up. At the end of the speech 'night's black agents to their preys do rouse'. In the banquet scene, Macbeth, terrified of the ghost, declares that he would not be afraid of bear, rhinoceros or tiger, and he speaks of the way 'maggot-pies and choughs and rooks' have 'brought forth the secret'st man of blood'.

In the scene of Lady Macduff's murder, she compares her children to baby wrens; and her son, alluding perhaps to the way the fowls of the air are fed by our heavenly father, declares that without an earthly father he will live as birds do. Finally, when Macduff encounters Macbeth, he addresses him as 'hell-hound' — and our thoughts return to the catalogue of dogs in the earlier scene:

> hounds, and greyhounds, mongrels, spaniels, curs,
> Choughs, water-rugs and demi-wolves.

The animal imagery is linked with the question of what constitutes manliness. In the first act of the play, the epithets applied to Macbeth all emphasize his courage. He is *brave*, *Valour's minion*, *valiant cousin*, *Bellona's bridegroom*, *noble*, *worthiest cousin*, and *peerless*. Lady Macbeth admits he is without the 'illness' (the evil) which should attend ambition. When she chastizes him with the valour of her tongue, her main argument is that only cowardice could prevent him from murdering Duncan:

> Art thou afeard . . . ?

> Wouldst thou . . .
> . . . live a coward in thine own esteem,
> Letting 'I dare not' wait upon 'I would',
> Like the poor cat i'the adage?

Macbeth protests:

> I dare do all that may become a man;
> Who dares do more is none.

Lady Macbeth asks scornfully:

> What beast was't then
> That made you break this enterprize to me?
> When you durst do it, then you were a man;
> And, to be more than what you were, you would
> Be so much more the man.

When Macbeth finally consents, he praises his wife's masculinity:

> Bring forth men-children only;
> For thy undaunted mettle should compose
> Nothing but males.

After the murder, when Macbeth is afraid to think on the deed, or to carry the daggers back to Duncan's chamber, Lady Macbeth upbraids his childishness in fearing a painted devil, and sneers at the whiteness of his heart. After this, it is natural that Macbeth should express the idea of 'Let us get dressed' as 'Let's briefly put on manly readiness', and that in his colloquy with the murderers of Banquo he should pretend that manliness meant willingness to commit murder. He asks ironically if they are 'so gospell'd To pray for this good man and for his issue'. The reference is to the Sermon on the Mount:

> Love your enemies; blesse them that curse you; doe good to them that hate you, and pray for them which hurt you, and persecute you.

The First Murderer replies: 'We are men, my liege'. Macbeth answers, as we have seen, that there are different sorts of men as there are different sorts of dogs. In the Banquet scene, Lady Macbeth tries to recall her husband to his senses by asking 'Are you a man?' and 'What! Quite unmann'd in folly?' Macbeth, echoing his previous boast, declares 'What man dare, I dare'; and, on the disappearance of the ghost, he says:

> Why, so; being gone,
> I am a man again.

At the end of the scene, Macbeth supposes that his delusions,
– his 'strange and self-abuse '– are due to his immaturity in
crime: 'We are yet but young in deed'. With greater experience, he thinks, he will become suitably tough and manly.

The theme of manliness is expressed by other characters.
When Macduff vows to avenge the death of his family,
Malcolm comments: 'This tune goes manly'; and Ross,
reporting Young Siward's death, tells his father that though
little more than a boy in years, 'like a man he died'. But the
manliness Lady Macbeth requires of her husband is not
bravery, but insensibility; not nobility, but imperviousness
to conscience; not to be more than a man, but less than a man.
It is appropriate, therefore, that near the end, as the avengers
close in, Macbeth should compare himself to a baited bear,
and that he should die like a hunted beast. His words –

> I dare do all that may become a man,
> Who dares do more is none –

are borne out by the event. Although to all but his wife he is
outstandingly brave, he becomes a haunted and terrified man
by performing the very deeds which were intended to demonstrate his bravery to his wife. When he hears the prophecy of
the witches he starts and seems to fear. He is terrified by the
temptation of murder,

> that suggestion
> Whose horrid image doth unfix my hair
> And make my seated heart knock at my ribs
> Against the use of nature.

His very fears are the reflection of his conscience. Lady
Macbeth is able to seduce him because he is afraid of being
thought afraid. It is only in the last act, when his conscience is
quite deadened, that Macbeth can speak of his fears in the
past tense:

> I have supp'd full with horrors:
> Direness, familiar to my slaughterous thoughts,
> Cannot once start me.

[7]

Blood will have Blood

John Masefield once remarked that the subject of *Macbeth* is blood; and from the appearance of the bloody sergeant in the second scene of the play to the last scene of all, we have a continual vision of blood. Macbeth's sword in the battle 'smok'd with bloody execution'; he and Banquo seemed to 'bathe in reeking wounds'; the Sergeant's 'gashes cry for help'. The second Witch comes from the bloody task of killing swine. The visionary dagger is stained with 'gouts of blood'. Macbeth, after the murder, declares that not all great Neptune's ocean will cleanse his hands:

> this my hand will rather
> The multitudinous seas incarnadine,
> Making the green one red.

Duncan is spoken of as the fountain of his sons' blood; his wounds

> look'd like a breach in nature
> For ruin's wasteful entrance.

The world had become a 'bloody stage'. Macbeth, before the murder of Banquo, invokes the 'bloody and invisible hand' of night. We are told of the twenty trenched gashes on Banquo's body and his ghost shakes his 'gory locks' at Macbeth, who is convinced that 'blood will have blood'. At the end of the banquet scene, he confesses wearily that he is 'stepp'd so far' in blood, that

> should I wade no more,
> Returning were as tedious as go o'er.

The Second Apparition, a bloody child, advises Macbeth to be 'bloody, bold, and resolute'. Malcolm declares that Scotland bleeds,

> and each new day a gash
> Is added to her wounds.

Lady Macbeth, sleep-walking, tries in vain to remove the 'damned spot' from her hands:

> Here's the smell of the blood still. All the perfumes of Arabia
> will not sweeten this little hand.

In the final scene, Macbeth's severed head is displayed on a pole. As Jan Kott has recently reminded us in *Shakespeare Our Contemporary*, the subject of the play is murder, and the prevalence of blood ensures that we shall never forget the physical realities in metaphysical overtones.

[8]

Time and Order

Macbeth is not the only one of Shakespeare's works in which time is particularly significant. It is the main theme of the *Sonnets*, where it is regarded as the enemy of love and beauty; it is the subject of Lucrece's tirade; and it is relevant to the interpretation of *Troilus and Cressida*. As several critics have recognized, Time is of central importance in *Macbeth*. He is promised by the Weird Sisters that he will be king 'hereafter' and Banquo wonders if they 'can look into the seeds of time'. Macbeth, tempted by the thought of murder, declares that 'Present fears / Are less than horrible imaginings' and decides that 'Time and the hour runs through the roughest day'. Lady Macbeth says she feels 'The future in the instant'. In his soliloquy in the last scene of Act I, Macbeth speaks of himself as 'here upon this bank and shoal of time', time being contrasted with the sea of eternity. He pretends that he would not worry about the future, or about the life to come, if he could be sure of success in the present; and his wife implies that the conjunction of time and place for the murder will never recur. Just before the murder, Macbeth reminds himself of the exact time and place, so that he can relegate (as Stephen Spender suggests)[15] 'the moment to the past from which it will never escape into the future'. Macbeth is troubled by his inability to say amen, because he dimly realizes he has forfeited the possibility of blessing and because he knows that he has become 'the deed's creature'. The nightmares of the guilty pair and the return of Banquo from the grave symbolize the haunting of the present by the past. When Macbeth is informed of his wife's death, he describes how life has become for him a succession of meaningless days, the futility he has brought upon himself by his crimes:

> To-morrow, and to-morrow, and to-morrow,
> Creeps in this petty pace from day to day
> To the last syllable of recorded time,
> And all our yesterdays have lighted fools
> The way to dusty death.

At the very end of the play, Macduff announces that with the death of the tyrant 'The time is free' and Malcolm promises, without 'a large expense of time' to do what is necessary ('which would be planted newly with the time') and to bring back order from chaos 'in measure, time, and place'.

From this last speech, it can be seen that *Macbeth* can be regarded as a play about the disruption of order through evil, and its final restoration.[16] It begins with what the witches call a hurly-burly and ends with the restoration of order by Malcolm. Order is represented throughout by the bonds of loyalty; and chaos is represented by the powers of darkness with their upsetting of moral values ('Fair is foul and foul is fair'). The witches can raise winds to fight against the churches, to sink ships and destroy buildings: they are the enemies both of religion and of civilization. Lady Macbeth invokes the evil spirits to take possession of her; and, after he murder of Duncan, Macbeth's mind begins to dwell on universal destruction. He is willing 'to let the frame of things disjoint, both the worlds suffer' merely to be freed from his nightmares. Again, in his conjuration of the witches in the cauldron scene, he is prepared to risk absolute chaos, 'even till destruction sicken' through surfeit, rather than not obtain an answer. In his last days, Macbeth is 'aweary of the sun' and he wishes 'the estate of the world' were undone. Order in Scotland, even the moral order in the universe, can be restored only by his death. G. R. Elliott contrasts[17] the threefold hail with which Malcolm is greeted at the end of the play with the threefold hail of the witches on the blasted heath: they mark the destruction of order and its restoration.

All through the play ideas of order and chaos are juxtaposed. When Macbeth is first visited by temptation his single state of man' is shaken and 'nothing is but what is not'. In the next scene Shakespeare presents ideas of loyalty, duty, and the reward of faithful service, in contrast both to the treachery of the dead Thane of Cawdor, and to the treacherous thoughts of the new thane. Lady Macbeth prays that 'no compunctious visitings of nature' shall prevent her fell purpose; and in the next scene in which Duncan appears he describes the beautiful setting of Macbeth's castle. The main purpose of this description is for dramatic irony – the setting contrasting with the deed which the audience know is about to be enacted there – but it also links up with the natural images of growth used by Duncan in the previous scene. We are reminded, as Lady Macbeth welcomes the King, of the duties of hospitality soon to be violated.

Before the murder, Macbeth reminds himself that he is the kinsman, the subject and the host of his intended victim; Duncan sends a diamond to his 'most kind hostess'; and Banquo speaks of his franchised bosom and clear allegiance. The vision of the dagger repeats in a more intense form the experience that in the first act had shaken Macbeth's single state of man; and later he is afraid that the stones will cry out against the unnaturalness of the murder. At the moment

when the murder is being committed, there is a violent
storm:

> Lamentings heard i' the air, strange screams of death,
> And prophesying with accents terrible
> Of dire combustion and confused events
> New hatch'd to the woeful time –

possibly an allusion to dire the combustion of the gunpowder
plot, but carrying also a more universal significance – an
unnatural darkness hides the sun, a falcon is killed by an owl,
and Duncan's horses eat each other. As Ross emphasizes,
the deed is against nature.

The third act is devoted to the murder of Banquo and the
appearance of his ghost at the banquet. In the first scene he is
invited as the chief guest to the solemn supper, the great
feast, with which Macbeth's coronation is being celebrated.

In the second scene Macbeth's mind begins to dwell on
universal destruction. He is willing to 'let the frame of
things disjoint, both the worlds suffer', rather than endure
the terrible dreams that shake him every night; and he envies
Duncan in his grave, safe from treachery and foreign in-
vasion. In the Banquet scene, stress is laid on its ceremonious-
ness. In the very first line Macbeth refers to the 'degrees' of
the guests, and this contrasts with his wife's abrupt dismissal
of the guests when the feast is broken up: 'Stand not upon
the order of your going'. Lady Macbeth reminds her husband that 'the sauce to meat is ceremony'. The 'twenty
trenched gashes' on Banquo's head are each 'a death to
nature' – enough to kill him and to upset the natural order.
As soon as Macbeth pretends to wish that Banquo were
present, the ghost appears on two occasions. When her
guests are dismissed, Lady Macbeth tells her husband:

> You have displac'd the mirth, broke the good meeting
> With most admir'd disorder.

The anonymous Lord who discusses the state of the realm
with Lennox prays for the return of normal conditions of
life, disrupted by Macbeth's tyranny:

> Give to our tables meat, sleep to our nights,
> Free from our feasts and banquets bloody knives,
> Do faithful homage and receive free honours:
> All which we pine for now.

In the scene in England Malcolm's self-accusations – in particular his pretence of wishing to uproar the universal peace and confound all unity on earth – are disorders contrasted with the virtues he pretends not to have, with the virtues he does have, and with the miraculous powers of the pious Edward. Order is restored by the overthrow of the tyrant.

[9]

The Hidden Links

One characteristic of the style of *Macbeth* remains to be noted. Concealed puns provide an illogical reinforcement of the logical sequence of thought, so that the poetic statement strikes us almost as a remembrance – as Keats said that poetry should do; such puns often link together unrelated imagery and act as solvents for mixed metaphors; and they make the listener aware of a complex of ideas which enrich the total statement, even though they do not come into full consciousness.[18]

A few examples may be given of the linking of images by means of hidden quibbles, of which the poet himself may have been unconscious. In Macbeth's address to night, just before the murder of Banquo –

> Come, seeling Night,
> Scarf up the tender eye of pitiful Day,
> And, with thy bloody and invisible hand,
> Cancel, and tear to pieces, that great bond
> Which keeps me pale! –

F

the word *seeling* — a term in falconry, referring to the
stitching up of hawks' eyelids — suggested the word *bond* by
way of *sealing*; and *bond* suggested *pale*, since Macbeth's
white face resembled parchment.

In the preceding scene Macbeth tells the murderers:

> Now, if you have a station in the file
> Not i' th' worst rank of manhood, say 't.

Here *file* in the old sense of catologue suggested *rank*, by way
of *file* in the military sense. There is another example in the
last act of the play when Macbeth remarks that

> this push
> Will cheer me ever, or dis-seat me now;

where *cheer* suggested *dis-seat* through the intermediate *chair*.
In the scene in England, Macduff tells Malcolm:

> A good and virtuous nature may recoil
> In an imperial charge.

This is generally taken to mean 'give way under pressure
from a monarch'. The image may be either that of retiring
before the onslaught of a superior force, or that of a gun
which recoils when the charge is great. *Charge* can thus mean
'duty', 'onslaught' or 'gunpowder' and was doubtless suggested to Shakespeare by the double meaning of 'recoil'.

A more complicated example is to be found in Act II, just
after the murder of Duncan:

> Macbeth does murder Sleep — the innocent Sleep;
> Sleep, that knits up the ravell'd sleave of care,
> The death of each day's life, sore labour's bath,
> Balm of hurt minds, great Nature's second course,
> Chief nourisher in life's feast; —

In the First Folio the word 'sleave' is spelt 'sleeve'. A few
commentators have therefore assumed that the clause means
'knits up the frayed sleeve'; but most editors have explained
'sleave' as 'a slender filament of silk obtained by separating
a thicker thread'. But the word also means 'coarse silk', for

Florio translates *sfilazza* as 'any kinde of ravelled stuffe' or 'sleave silke'. Macbeth's phrase would then mean simply 'knits up the tangled silk'. Another phrase in this passage is ambiguous. 'Great Nature's second course' means the second race or career after the death of each day; but, by a quibble, it suggested to the poet the joint or roast, the second course of a meal. The succeeding phrase, 'Chief nourisher in life's feast', was probably suggested by another meaning of *ravell'd*: ravelled bread was made from flour and bran; and wholemeal bread, the staff of life, could be regarded as the chief nourisher.

A still more complicated example is afforded by Macbeth's soliloquy in Act I, Scene 7:

> If it were done, when 'tis done, then 'twere well
> It were done quickly: if th'assassination
> Could trammel up the consequence, and catch
> With his surcease success; that but this blow
> Might be the be-all and the end-all – here,
> But here, upon this bank and shoal of time,
> We'd jump the life to come.

These seven lines contain a large number of ambiguities. 'Trammel up' can mean 'entangle, as in a net', 'fasten the legs of horses together, so that they cannot stray', or possibly 'hang up', a trammel being an iron device for suspending pots over a fire. 'Surcease' may be a legal term, derived from the Old French *sursis*, meaning the stay of proceedings – in which case the pronoun *his* refers to *consequence*; but as Shakespeare elsewhere uses the word as a euphemism for *die* –

> If they surcease to be that should survive –

t may mean *death* here, the pronoun referring to Duncan. (In *Romeo and Juliet* and *Coriolanus*, 'surcease' is used simply as a synonym for cease.) 'Success' may be used in its ordinary modern sense, as usually in Shakespeare, or it may mean *consequence* or *succession* (to the throne). Although editors have plumped for a single meaning of each of these

words, Shakespeare and his audience would have had alternative meanings at the back of their minds.

A more significant phrase is 'bank and shoal of time'.
Shoal is Theobald's generally accepted emendation for the
Schoole of the First Folio. He explained: 'This Shallow, this
narrow Ford, of humane Life, opposed to the great Abyss of
Eternity'. One of two critics, however, have defended the
Folio reading, taking *bank* to mean school bench. Elwin, for
example, paraphrased the lines:

> If here only, upon this bench of instruction, in this school of
> eternity, I could do this without bringing these, my pupil days,
> under suffering, I would hazard its effect on the endless life to
> come.

The late S. L. Bethell, who was one of the few modern critics
to defend the Folio reading, assumed that *bank* was the
judicial, not the school, bench (O.F. *banc*). He argued that
'Time is thus seen as the period of judgment, testing, or
"crisis", and as a school'.[19] If we reject this interpretation, as
I think we must, it is because, despite Bethell's denial,
Shakespeare often couples words together of similiar meaning
like 'bank and shoal' and because the preposition 'upon' fits
bank, but not *school*. The true explanation is that we have here
another example of a hidden quibble. Shakespeare intended
shoal rather than school; but the spelling *Schoole* would
lead naturally to *teach*, *instructions* and *taught* a few lines
later, while the alternative meaning of *bank* would suggest
judgment:

> But in these cases
> We still have judgment here, that we but teach
> Bloody instructions, which being taught, return
> To plague th'inventor.

In the same soliloquy the 'Angels, trumpet-tongued' are
closely followed by the image of

> Pity, like a naked new-born babe,
> Striding the blast;

here the blast of the storm was clearly suggested by the blast of the trumpet.

A few other examples may be given. When Macbeth describes the discovery of Duncan's murder, the phrase 'breach in nature' suggested the word used to describe the daggers, 'Unmannerly breech'd with gore'. In the scene in England, Macduff, hearing of Malcolm's distrust, exclaims:

> Bleed, bleed, poor country
> Great tyranny, lay thou thy basis sure,
> For goodness dare not check thee: wear thou thy wrongs
> The title is affear'd.

The last word is nearly always emended to 'affeer'd', meaning *confirmed*; and no doubt the primary meaning of the passage is that the title of Macbeth is confirmed by the cowardice of the good. But 'the title is affear'd' may also bear the meaning 'Malcolm, the rightful king, is afraid'. Finally in, Act V, Scene 2, Menteith speaks of the army of liberation:

> Revenges burn in them: for their dear causes
> Would to the bleeding and the grim alarm
> Excite the mortified man.

The word *burn*, associated with fever, suggested *dear causes*; for this phrase could mean 'sore diseases' as well as 'grievous wrongs' or 'grounds of action'.

Macbeth is not the only play in which images are linked by hidden puns. Examples can be found as early as *Romeo and Juliet* and as late as *The Tempest*; yet the peculiar density of the style of Macbeth, recognized by many critics, appears to be due to this characteristic of Shakespeare's style.

9 The High Roman Fashion

Antony and Cleopatra has been interpreted in radically different ways. On the one hand, Morley, Quiller-Couch, Kolbe and Dickey assume that the theme of the play is *All for Lust: or the World Ill-Lost*, though some of these critics would agree with Professor L. C. Knights when he admits that Shakespeare evokes sympathy and admiration for what, 'in his final judgment, is discarded or condemned'. He adds 'it is perhaps this that makes the tragedy so sombre in its realism, so little comforting to the romantic imagination'. Other critics – G. Wilson Knight, John Dover Wilson and Harold S. Wilson – regard the play as an affirmation of love. Bernard Shaw and L. L. Schücking argued that the characterization is inconsistent and that the Cleopatra of the last act has undergone an impossible transformation. Lastly, John F. Danby and Ernest Schanzer have tried to show that *Antony and Cleopatra* is a problem play in which two conflicting views, the Roman and the Egyptian, are juxtaposed.[1]

A consideration of the imagery may help us to decide between these rival interpretations. The four main groups of images in the play are concerned with (1) the world and the heavenly bodies; (2) eating; (3) bodily movement; (4) melting. These groups are reinforced by the iteration of words relating to nobility, to the gods, to serpents' poison, to kingship, and to fortune.[2]

The main function of the cosmic imagery is to show that on the action of the play depends the fate of the Roman

world, and hence the whole course of history. Whether the
world was well, or ill, lost remains to be discussed, but
Antony certainly loses the world. The theme is sounded in
the very first scene both by Antony's critics and by himself.
Philo announces Antony's first entrance with the words:

> Take but good note, and you shall see in him
> The triple pillar of the world transform'd
> Into a strumpet's fool

Antony in his second speech tells Cleopatra that if she is to
set a bourn how far to be beloved, she must 'needs find out
new heaven, new earth'; and a few lines later he dismisses the
Roman world:

> Let Rome in Tiber melt, and the wide arch
> Of the rang'd empire fall! Here is my space.
> Kingdoms are clay; our dungy earth alike
> Feeds beast as man.

In the same speech he binds the world to witness that their
mutual love is peerless.

In the next scene, Antony decides to leave Egypt because
of the danger of Sextus Pomeius to 'the sides of the world'.
Cleopatra in the third scene speaks of Antony as 'the greatest
soldier of the world', and in the fifth scene she calls him 'the
demi-Atlas of this earth', bearing half the world on his
shoulders.

In Act II Antony tells Caesar:

> The third o' the world is yours, which with a snaffle
> You may pace easy;

and Caesar wishes he could find a hoop

> should hold us stanch, from edge to edge
> O' the world.

Antony tells Octavia that the world will sometimes part them
and begs her not to read his blemishes in the world's report.
Lepidus, the third of the triumvirate, is described as being
'called into a huge sphere, and not to be seen to move in't'.

Menas asks Pompey if he would be Lord of the whole world, by the murder of Caesar and Antony. Lepidus is carried off drunk by a servant who 'bears the third part of the world'. Even the drinking song on Pompey's galley speaks of the world going round.

In the third act, Octavia tells Antony that wars between him and her brother would be

> As if the world should cleave, and that slain men
> Should solder up the rift.

Enobarbus, referring to Lepidus's dismissal from the triumvirate, says:

> Then, world, thou hast a pair of chaps – no more;
> And throw between them all the food thou hast,
> They'll grind the one the other.

In these lines the cosmic imagery is linked with that derived from eating. Antony levies the kings of the earth for war. Scarus laments that

> The greater cantle of the world is lost
> With very ignorance.

Antony, defeated at Actium, tells his soldiers:

> I am so lated in the world, that I
> Have lost my way for ever.

And he tells Cleopatra that once 'With half the bulk o' the world' he 'played as he pleased'. He swears by the moon and the stars, and confesses to Thyreus that his good stars

> Have empty left their orbs and shot their fires
> Into th'abysm of hell;

and he confesses to Cleopatra that

> our terrene moon
> Is now eclips'd, and it portends alone
> The fall of Antony.

The terrene moon, it seems, refers partly to the earth's moon, and partly, perhaps, to Cleopatra herself in her role as

Isis.[3] She is eclips'd, as Antony explains in his next words, because she, the great queen, has stooped to flatter Caesar.

In Act IV, before the battle, Caesar says that if he wins, 'the three-nook'd world Shall bear the olive freely'. Enobarbus, on receiving his treasure from Antony, declares himself to be 'the villain of the earth'. Antony, after his last unexpected victory, addresses Cleopatra as 'thou day o'th'world', and she replies:

> Lord of lords!
> O infinite virtue, com'st thou smiling from
> The world's great snare uncaught?

This passage should warn us against adopting a simple interpretation of the cosmic imagery. Although Antony's passion makes him lose the world, there are some indications that the world and its affairs are the enemy. At the end of the same scene Antony celebrates his last triumph with trumpets and tambourines,

> That heaven and earth may strike their sounds together
> Applauding our approach.

Enobarbus, as his heart breaks, prays to the blessed moon and asks the world to rank him as a master-leaver. Antony, enraged with Cleopatra, compares himself to Alcides, his ancestor, wearing the poisoned shirt of Nessus:

> Let me lodge Lichas on the horns of the moon.

The image helps to convey the idea of Antony as a semidivine figure.

When he hears of Cleopatra's supposed death he tells how his sword 'Quarter'd the world'; and Eros speaks of his master's 'noble countenance, Wherein the worship of the whole world lies'. One of Antony's guard, seeing him lying wounded, exclaims, 'The star is fallen'. Cleopatra, as the dying body of Antony is brought in, cries:

> O sun,
> Burn the great sphere thou mov'st in! Darkling stand
> The varying shore o' th' world.

Antony, in his last speech, calls himself 'the greatest prince o'th'world'. Cleopatra asks:

> Shall I abide
> In this dull world, which in thy absence is
> No better than a sty?

Now Antony, 'the crown of the earth', is dead,

> there is nothing left remarkable
> Beneath the visiting moon.

She wishes to tell the gods

> that this world did equal theirs
> Till they had stol'n our jewel.

Caesar, hearing of Antony's death, twice mentions the world-shaking importance of the event:

> The breaking of so great a thing should make
> A greater crack. The round world
> Should have shook lions into civil streets
> And citizens to their dens. The death of Antony
> Is not a single doom: in the name lay
> A moiety of the world.

A few lines later he confesses that they 'could not stall together In the whole world', because their stars were irreconcilable.

In the last scene of the play the cosmic imagery appears again and again. Proculeius urges Cleopatra to let the world see Caesar's 'nobleness well acted'. Her description of Antony uses the sun and moon, earth and ocean for comparisons:

> His face was as the heav'ns, and therein stuck
> A sun and moon, which kept their course and lighted
> The little O, the earth . . .
> His legs bestrid the ocean; his rear'd arm
> Crested the world.

Later, she addresses Caesar, now Antony is dead, as 'sole sir o'th'world', who may take his leave 'through all the world'. When Iras dies peacefully, it is as though she told 'the world It is not worth leave-taking'. Charmian addresses Cleopatra as 'O Eastern star' and completes her question: 'What should I stay − ' 'In this vile world?' As she closes the 'downy windows' of her mistress's eyes, she says:

> golden Phoebus never be beheld
> Of eyes again so royal.

Finally Caesar declares that

> No grave upon the earth shall clip in it
> A pair so famous.

The effect, therefore, of the cosmic imagery is twofold. On the one hand it underlines the stakes for which Antony and Caesar are playing, and the power which Antony is sacrificing by his continuing passion for Cleopatra; on the other hand, and particularly towards the end of Antony's life and afterwards, it stresses his superhuman qualities.

The imagery connected with feeding − as in *Troilus and Cressida*, where the same imagery is predominant − is to show the love of Antony and Cleopatra as based on a natural appetite which, like any other, can be indulged to excess. Cleopatra, speaking of her liaison with Julius Caesar, says that he was 'a morsel for a monarch', though these were her 'salad days' when she was 'green in judgment'. A similar expression is used in a later scene by Antony in his jealous rage:

> I found you as a morsel cold upon
> Dead Caesar's trencher. Nay, you were a fragment
> Of Cneius Pompey's.   (III. xiii. 116)

In Act II we are told that Antony 'sits at dinner'− the phrase is not used literally − and Pompey hopes that 'Epicurean cooks' will 'sharpen with cloyless sauce his appetite'. The same idea is used metaphorically later in the same act when Enobarbus says of Cleopatra:

> Other women cloy
> The appetites they feed, but she makes hungry
> Where most she satisfies.

Pompey calls Antony 'this amorous surfeiter'. At his first meeting with Cleopatra, Enobarbus tells us, Antony paid with his heart for 'what his eyes eat only' and he prophecies that Antony, in spite of his marriage to Octavia 'will to his Egyptian dish again'. Enobarbus, again acting as chorus, in a speech significantly at the very end of Act III, say that

> When valour preys on reason,
> It eats the sword it fights with.

In the last act the countryman who brings the asps to Cleopatra tells her that 'a woman is a dish for the gods, if the devil dress her not'; and Cleopatra, meditating suicide, declares:

> it is great
> To do that thing that ends all other deeds,
> Which shackles accidents and bolts up change,
> Which sleeps, and never palates more the dung,
> The beggar's nurse and Caesar's.

In the food imagery, as with the cosmic imagery, there is a certain ambiguity. It is used to emphasize the force of the sexual instinct in Antony and to reduce his love to a mere appetite, a passion uncontrolled by will; but, after Antony's death, the imagery seems to be used with a different purpose.

The sense of conflict and rapid movement in the play is partly caused by the numerous battles in the third and fourth acts, and partly by the frequent changes of scene from Egypt to Rome, from Rome to Athens, from Athens to Egypt and from Egypt to Parthia. But it is reinforced by the imagery. Cleopatra says that a Roman thought has struck Antony. Antony resolves to break 'these strong Egyptian fetters'; and, speaking of Fulvia's death, he says:

> What our contempts doth often hurl from us,
> We wish it ours again . . .
> The hand could pluck her back that shov'd her on.

Enobarbus remarks that it would be a pity to 'cast away' women for nothing; and Antony says that the people begin to 'throw' the dignities of Pompey the Great on his son. Cleopatra speaks of 'sweating labour'. Caesar complains that Antony 'tumbles on the bed of Potolemy', that he 'reels the streets at noon' and 'stands the buffet With knaves that smell of sweat'. Cleopatra describes herself as black with Phoebus's 'amorous pinches' and she proposes to 'pluck' his tidings from Alexas. Pompey professes to be pleased that he has been able to 'pluck the ne'er-lust-wearied Antony' from Cleopatra's lap. Lepidus urges Antony and Caesar not to allow a leaner action to 'rend' them; and when Caesar agrees to the marriage of Antony and Octavia, he prays: 'Never fly off our loves again'. The oars which propelled Cleopatra's barge made

> The water which they beat to follow faster,
> As amorous of their strokes;

and from the barge

> A strange invisible perfume hits the sense
> Of the adjacent wharfs.

Cleopatra urges the messenger to 'ram' his fruitful tidings in her ears, and, on hearing that Antony is married, she threatens to spurn the messenger's eyes like balls. Enobarbus prophesies that the band which seems to tie Antony and Caesar together 'will be the very strangler of their amity'. Caesar, fearful of the same thing, urges Antony not to let Octavia be the 'ram to batter the fortress of' their love. Antony tells Caesar:

> I'll wrestle with you in my strength of love.

Eros tells Antony in Act III that 'death will seize' Cleopatra; and Antony says that he scorns Fortune 'most when most she offers blows'. Enobarbus remarks that Caesar has subdued Antony's judgment too, and that his own honesty begins to square (i.e. quarrel) with himself. Thyreus speaks of 'wisdom and fortune combating together'. Antony laments that he has left his pillow 'unpressed' in Rome.

In Act IV Enobarbus speaks of those who have fallen away from Antony; Antony's generosity 'blows' his heart; and he declares that

> If swift thought break it not, a swifter mean
> Shall outstrike thought.

Antony, after his last victory, wishes the echo of the trumpets should mix with the noise of the tambourines,

> That heaven and earth may strike their sounds together.

Enobarbus, in his remorse, wishes to throw his heart 'Against the flint and hardness' of his fault. Charmian tells Cleopatra:

> The soul and body rive not more in parting
> Than greatness going off.

In the last act, Dolabella, feeling Cleopatra's grief on the rebound, is smitten to the very heart by it. Cleopatra speaks to Caesar of her 'wounding shame' which 'smites' her beneath her fall. When Iras falls dead, Cleopatra exclaims that

> The stroke of death is as a lover's pinch
> Which hurts, and is desired.

And, in his concluding speech, Caesar says that

> High events as these
> Strike those that make them.

There are a number of images which were suggested by the overflowing of the Nile, and the ebbing and flowing tide. We hear of the overflowing of Antony's dotage; Iras's palm is said to presage chastity, as the 'o'erflowing Nilus presageth famine'. There are two striking images relating to things floating on the stream:

> This common body,
> Like to a vagabond flag upon the stream
> Goes to and back, lackeying the varying tide,
> To rot itself with motion.

Antony, similarly, describes Octavia:

> Her tongue will not obey her heart, nor can
> Her heart inform her tongue, the swan's-down feather,
> That stands upon the swell at full of tide
> And neither way inclines.

More significant are the images relating to melting. The first of them expresses the relative importance to Antony of Cleopatra and Rome: 'Let Rome in Tiber melt!' In Act II Cleopatra speaks of melting gold and pouring it down the messenger's throat, and she echoes Antony's 'Authority melts from me'. Here, and in the following image, the melting is associated with flattery, as so often in Shakespeare. Antony reproaches Cleopatra for her flattery of Caesar, and she replies:

> As it determines, so
> Dissolve my life! The next Caesarion smite!
> Till by degrees the memory of my womb,
> Together with my brave Egyptians all,
> By the discandying of this pelleted storm
> Lie graveless . . .

In the next act Antony introduces the third factor in this image-cluster — dogs:

> The hearts
> That spaniel'd me at heels, to whom I gave
> Their wishes, do discandy, melt their sweets
> On blossoming Caesar.

In the next scene, he compares himself to a melting cloud of which 'the rack dislimns'. When he dies Cleopatra cries 'The crown of the earth doth melt'. As Cleopatra herself dies, becoming all air and fire, Charmian prays the thick cloud to dissolve, and rain. The melting of the world of power is thus paralleled with a dissolving of life itself.

There are some fifty references to Fortune in the course of the play. Many of them, naturally enough, are contained in the two scenes in which the Soothsayer appears; and he prophesies, somewhat obscurely, what is going to happen

later. Some of the references seem to refer back to the idea
expressed in *Julius Caesar* that

> There is a tide in the affairs of men,
> Which taken at the flood leads on to fortune.

Menas tells Enobarbus that Pompey, politically inept,
'doth this day laugh away his fortune'; and when Pompey
refuses the chance of being lord of all the world by murdering
Antony and Caesar, Menas says:

> I'll never follow thy pall'd fortunes more.

So, after the battle of Actium, Canidius declares:

> Our fortune on the sea is out of breath,
> And sinks most lamentably. Had our general
> Been what he knew himself, it had gone well.

Antony boasts that once he could make and mar fortunes,
but that now he scorns Fortune most when she is adverse. In
the next scene he sends his schoolmaster as ambassador to
Caesar, saluting him as 'Lord of his fortunes' and Euphron-
ius takes his leave of Caesar with the words 'Fortune pursue
thee!' — which is intended as a compliment, but could be
regarded as ambiguous. Enobarbus, seeing Antony's blind-
ness, remarks that 'men's judgments are A parcel of their
fortunes'. Thyreus tells Cleopatra that Caesar would like her
to make a staff of his fortunes for her to lean upon. Antony,
making ready for his last battle, proposes to brave fortune;
and, on hearing of Enobarbus's desertion, he laments that
his fortunes have corrupted honest men. Scarus says that
Antony's fortunes are fretted; and in the same scene Antony
declares that he and Fortune part. Cleopatra hopes that the
'false housewife, Fortune' will break her wheel; and this
reference to the wheel of fortune is reinforced by Antony's
dying words about his former fortunes,

> Wherein I liv'd, the greatest prince o' the world.

Cleopatra, in the last scene, speaks scornfully of Caesar:

> 'Tis paltry to be Caesar:
> Not being Fortune, he's but Fortune's knave.

But later she speaks of herself as 'his fortune's vassal' and threatens to

> show the cinders of my spirits
> Through the ashes of my chance.

Finally, as she prepares for death, she thinks she hears Antony mock

> The luck of Caesar, which the gods give men
> To excuse their after-wrath;

and she wishes the asp could speak,

> That I might hear thee call great Caesar ass
> Unpolicied!

Antony had previously complained of Caesar's luck at games.

From one point of view, therefore, we watch the operations of the wheel of fortune bringing Antony down from greatness to ruin: but these are presented not without irony, since Antony is the real architect of his own destruction. From another point of view, we watch Antony and Cleopatra emancipating themselves from their fortunes, and in their defeat scorning the fortunate Caesar.

There are more than fifty references to nobility and honour, which are partly concerned with Antony's genuine nobility and partly with the dishonourable actions of which he is frequently guilty — his shabby treatment of his two wives, his annoyance when his subordinates win victories, and his suggestion that Caesar should whip a prisoner in retaliation for the flogging of Thyreus.

In the concluding scenes of the play the word 'noble' is used without irony. Antony calls Eros 'thrice-nobler' than himself, and in his last speech he claims that he was the noblest prince of the world. Cleopatra calls him 'noblest of men' and calls her projected suicide 'what's brave, what's noble'. She speaks again in the last scene of being noble to herself, and of her suicide as a noble deed, a noble act. This nobility is associated with royalty. Iras calls Cleopatra 'Royal Egypt' and 'Royal queen', and Cleopatra calls Charmian 'noble'. Charmian in turn closes her mistress's eyes with the words:

> Golden Phoebus never be beheld
> Of eyes again so royal!

and she tells the guard:

> It is well done, and fitting for a princess
> Descended of so many royal kings.

Even Caesar says that Cleopatra, 'being royal, Took her own way'.[4]

By the numerous references to gods and demi-gods, Shakespeare associates Antony with Mars, Bacchus and with his reputed ancestor Hercules; while Cleopatra is associated both with Venus and Isis. Indeed, when Cleopatra dresses up as Isis, we do not feel, as Caesar obviously does, that she is committing sacrilege.[5]

The imagery we have examined can be used in support of any of the interpretations mentioned at the beginning of this chapter and it would therefore be dangerous to use it to support any. When the sickness images in *Hamlet* are considered in their context, as we have seen, there is only one valid conclusion to be drawn from them; and Robert B. Heilman's analysis of the patterns of imagery in *King Lear*, however we may differ on details, is generally convincing. The ambiguity that runs through the imagery of *Antony and Cleopatra* may therefore be taken to mean that Shakespeare presented the facts about the situation and left the members of his audience to draw their own conclusions.

10 *Venus and Adonis*: Comedy or Tragedy?

William Hazlitt tells us that his idolatry of Shakespeare ended with the plays. In the poems he is 'a mere author, though not a common author. The poems were splendid patch-work, with striking images and beautiful thoughts which were lost in the welter of fine-spun allegory and verbal quibbling.'[1] A later critic, Samuel Butler, recorded in his note-book:[2]

> I have been trying to read *Venus and Adonis* and *The Rape of Lucrece* but cannot get on with them. They teem with fine things, but they are got-up fine things. I do not know whether this is quite what I mean but, come what may, I find the poems bore me. Were I a schoolmaster I should think I was setting a boy a very severe punishment if I told him to read *Venus and Adonis* through in three sittings. If, then, the magic of Shakespeare's name, let alone the great beauty of occasional passages, cannot reconcile us (for I find most people of the same mind) to verse, and especially rhymed verse as a medium of sustained expression, what chance has any one else?

Butler blurted out what others have thought privately; but in Shakespeare's lifetime the poems were apparently more popular than the plays. There were no less than ten editions of *Venus and Adonis* before Shakespeares' death: it was widely imitated and frequently quoted. An undergraduate in *The Return from Parnassus* keeps a copy of the poem under his pillow; Harebrain is shocked to find his bride reading such a poem, calling it a luscious marrow-bone pie; and Richard Braithwaite made a similar complaint. Right down to our own day critics have expressed a good deal of uneasiness with regard to the poem. In 1819 Ezekiel Sanford, though admitting its poetic merits, remarked that 'so long as we are concerned for the interests of morality, we cannot wish that it may again become popular'.[3] Professor Douglas Bush, in his admirable book, *Mythology and the Renaissance Tradition*, while admitting that Shakespeare was wholly successful in what he set out to do, asks 'Was it worth doing?'.[4] He complains that Shakespeare, unlike Marlowe, is content with prettiness, 'and the poem, though far from languid, is sicklied o'er with effeminacy'; it has a fatal lack of emotion; it 'is a tissue of bookish conventions'; it lacks 'that genius for packing a world of meaning into a phrase' characteristic of the mature Shakespeare; and Shakespeare (he complains)

> seems quite satisfied and happy in seriously exploiting the popular conceits, decoration, rhetorical wooing, rhetorical declamation . . . If *Venus and Adonis* were wholly bookish, a piece of pure tapestry, all would be well, in a limited sense. But for an orgy of the senses it is too unreal, for a decorative pseudo-classic picture it has too much homely realism.

Professor C. S. Lewis is even more damning. He declares that we do not know how to take the poem. If it was intended to be written against lust, 'the story does not point the moral at all well' and Venus is 'a very ill-conceived temptress'. On the other hand, if the poem was meant to be an aphrodisiac, it fails egregiously:[5]

> Words and images which . . . ought to have been avoided keep on coming in and almost determine the dominant mood of the reader — 'satiety,' 'sweating,' 'leaden appetite,' 'gorge,' 'stuff'd,' 'glutton.' . . . And this flushed, panting, perspiring, suffocating, loquacious creature is supposed to be the goddess of love herself, the golden Aphrodite. It will not do. If the poem is not meant to

arouse disgust it was very foolishly written: if it is, then disgust
. . . is not, either aesthetically or morally, the feeling on which a
poet should rely in a moral poem.

It is a formidable indictment: pretty, effeminate, artificial,
heartless, bookish, rhetorical and ultimately disgusting. One
hesitates to disagree with two such admirable critics; but
not one of these epithets seems to be appropriate, at least
in their derogatory senses. Imperfect sympathies with the
poem have often been caused by an unavowed or unconscious
puritanism, but with Bush and Lewis one suspects that their
hostile verdicts are the result of a misunderstanding of the
poet's intentions.

Professor M. C. Bradbrook has recently argued[6] that
Shakespeare wrote the poem to obliterate the impression
Greene had tried to make that his rival was an upstart crow,
beautified with the feathers of the University Wits:

> *Venus and Adonis* is at once a claim to social dignity for its
> author, a justification of the natural and instinctive beauty of the
> animal world against sour moralists and scurrilous invective . . .
> The player had shown his capacity to move in a world of gorgeous
> paganism, to write upon a noble model, and to deal with love in
> aristocratic boldness and freedom.

We cannot, in fact, know whether Shakespeare wrote the
poem because of Greene's attack: but Dr Bradbrook seems to
characterize the tone of the poem more successfully than the
other critics we have quoted. The poem was dedicated to the
Earl of Southampton[7]; and, if we are to judge from the
poem dedicated to him by Nashe, he enjoyed obscenity. It
was natural, therefore, for Shakespeare to choose an erotic
subject as the first heir of his invention and as his first bid
for aristocratic patronage. But just as he was able to satisfy
the demands of James I or of the groundlings without
sacrificing his artistic integrity, so he was able to write a
poem which would appeal to Southampton and yet be an
expression of his own creative imagination. He went, as
Lodge and others before him, to Ovid's *Metamorphoses*, in

which Adonis – a man in the original, a 'sweet boy' in Golding's translation – is not at all averse to Venus's love. Golding thought that the purpose of the story was to reprove 'prodigious lust', that Venus represents 'such as of the flesh to filthy lust are bent', and that the fate of Adonis shows that 'beauty . . . ay doth men in danger throw'.[8] There is no evidence that Shakespeare took this moral very seriously, for his Adonis rejects the advances of the goddess. The bashfulness of Adonis is not, however, peculiar to Shakespeare's treatment of the story. Marlowe, in the great poem which Shakespeare was obviously trying to emulate, describes a picture in which

> Venus in her naked glory strove
> To please the careless and disdainful eyes
> Of proud Adonis that before her lies.

Greene had two songs (in *Never too Late* and *Permides*) in both of which Venus woos a blushing and bashful Adonis.[9] Shakespeare may have been influenced too by Ovid's stories of Salmacis and Echo, who both fall in love with coy youths, and by Lodge's adaption of the story of Glaucus and Scylla, in which Glaucus repulses the amorous advances of a lustful Scylla, and not, as in Ovid, woos a reluctant Scylla. There would be no sustained interest in the description of a love affair brought to an end by death, unless it was treated allegorically. It was natural, therefore, for Shakespeare to follow those versions of the story in which Adonis was coy.

Professor T. W. Baldwin[10] has suggested that three of the four sonnets on the Venus and Adonis theme which were included in *The Passionate Pilgrim* were written by Shakespeare before his narrative poem on the same subject. In one of them, 'sweet Cytherea' courts Adonis and he runs away; in the second, she watches Adonis bathing in a brook; in the third she warns him against hunting the boar; and in the fourth (written by Griffin) she describes to him how Mars had wooed her:

> Venus, with Adonis sitting by her
> Under a myrtle shade, began to woo him.
> She told the youngling how god Mars did try her,
> And as he fell to her, she fell to him.
> "Even thus," quoth she, "the warlike god embrac'd me."
> And then she clipp'd Adonis in her arms.
> "Even thus," quoth she, "the warlike god unlac'd me,"
> As if the boy should use like loving charms.
> "Even thus," quoth she, "he seized on my lips,"
> And with her lips on his did act the seizure:
> And as she fetched breath, away he skips,
> And would not take her meaning nor her pleasure.
>   Ah! that I had my lady at this bay,
>   To kiss and clip me till I run away!

The other three sonnets might, perhaps, have been written by Shakespeare in his extreme youth; but it seems much more likely that they were written by an imitator — perhaps Griffin too — who had admired lines 97–114 of Shakespeare's poem. The only poems certainly by Shakespeare in *The Passionate Pilgrim* were taken from the quarto of *Love's Labour's Lost* and from the Sonnets which were circulating in manuscript before 1598.

The Elizabethans interpreted the Adonis story in several different ways. In Book III of *The Faerie Queene*, Spenser makes the love of Venus and Adonis sustain all creation. Greene, in *Perimides*, makes the boar symbolize lust, and Adonis is slain because he yields to Venus. Abraham Fraunce, in *The Countess of Pembroke's Ivy-church*, published in the year before Shakespeare's poem, interprets the story as an allegory of the seasons:[11]

By *Adonis*, is meant the sunne, by *Venus*, the vpper hemisphere of the earth (as by *Proserpina* the lower) by the boare, winter: by the death of *Adonis*, the absence of the sunne for the sixe wintrie moneths; all which time, the earth lamenteth: *Adonis* is wounded in those parts, which are the instruments of propagation: for, in winter the sun seemeth impotent, and the earth barren: neither that being able to get, nor this to beare either fruite or flowres: and therefore *Venus* sits, lamentably hanging downe her head, leaning on her left hand, her garments all ouer her face.

We can see from these different treatments of the Adonis story that Shakespeare could have used it for various purposes. But there is no sign in his poem that he was following Spenser in making the love of Venus and Adonis sustain all creation, for their love is never consummated, and he makes no reference to the resurrection of Adonis. Although, at the end of his career, perhaps influenced by Leonard Digges who afterwards translated Claudian, Shakespeare seems to have been aware of the allegorical treatment of the Proserpine story, there is no evidence that he regarded the story of Venus and Adonis as a vegetation myth. Nor, surely, could he have intended the Boar to symbolize lust, since Adonis is anything but lustful.

According to Dr L. E. Pearson 'Venus is shown as the destructive agent of sensual love; Adonis, as reason in love'.[12] Most critics, indeed, seem to assume that the moral of the poem – if it has a moral – is to be found in the distinction made by Adonis between love and lust:

> Call it not love, for love to heaven is fled,
> Since sweating lust on earth usurp'd his name,
> Under whose simple semblance he hath fed
> Upon fresh beauty, blotting it with blame;
>> Which the hot tyrant stains, and soon bereaves,
>> As caterpillars do the tender leaves.
> Love comforteth like sunshine after rain,
> But Lust's effect is tempest after sun;
> Love's gentle spring doth always fresh remain
> Lust's winter comes ere summer half be done:
>> Love surfeits not, Lust like a glutton dies:
>> Love is all truth, Lust full of forged lies.

T. W. Baldwin seems to agree in part with this interpretation, for he suggests that Venus's pretended love is lust because, unlike the true Neoplatonic lover, she wants to touch Adonis. He goes on to quote Ficino to the effect that 'the lust to touch the body is not a part of love'.[13] But Shakespeare's plays are singularly free from such Neoplatonic nonsense. It is difficult to imagine him blaming Romeo because he wanted to touch Juliet, or blaming Juliet because she was anxious to 'lose a winning match'. He knew, as well as Donne, 'the right, true end of love'. There are, moreover, other stanzas in the poem which prevent us from accepting Adonis's moral without qualification. Venus compares Adonis to the self-lover, Narcissus, who 'died to kiss his shadow in the brook'. She points out the dangers of self-sufficiency:

> Torches are made to light, jewels to wear,
> Dainties to taste, fresh beauty for the use,
> Herbs for their smell, and sappy plants to bear:
> Things growing to themselves are growth's abuse.
>> Seeds spring from seeds, and beauty breedeth beauty.
>> Thou wast begot – to get it is thy duty.
>
> Upon the earth's increase why shouldst thou feed,
> Unless the earth with thy increase be fed?
> By law of nature thou art bound to breed,
> That thine may live when thou thyself art dead;
>> And so in spite of death thou dost survive,
>> In that thy likeness still is left alive.

Later in the poem she asks Adonis:

> What is thy body but a swallowing grave,
> Seeming to bury that posterity
> Which by the rights of time thou needs must have,
> If thou destroy them not in dark obscurity?
>> If so, the world will hold thee in disdain,
>> Sith in thy pride so fair a hope is slain.

We are inevitably reminded of the first fourteen sonnets in which Shakespeare urges his friend to marry, so as to ensure the survival of his beauty in his children. The theme is repeated over and over again. 'From fairest creatures we desire increase', so as to cheat the grave; after the friend has lost his beauty, he will be able to say 'This fair child of mine Shall sum my count, and make my old excuse'; his mother, looking at him, 'Calls back the lovely April of her prime', and so might the friend do with his son; not to marry is to be guilty of the sin of self-will; and the only protection against the scythe of Time is breed:[14]

> Who lets so fair a house fall to decay,
> Which husbandry in honour might uphold
> Against the stormy gusts of winter's day
> And barren rage of death's eternal cold?

We are reminded, too, of passages in the mature plays in which Shakespeare's spokesmen attack self-sufficiency. Duke Vincentio, for example, in the first scene of *Measure for Measure* tells Angelo:

> Thyself and thy belongings
> Are not thine own so proper as to waste
> Thyself upon thy virtues, they on thee.
> Heaven doth with us as we with torches do,
> Not light them for themselves; for if our virtues
> Did not go forth of us, 'twere all alike
> As if we had them not.

He is preaching on the text of 'Let your light so shine before men'; and Ulysses in *Troilus and Cressida* has variations on the same theme:[15]

> No man is the lord of anything,
> Though in and of him there be much consisting,
> Till he communicate his parts to others;
> Nor doth he of himself know them for aught . . .

Of course, we might argue that Shakespeare puts good arguments into Venus's mouth, as Milton puts an eloquent plea into the mouth of Comus. Adonis himself points out that 'Reason is the bawd to lust's abuse' as Hamlet was later to declare that 'Reason panders will'. But, in fact, there are several reasons why we should not take Adonis's moralizing as an objective statement of the situation. First, it reads too much like an afterthought on his part. In the first half of the poem he is bashful, but he seems to feel no moral objections

to Venus's suit: he merely declares that he is too young and
implies that Venus is a 'baby-snatcher':

> Who wears a garment shapeless and unfinish'd?
> Who plucks the bud before one leaf put forth?
> If springing things be any jot diminish'd,
> They wither in their prime, prove nothing worth.
> The colt that's back'd and burden'd being young
> Loseth his pride and never waxeth strong.

Here he is concerned with the maintenance of his own
strength, not with Venus's sensuality; and later he ascribes
his reluctance to his youth:

> Fair Queen . . . if any love you owe me,
> Measure my strangeness with my unripe years;
> Before I know myself, seek not to know me;
> No fisher but the ungrown fry forbears.
> The mellow plum doth fall, the green sticks fast,
> Or being early pluck'd is sour to taste.

He is implying that he would make an unsatisfactory lover.
Between these two passages Adonis kissed Venus when she
fainted, and we may suspect that this was not merely a method
of First Aid.

Secondly, as we see everything through Venus's eyes, we
cannot help feeling that Adonis is guilty of pride and self-
sufficiency. He is a kind of Hippolytus, a follower of Artemis
and a scorner of Aphrodite, as he himself admits:

> I know not love . . . nor will not know it,
> Unless it be a boar, and then I chase it.
> 'Tis much to borrow, and I will not owe it.
> My love to love is love but to disgrace it.

It is not virtue which makes him repulse Venus, but an
unwillingness to give himself. He is like the friend as
depicted in the 94th sonnet:

> Who, moving others, are themselves as stone,
> Unmoved, cold, and to temptation slow —
> They rightly do inherit Heaven's graces,

> And husband nature's riches from expense;
> They are the lords and owners of their faces,
> Others but stewards of their excellence.

The boar, loved by Adonis, symbolizes death and mutability. Beauty which refuses Love is doomed to destruction and decay.

Thirdly, Shakespeares's epithets should surely prevent us from adopting a moral attitude to Venus's behaviour. After her final failure to obtain her desire, the poet comments: 'But all in vain; *good* queen, it will not be'. And just before this Adonis is called 'the poor fool'.

Fourthly, at the end of the poem, after Adonis's death, Venus prophecies the corruption of love:

> Since thou art dead, lo, here I prophesy
> Sorrow on love hereafter shall attend:
> It shall be waited on with jealousy,
> Find sweet beginning but unsavoury end,
>   Ne'er settled equally, but high or low,
>   That all love's pleasure shall not match his woe.
>
> It shall be fickle, false, and full of fraud,
> Bud and be blasted in a breathing while,
> The bottom poison, and the top o'erstraw'd
> With sweets that shall the truest sight beguile;
>   The strongest body shall it make most weak,
>   Strike the wise dumb, and teach the fool to speak.
>
> It shall be sparing, and too full of riot,
> Teaching decrepit age to tread the measures;
> The staring ruffian shall it keep in quiet,
> Pluck down the rich, enrich the poor with treasures;
>   It shall be raging mad, and silly mild,
>   Make the young old, the old become a child.
>
> It shall suspect where is no cause of fear;
> It shall not fear where it should most mistrust;
> It shall be merciful, and too severe,
> And most deceiving when it seems most just;
>   Perverse it shall be where it shows most toward,
>   Put fear to valour, courage to the coward.

> It shall be cause of war and dire events,
> And set dissension 'twixt the son and sire,
> Subject and servile to all discontents,
> As dry combustious matter is to fire.
> Sith in his prime death doth my love destroy,
> They that love best their loves shall not enjoy.

Compared with this state of affairs, the straightforward sensuality of Venus's love for Adonis represents a state of innocence. Although Adonis claims that love to heaven is fled, Love has not fled, as Mr A. C. Hamilton points out, for she is with him now:[16]

> Only with his death, as Venus prophesies, will discord, dissension, and hatred – that is, lust – usurp the name of love. And only after his death does Love, that is, Venus, flee to heaven.

This, however, is not the whole truth about the poem. Although an interpretation that seeks to show that Shakespeare was writing a sermon against lust is clearly impossible, it is equally impossible to assume that the poem is a straightforward eulogy of sexual love. Almost everything in the poem appears to be ambivalent. The famous description of Adonis's stallion pursuing the mare can be taken either as an emblem of the naturalness of desire, as Venus herself points out, or as an emblem of uncontrolled desire, or lust, as it frequently was.

Some modern critics, of whom Mr Rufus Putney is perhaps the most persuasive,[17] have argued that the poem is meant to be comic throughout and that it belongs to the popular genre of erotic narratives, mostly derived from Ovid. They had several characteristics in common: they all had elaborate sensuous descriptions; they tended to be realistic in their treatment of mythological love-stories; they used wit to offset the sensuous atmosphere; they introduced, as Ovid has done, sententious generalizations about love; and most of them were steeped in irony.[18] The masterpiece in this kind was Marlowe's *Hero and Leander* which illustrates all the characteristics outlined by Putney. The description of

Leander could be given as an example of sensuous description; the pictures in Venus's temple exemplify the grotesque realism of his treatment of mythology, with Jupiter

> for his love Europa bellowing loud,
> And tumbling with the Rainbow in a cloud;

Marlowe's wit is ubiquitous; and his poem is full of generalizations about love:

> Who ever lov'd, that lov'd not at first sight? ...
> Love is not full of pity, as men say,
> But deaf and cruel where he means to prey.

Another resemblance between *Hero and Leander* and *Venus and Adonis* is that both Marlowe and Shakespeare put into the mouths of their characters long sophistical speeches, arguing against virginity:

> Like untun'd golden strings all women are,
> Which long time lie untouch'd, will harshly jar,
> Vessels of brass, oft handled, brightly shine:
> What difference betwixt the richest mine
> And basest mould, but use? for both, not us'd,
> Are of like worth. Then treasure is abus'd,
> When misers keep it: being put to loan,
> In time it will return us two for one.
> Rich robes themselves and others do adorn;
> Neither themselves nor others, if not worn.
> Who builds a palace, and rams up the gate,
> Shall see it ruinous and desolate:
> Ah, simple Hero, learn thyself to cherish!
> Lone women, like to empty houses, perish.
> Less sins the poor rich man, that starves himself
> In heaping up a mass of drossy pelf,
> Than such as you: his golden earth remains,
> Which after his decease some other gains;
> But this fair gem, sweet in the loss alone,
> When you fleet hence, can be bequeath'd to none ...

Certainly *Venus and Adonis* displays many of the same characteristics. It contains some lovely descriptions. Some stanzas are frankly erotic and Shakespeare provides plenty of realistic touches, so that Venus at times appears to be an amorous country girl in the pastoral tradition. Although she is as beautiful as Titian's painting of her, she sweats, weeps, hurts Adonis's hand by grasping it too hard, and, though she compares herself to a fairy and nymph and claims that she does not leave footprints on the sand, she is substantial enough to pluck Adonis from his horse. Shakespeare introduces plenty of generalizations about love:

> Love is a spirit, all compact of fire . . .

> The sea hath bounds, but deep desire hath none . . .

> Foul words and frowns must not repel a lover . . .

And Shakespeare, like Marlowe, qualifies his eroticism with wit.

But, all the same, Putney's account of the poem does not quite fit in with one's own experience of it. Even the total impression of *Hero and Leander* is not primarily comic, but rather of a mingling of wit and sensuousness such as we find in the best of the Metaphysicals; and the dominant impression of *Venus and Adonis* is not really of 'jocosity'. Putney thinks that the stanzas describing the imprisonment of Adonis by the locking of Venus's lily fingers must have seemed very funny to the Elizabethans:

> "Foundling," she saith, "since I have hemm'd thee here
> Within the circuit of this ivory pale,
> I'll be a park, and thou shalt be my deer;
> Feed where thou wilt, on mountain or in dale;
>   Graze on my lips; and if those hills be dry,
>   Stray lower, where the pleasant fountains lie.

> "Within this limit is relief enough,
> Sweet bottom-grass, and high delightful plain,
> Round rising hillocks, brakes obscure and rough,
> To shelter thee from tempest and from rain . . .

The erotic imagery and the pun on 'deer' are not 'funny', but rather sensuousness tempered with wit; and the later comparison of the echoes of Venus's laments to

> shrill-tong'd tapsters answering every call,
> Soothing the humour of fantastic wits,

although we are reminded of the cruel baiting of Francis by Prince Hal, is grotesque rather than funny. Even the comparison of Adonis lying on Venus to a man on a horse is brilliant rather than erotic, grotesque rather than jocose. It is, moreover, difficult to believe with Putney that the lament of Venus at the conclusion of the poem is intended to be 'a diverting parody of mourners, zoological, inanimate and disembodied'. It seems rather to be the expression of real, if distanced, emotion.

There is, after all, a large amount of imagery in the poem, and many lines and stanzas, which no one could regard as comic:

> Leading him prisoner in a red-rose chain . . .

> A lily prison'd in a gaol of snow . . .

> Hot, faint, and weary, with her hard embracing,
> Like a wild bird being tam'd with too much handling,
> Or as the fleet-foot roe that's tir'd with chasing,
> Or like the froward infant still'd with dandling . . .

> Look how a bright star shooteth from the sky,
> So glides he in the night from Venus' eye.

> Or as the snail, whose tender horns being hit,
> Shrinks backward in his shelly cave with pain,
> And there, all smoth'red up, in shade doth sit,
> Long after fearing to creep forth again. . . .

Some of the imagery, as in Shakespeare's mature work, is derived from books rather than from nature. The description of the boar, for example, is derived from Golding and Brooke; and even the description of Adonis's stallion is based not merely on observation.[19] But *Venus and Adonis* has more natural imagery than *Lucrece*; and in the description of the hunted hare, which begins as an argument for hunting it, Shakespeare's own sympathies with the hare militate against the argument.

There are traces of iterative imagery in the poem, a year or two before Shakespeare began to use it in his plays. There is, for example, a frequent recurrence of red and white, the colours of love, combined in Adonis's cheeks, and in his lips after they have been kissed, and separate in the red of Adonis's shame and of Venus's desire, and in the white of Adonis's anger and of Venus's fear. There are some thirty references to burning and cooling, used both metaphorically and literally, and symbolizing desire and chastity. Equally important is the iteration of words denoting sweetness – sweet boy, sweet kiss, sweet look, sweet desire, sweet lips, deep-sweet music, honey secrets, honey fee and nectar. The atmosphere of the poem would be cloying and enervating without the frequent touches of realism.

We are driven to conclude that the poem cannot easily be categorized. It is not straightforwardly didactic, designed, like *Lucrece*, as a warning against lust or in praise of chastity. It is not, on the other hand, a straightforward paean in praise of sexual love or of 'breed', since Venus – not merely in the eyes of Adonis, but in the eyes of Shakespeare himself – allows passion to usurp the place of reason. She is compared to a famished eagle and a vulture, sweating, reeking, smoking, boiling,

> beating reason back,
> Forgetting shame's pure blush, and honour's wrack.

Nor, as we have seen, can the poem be regarded as 'comic', for its frequent touches of wit are offset by the tragic ending, in which the boar symbolizes death rather than lust.

Shakespeare, we may suppose, set out to write a poem, based on Ovid, with Lodge as his closest model for form, and Marlowe for style. The theme gave him opportunities for rivalling some of the effects of Renaissance painting, and

G

of repudiating the denial of the flesh by puritan moralists and Neoplatonic theorists. At the same time, it enabled him to express through the mouth of Venus the theme of 'breed' he was afterwards to develop in the early sonnets – if indeed the sonnets were not written earlier. In accordance with the conventions of the *genre* he was committed to a realistic treatment of mythology, so that Venus, though surpassingly beautiful, has the physiological characteristics of an ordinary woman; and a woman who takes the sexual initiative is apt to seem like a Colette heroine engaged in the seduction of a boy. In Sonnet 41 Shakespeare asks:

> And when a woman woos, what woman's son
> Will sourly leave her till she have prevailed?

Adonis sourly leaves Venus, preferring hunting the boar to being hunted by her. As his objections to her promiscuity are an afterthought, we cannot help thinking that he preserves his virginity more because of his self-centredness than because of his virtue; and Venus arouses our pity as any woman will whose passion is not reciprocated. As Dr Bradbrook says,[20] 'a lofty form and classic authority is invoked to display the continuity of animal, human and divine passion'.

The ambivalence of the poem is caused partly by the poet's own acceptance of conflicting feelings about love, and partly by the essentially dramatic nature of his imagination. Just as he had as much delight in depicting an Iago as an Imogen, he had as much delight in depicting a Venus as an Adonis. He sees the situation from both points of view, so that we feel the force of Venus's arguments for love, as well as the reluctance of the unawakened adolescent. Both use reason to justify an irrational position.

II *The Rape of Lucrece*

Lucrece was the 'graver labour' promised by Shakespeare in the Dedication to *Venus and Adonis*. It is written in rhyme royal, the stanza form employed by Chaucer in *Troilus and Criseyde* and by Sackville in his Induction to the *Mirror for Magistrates*, and it has a slower, graver movement than the six-line stanza of *Venus and Adonis*. There may have been a draft in the six-line stanza of *Venus and Adonis*, since Suckling quoted several stanzas in this form.

In *Venus and Adonis* Shakespeare had written of a chaste youth repelling the assaults of an amorous goddess. In the companion poem he writes of a chaste wife violated by a lustful guest. Adonis is successful in preserving his chastity, but he is slain by a boar, and bewailed by Venus; Lucrece, unable to endure the shame, commits suicide.

By providing a prose 'argument' – concerned partly with previous events – Shakespeare was able to plunge into the middle of the story, and to concentrate on the struggle in Tarquin's mind before the rape, on Lucrece's appeal to him to spare her, and on her lament afterwards.

Lucrece is interesting as a forerunner and there are many links between it and later plays. One of the most significant is with *Macbeth*. Just before the murder of Duncan, Macbeth has a soliloquy describing an imaginary dagger which seems to lead him to Duncan's chamber, inciting him to the deed. The speech continues:

> Now o'er the one half world,
> Nature seems dead and wicked dreams abuse

The curtained sleep. Witchcraft celebrates
Pale Hecate's offerings; and withered murder,
Alarumed by his sentinel the wolf
Whose howl's his watch, thus with his stealthy pace
With Tarquin's ravishing strides, towards his design
Moves like a ghost.

Shakespeare's mind went back some twelve years to the
earlier scene in *Lucrece*, to that other deed of darkness – a rape
being a symbolic murder. Many editors have observed that
a large number of details of the two scenes are identical,
whether because Shakespeare was consciously drawing on his
narrative poem, or because the various scenic properties are
natural concomitants of the violent deeds – the starless
night, the noise of owls and wolves:

Now stole upon the time the dead of night,
When heavy sleep had clos'd up mortal eyes;
No comfortable star did lend his light,
No noise but owls' and wolves' death-boding cries;
Now serves the season that they may surprise
    The silly lambs. Pure thoughts are dead and still,
    While lust and murder wake to stain and kill.

Baldwin points out[1] that this is partly derived from Ovid's
description of the rape beginning *Nox erat*, and this would
send Shakespeare's mind to a similar passage in Virgil,
Book IV, describing Dido's sleeplessness in the toils of
love.[2]

More significant than the background of the two scenes
is the fact that Tarquin is, in a sense, the first of Shakespeare's tragic heroes. Richard III is a tragic villain, conscious
of the evil he commits, but not seeking to repent until the
last act of the play. Tarquin is fully conscious of the sin he
contemplates and the first 51 stanzas are devoted to the
conflict in his mind before he definitely succumbs to evil. In
this respect he is much closer to Macbeth than he is to
Richard.

Like Angelo, whose passions are aroused by the sight of

the novice, Isabella, Tarquin is sexually stirred by the
reputed chastity of the heroine:

> Haply that name of 'chaste' unhaply set
> This bateless edge on his keen appetite . . .

> Perchance his boast of Lucrece' sovereignty
> Suggested this proud issue of a king;
> For by our ears our hearts oft tainted be.
> Perchance that envy of so rich a thing,
> Braving compare, disdainfully did sting
> His high-pitched thoughts that meaner men should vaunt
> That golden hap which their superiors want.

When Tarquin goes to his bedroom, he weighs 'the sundry
dangers of his will's obtaining'. He realizes, as Macbeth was
later to realize, that he is liable to forfeit the things that
should accompany old age, 'As honour, love, obedience,
troops of friends', but his desire brushes these unpleasant
facts on one side.

> And when great treasure is the meed proposed,
> Though death be adjunct, there's no death supposed.

> Those that much covet are with gain so fond
> That what they have not, that which they possess
> They scatter and unloose it from their bond,
> And so, by hoping more, they have but less;
> Or, gaining more, the profit of excess
> Is but to surfeit, and such grief sustain
> That they prove bankrupt in this poor-rich gain.

> So that in vent'ring ill, we leave to be
> The things we are for that which we expect;
> And this ambitious foul infirmity,
> In having much, torments us with defect
> Of that we have; so then we do neglect
> The thing we have and, all for want of wit,
> Make something nothing by augmenting it.

(It will be noted that considered as poetry such passages of
argumentation are inferior to the passages of description in
the poem.)

Even when Tarquin leaps from his bed to go to Lucrece's chamber, he is still 'madly tossed between desire and dread', but 'honest fear' is 'bewitched with lust's foul charm'. He upbraids his own lust. He knows perfectly well that he should 'offer pure incense to so pure a shrine', and that 'fair humanity' abhors the deed he contemplates. He knows that it is a shame to knighthood, a slur on his own ancestry, a disgrace to bravery, and a scandal to his descendants.

> What win I if I gain the thing I seek?
> A dream, a breath, a froth of fleeting joy.
> Who buys a minute's mirth to wail a week?
> Or sells eternity to get a toy?
> For one sweet grape who will the vine destroy?
> Or what fond beggar, but to touch the crown,
> Would with the sceptre straight be strucken down?

Moreover, Collatinus, Lucrece's husband, is not his enemy, but his dear friend and kinsmen. So Macbeth reminds himself that he is Duncan's kinsman. Then, like Lady Macbeth, telling her husband that it is the eye of childhood that fears a painted devil, Tarquin answers his own scruples:

> Who fears a sentence or an old man's saw
> Shall by a painted cloth be kept in awe.

St Thomas Aquinas says somewhere that no man can deliberately choose evil; he has first to delude himself that the choice is good for him. So, in the disputation between frozen conscience and hot-burning will, Tarquin persuades himself that the temporary possession of Lucrece is a 'good' which outweighs all other considerations. 'What is vile shows like a virtuous deed'.

I have stressed the importance of Tarquin as a forerunner of later dramatization of sin, although the demands of the narrative form, while allowing for more direct commentary by the poet, are different from those of the drama; and Shakespeare never forgets that he is writing a narrative poem.

The next section of the poem (stanzas 52–98) deals with

the debate between Tarquin and Lucrece and the actual
violation by means of blackmail. He tells her that if he kills
her under the pretence that he had caught her committing
adultery with a servant, her reputation will be blasted, her
children will be bastardized, and her husband will suffer
more than if she submits to Tarquin's will:

> But if thou yield, I rest thy secret friend:
> The fault unknown is as a thought unacted;
> A little harm done to a great good end
> For lawful policy remains enacted.

The choice for Lucrece is not a simple one between death
and dishonour, but between death and apparent dishonour
on the one hand, and life and secret dishonour on the other.
The arguments Lucrece uses to plead with Tarquin are
those he had himself used. She appeals to religion, knighthood, friendship, pity, laws human and divine, hospitality,
his own royal birth since the man who rules a country should
be able to govern his passions.

After the rape and Tarquin's departure, Shakespeare
switches attention from criminal to victim, and from victim
to criminal, in alternate lines, and it has the effect of alternating shots in a film.

> She bears the load of lust he left behind,
> And he the burthen of a guilty mind.
>
> He like a thievish dog creeps sadly hence,
> She like a wearied lamb lies panting there;
> He scowls and hates himself for his offence,
> She, desperate, with her nails her flesh doth tear.
> He faintly flies, sweating with guilty fear;
>   She stays, exclaiming on the direful night;
>   He runs, and chides his vanish'd loath'd delight.
>
> He thence departs a heavy convertite,
> She there remains a hopeless castaway;
> He in his speed looks for the morning light;
> She prays she never may behold the day.

Coleridge said that in *Lucrece* Shakespeare 'gave ample proof of his possession of a most profound, energetic, and philosophical mind'. The evidence for this is mostly contained in the long soliloquy in which the heroine rails at Night and Time and Opportunity (stanzas 113–147). It is a foretaste of the tirades of the early Histories, and it looks forward to the soliloquies of the mature plays. It exemplifies Shakespeare's amazing facility of expression, and his daring virtuosity in utilizing and displaying all the resources of rhetoric, and contains passages as great as anything in Elizabethan non-dramatic poetry.

Lucrece begins with an invocation of Night, in which there is an accumulation of epithets and images. Night is associated with hell, with tragedies performed on the Elizabethan stage, with chaos, prostitution, death, conspiracy, fog, poison, sickness and impurity, because Night was an accomplice of Tarquin in his crime. This leads Lucrece to a reflection on his hypocrisy, the contrast between the virtue he talked of and the deed he committed. This is followed by a whole catalogue of examples of similar contrasts, all convential, but obtaining their effect by accumulation: worm in the bud, cuckoo in the nest, toads fouling fountains, misers who suffer from gout, unruly blasts in the spring, weeds growing side by side with flowers, the adder hissing while birds are singing. This again leads on to a diatribe against Opportunity, probably suggested by these remarks of Erasmus:[2]

> So much force has opportunity as to turn honesty into dishonesty, debt into wealth, pleasure into heaviness, a benefit into a curse, and vice versa; and, in short, it changes the nature of everything.

But Shakespeare is concerned only with the evil effects of Opportunity, not with their opposite. Opportunity is the cause of treachery, fornication, murder, incest, nay

> all sins past, and all that are to come
> From the creation to the general doom.

Opportunity is Time's servant, as Time is copesmate of Night; so Lucrece proceeds to address Time, 'Thou ceaseless lackey to Eternity', in lines partly inspired by the last book of Ovid's *Metamorphoses*. Time, though he is the destroyer and overturner of the works of man and nature, is also the power which brings truth to light; and Lucrece appeals to him to overthrow Tarquin and bring him to despair.

T. W. Baldwin, in his account of what he calls the literary genetics of *Lucrece*, has a number of examples of Shakespeare's method of composition in the stanzas we have been discussing. Perhaps the neatest example is the stanza about the miser.[3]

> The aged man that coffers up his gold
> Is plagu'd with cramps and gouts and painful fits,
> And scarce hath eyes his treasure to behold,
> But like still-pining Tantalus he sits,
> And useless barns the harvest of his wits,
>> Having no other pleasure of his gain,
>> But torment that it cannot cure his pain.

Ovid refers briefly to the story of Tantalus in the *Metamorphoses* (IV), and in a note on the passage (probably in the edition used by Shakespeare) Regius suggests that Tantalus is a type of avarice. The connection between the story of Tantalus and avarice is also brought out in Horace's first satire, a passage quoted by Erasmus in his *Adagia*. The same point is made in one of Sidney's sonnets, but that Erasmus was the source is supported by another quotation from one of Horace's odes:

> magnas inter opes inops.

If Shakespeare knew the ode, or looked it up, he would know that the stanza which this line concludes runs:

> contemptae dominus splendidior rei,
> quam si quicquid arat impiger Apulus
> occultare meis dicerer horreis . . .

Baldwin does not point out that these granaries are the link between avarice and the parable of the covetous rich man in the Bible, Luke XII. The rich man proposed building greater barns only to be told 'O fool, this night will they fetch thy soul from thee'. On this parable, the Genevan version has the marginal note:

> Christ condemneth the arrogancy of the rich worldlings, who as though they had God locked up in their coffers and barns, set their whole felicity in their goods, not considering that God gave them life and also can take it away when he will.

The coffers and barns, used as nouns in this note, are taken over by Shakespeare and used as verbs:

> The aged man that coffers up his gold . . .
> And useless barns the harvest of his wits.

The 31 stanzas describing the painting of the destruction of Troy are partly based on Virgil's account in the first two books of the *Aeneid*; but, as Professor Root has shown,[4] the Virgilian account is amplified by details derived from the 13th book of the *Metamorphoses* in which Ovid describes the contest between Ajax and Ulysses, and gives an account of Hestor and Hecuba. The order of the scene – Ajax, Ulysses, Nestor, Hecuba – is the same as Ovid's. The idea of introducing the painting was perhaps suggested by the similar device in Samuel Daniel's *Complaint of Rosamund*, in which the heroine, just before her seduction, contemplates a casket decorated with mythological pictures, given her by her royal lover.

Nine of the stanzas describe the crafty Sinon, who is compared by Lucrece to Tarquin. Both men united 'outward truth and inward guile . . . saintly seeming and diabolical purpose':

> For even as subtle Sinon here is painted,
> So sober-sad, so weary, and so mild,
> As if with grief or travail he had fainted,
> To me came Tarquin armed; so beguil'd

> With outward honesty, but yet defil'd
> With inward vice. As Priam him did cherish,
> So did I Tarquin; so my Troy did perish.

Shakespeare knew from his reading of Livy, although curiously enough he did not mention it, that Tarquin had engaged in a stratagem which makes the comparison with Sinon more relevant. Like Sinon, he had gone to the besieged inhabitants of Gabii

> as a suppliant outcast, with a forged tale of woe, and displaying in his person the marks of cruel usage, Tarquin had roused their sympathy, and secured a welcome he turned to account by conspiring against his friends and benefactors, and compassing their speedy destruction.

Lucrece also inveighs against Helen and Paris, whose lust was the cause of the war. She asks:

> Why should the private pleasure of some one
> Become the public plague of many moe?
> Let sin, alone committed, light alone
> Upon his head that hath transgressed so;
> Let guiltless souls be freed from guilty woe.
> For one's offence why should so many fall,
> To plague a private sin in general.

These stanzas are also interesting on two other grounds. They throw light on Shakespeare's views on painting which he shared with most of his contemporaries. In *Venus and Adonis*, there is a stanza describing Adonis's horse:

> Look when a painter would surpass the life
> In limning out a well-proportioned steed,
> His art with nature's workmanship at strife,
> As if the dead the living should exceed;
> So did this horse excel a common one
> In shape, in courage, colour, pace, and bone.

So in the painting of Troy Lucrece admires the way

> In scorn of nature, art gave lifeless life.

The panoramic view of the siege is filled with hundreds
of vivid details which seem to be painted from life; but
Lucrece (or Shakespeare) admires the psychological truth
even more than outward verisimilitude – the ashy lights in
dying eyes, other eyes seen through loopholes, and eyes in
the distance looking sad, pale cowards with trembling paces,
the triumphant faces of great commanders, the art of physiog-
nomy in the portraits of Ajax and Ulysses, Nestor's beard
wagging up and down, and Hecuba gazing on Priam's
wounds:

> In her the painter had anatomiz'd
> Time's ruin, beauty's wrack, and grim care's reign;
> Her cheeks with chaps and wrinkles were disguis'd;
> Of what she was no semblance did remain:
> Her blue blood chang'd to black in every vein,
>   Wanting the spring that those shrunk pipes had fed,
>   Show'd life imprison'd in a body dead.

These stanzas also show that Shakespeare's attitude to the
Trojan war did not change substantially during the next ten
years. His treatment of the subject in the Dido play in
Hamlet and Troilus and Cressida is essentially the same. It
may well be that the time-theme, which is so prominent in
Troilus and Cressida, was suggested by Lucrece's tirade
against time which comes just before the description of the
painting.

It is true that in the Sonnets we have a forerunner of the
Troilus situation – an obsessive concern with the power of
Time and a realization of the vulnerability of constancy. But
in Lucrece, written before many of the Sonnets, the heroine's
tirade against Time precedes, as we have seen, the description
of the painting of Troy. Time is described as 'carrier of
grisly care', 'eater of youth', 'virtue's snare' and 'the ceaseless lackey to eternity'. Some of the imagery used in the poem
links up with four famous speeches in Troilus and Cressida:

Thou grant'st no time for charitable deeds . . .   (l. 908)

Time's glory is to calm contending kings . . .   (l. 939)

To ruinate proud buildings with thy hours,
And smear with dust their glitt'ring golden towers ... (ll. 944–5)

To feed oblivion with decay of things . . .   (l. 947)

Let him have time a beggar's orts to crave,
And time to see one that by alms doth live
Disdain to him disdained scraps to give.   (ll. 985–7)

Ulysses's speech on Time is spoken in answer to Achilles's question: 'What, are my deeds forgot?' And in the course of his reply Ulysses mentions 'good deeds past', the scraps which are 'alms for oblivion', the charity which is subject to 'envious and calumniating time', and the 'gilt o'er-dusted' which is no longer praised. In the next act, when Troilus parts from Cressida, he makes use of Lucrece's epithet:

> Injurious time now with a robber's haste
> Crams his rich thievery up, he knows not how:
> As many farewells as be stars in heaven,
> With distinct breath and consign'd kisses to them,
> He fumbles up into a loose adieu,
> And scants us with a single famish'd kiss,
> Distasted with the salt of broken tears. (IV. iv. 44–50)

Here we have the same image of Time with a wallet, and also the cooking imagery first pointed out by Walter Whiter,[5] to the significance of which we shall have occasion to return. When Ulysses prophesies the destruction of Troy, Hector replies:[6]

> the end crowns all,
> And that old common arbitrator, Time,
> Will one day end it.

The fourth speech having links with the lines quoted from *Lucrece* is spoken by Troilus after he has witnessed Cressida's unfaithfulness:

> The fractions of her faith, orts of her love,
> The fragments, scraps, the bits and greasy relics
> Of her o'er-eaten faith, are bound to Diomed.
>
> (V. ii. 158–60)

Some of the food images in *Lucrece* and the *Sonnets* are connected with the Ovidian idea of devouring Time; the remainder associate sexual desire with feeding, and its satisfaction with surfeiting. The association is a natural extension of the various meanings of the word *appetite*. Tarquin considers that

> the profit of excess
> Is but to surfeit;

his lust is compared to the 'sharp hunger' of a lion; and he is described after his crime as 'surfeit-taking':

> His taste delicious, in digestion souring,
> Devours his will, that liv'd by foul devouring.

A few lines later, we have another image of surfeiting:[7]

> Drunken Desire must vomit his recept,
> Ere he can see his own abomination.

There are some twenty-five food images in *Lucrece* and more than three times that number in *Troilus and Cressida*. In the poem there is a link between the Time imagery and the Food imagery: Time is not merely a devourer, but also a bloody tyrant; and the ravisher is not merely a devourer of innocence, but a tyrant as well.

The analogy between love and war is to be found in the work of numerous poets between Ovid and Shakespeare. In one of Ovid's *Elegies*, there is a detailed comparison between the lover and the soldier:[8]

> Lovers are always at war, with Cupid watching the ramparts:
> Atticus, take it from me: lovers are always at war.
> What's the right age for love? – the same as that for a soldier.
> What the captains demand, agressiveness, ardor of spirit,
> That's what a pretty girl wants when a man's on the hunt.
> The soldier's service is long; but send a girl on before him,
> And the unfaltering lover plods the road without end.

In the middle ages, the siege of Love's castle was common enough; and it is natural that Tarquin should be compared to a soldier entering a breach in the walls, that Shakespeare should speak of honour and beauty being 'weakly fortressed'; that in the account of the actual rape, Tarquin's hand should be compared to a 'Rude ram, to batter such an ivory wall'; that Lucrece's breasts should be called 'round turrets'; that her white face should look like a flag of surrender; and that Tarquin should say he comes to scale her 'never-conquer'd fort'. As Professor Allen points out,[9] the image is turned against Tarquin when, after the crime, his soul complains that her walls have been demolished by his deed:

> She says her subjects with foul insurrection
> Have battered down her consecrated wall,
> And by their mortal fault brought in subjection
> Her immortality, and made her thrall
> To living death and pain perpetual.

Whereas the walls of Tarquin's soul are battered down – we are reminded of the sonnet 'Poor soul the centre of my sinful earth, Hemmed by these rebel powers that thee array' – the house of Lucrece's soul is sacked,

> Her mansion batter'd by the enemy,
> Her sacred temple spotted, spoil'd, corrupted,
> Grossly engirt with daring infamy.

She wishes therefore to leave her body – 'this blemish'd fort' – by killing herself.

Brutus, at the end of the poem, comments on Lucrece's suicide:

> Thy wretched wife mistook the matter so,
> To slay herself that should have slain her foe.

Is Brutus right? Professor Don Cameron Allen in the article to which I have referred (*Shakespeare Survey* 15), shows how there was a long controversy about Lucrece's suicide which dates back to the Fathers of the Church. Tertullian praised her as a 'splendid example of domestic virtue'. But St Augustine argued that 'if suicide is extenuated, adultery is proved ... If she was adulterous, why is she praised? If she was chaste, why was she killed?'

Camerarius expressed the same idea in verse (as translated by an Elizabethan poet)

> Were that unchaste mate welcome to thy bed,
> *Lucrece*, thy lust was justly punished.
> But if foul force defil'd thine honest bed,
> His only rage should have been punished.

A really chaste woman would have died rather than surrender.

Professor Allen thinks that Shakespeare read the story of Lucrece in its Christian context. 'Lucrece should have defended herself to the death, or, having been forced, lived free of blame with a guiltless conscience'.

Professor Roy Battenhouse in his *Shakespearean Tragedy* (1969) likewise argues that the poet was writing from St Augustine's standpoint. The 'pearly sweat' on Lucrece's 'hand that is lying the outside the coverlet' is a sign of her unchaste nature. When Tarquin warns her that if she refuses to yield, he will use force, 'deny she does – as if subconsciously she wished force to work his way'. Surely, Battenhouse continues,

> if Lucrece really wishes rescue, she has plenty of time to cry out for it; for Shakespeare, in contrast to Ovid, makes much of Tarquin's long dallying. And surely there are servants in the house to answer calls for help . . . Shakespeare is but giving his reader time to realize that actually Lucrece's resort to complaints is her way of escaping from calling for help.

Her grief is put down to her fear 'for loss of social status'. Her suicide is 'paganism's dark substitute for the Christian Passion story'.

Such an interpretation seems to conflict with the obvious meaning of the text, and is not really supported by the fact that Middleton in his feeble imitation of Shakespeare makes the ghost of Lucrece come from hell.

Both Allen and Battenhouse seem to leave out of account,

or at least to gloss over, the reason for Lucrece's capitulation, and also the reasons she gives for her suicide. It was not fear of death that made her give up the struggle, but fear for her reputation after death. For Tarquin blackmailed her with the threat that he would kill her and a servant and say he had caught her in the act of adultery. When one considers the high value set by the Elizabethans on reputation, and also that this story would be more damaging to her husband than her actual rape, one can see that in the circumstances Lucrece's duty was not clear, even if she had been in a position to think clearly. Just before she kills herself, Lucrece asks the bystanders:

> What is the quality of my offence,
> Being constrain'd with dreadful circumstance?
> May my pure mind with the foul act dispense,
> My low-declined honour to advance?
> May any terms acquit me from this chance?
>   The poisoned fountain clears itself again;
>   And why not I from this compelled stain?

She is assured by Brutus and Collatine that

> Her body's stain her mind untainted clears.

But she cannot accept this assurance:

> "No, no," quoth she, "no dame hereafter living
> By my excuse shall claim excuse's giving".

She felt, rightly or wrongly, that she could only prove that she had not consented to rape — that the rape was not half-desired — if she refused to go on living. She wished to set an example to women who came after, who might pretend that they had been forced when they had welcomed the opportunity of committing adultery with a clear conscience. I am reminded of two modern French plays. In Giraudoux's *La Guerre de Troie N'Aura Pas Lieu*, Hector asks Paris if Helen consented to the rape. Paris replies that all women in such circumstances resist, but they afterwards consent with enthusiasm. The other play is André Roussin's farce, *La petite hutte*, in which the heroine allows herself to be seduced by a supposed native of the isle on which she is shipwrecked, ostensibly to save the life of her husband, who has been tied up by the native. Roussin makes clear that her real motive, or at least her unconscious motive, is different from her avowed one.

On the whole, it must be admitted, *Lucrece* has been less popular among the critics as well as with the general reader than *Venus and Adonis*. It lacks something of the freshness of the earlier poem. It is as though Shakespeare felt hampered by the necessity of producing a graver labour for his patron. It is obvious that he took immense pains with it. He showed that he could surpass all his contemporaries in the tragic lament. It is better than Daniel, better even than Spenser. It is a beautifully composed poem. It could be used to illustrate a text-book on rhetorical devices. Every stanza exhibits a rhetorical figure. Shakespeare ransacked the work of his predecessors and amplified the various themes and topics in accordance with the best critical opinion. The verse is for the most part melodious and varied, the rhymes unforced except some of the feminine ones. There are some lines as magnificent as any he ever wrote, and even when they are not magnificent, they frequently exhibit considerable art. For example, if one takes the commonest of all rhetorical figures – alliteration – one finds that Shakespeare never overdoes it.

> To blot old books and alter their contents . . .
> Thy violent vanities can never last . . .
> Muster thy mists to meet the eastern light . . .
> Cave-keeping evils that obscurely sleep . . .
> For men have marble, women waxen minds . . .

The two halves of the line are frequently bound together by this subtle, and not obtrusive, alliteration.

It could be argued that although the poem is less attractive than *Venus and Adonis*, it shows greater dramatic power. It remains a narrative poem, a 'complaint' (one of the most popular forms in the 1590s); but Shakespeare would never have made a play on the subject, as Heywood was afterwards to do. How sound his instinct was can be seen from Obey's *Viol de Lucrèce* which is very closely based on Shakespeare's poem. Obey, indeed, translates many of Shakespeare's stanzas and puts them into the mouth of his chorus. The play is impressive in its way; but the long period between the rape and the suicide in which we see a voluble and suffering innocence is pathetic rather than tragic, and static rather than dramatic.

12 'A Lover's Complaint'
A Reconsideration

[1]

'A Lover's Complaint', published in Shakespeare's *Sonnets* (1609), has been comparatively neglected by the critics. Some, indeed, have assumed that Shakespeare was probably not responsible for the poem. These include Hazlitt, Lee, Saintsbury, Kittredge, Parrott, C. S. Lewis, and also apparently, Rollins. Robertson ascribed it to Chapman,[1] and Murry concurred in this ascription.[2] J. W. Mackail, in what is otherwise the best essay on the poem, suggested that it was written by the Rival Poet of the Sonnets.[3] Those who have thought that Shakespeare was the author have been somewhat perfunctory in their comments. Malone called it a 'beautiful poem, in every part of which the hand of Shakespeare is visible'. Swinburne remarked that 'it contains two of the most exquisitely Shakespearean verses ever vouchsafed to us by Shakespeare, and two of the most execrably euphuistic or dysphuistic lines ever inflicted on us by man'. Samuel Butler considered it to be a 'wonderful poem'. John Dover Wilson regarded it as a deliberate parody by Shakespeare of Chapman. George Rylands speaks of it as 'that little-appreciated Elizabethan masterpiece', declaring that it 'shows an advance on the lyrical *Venus and Adonis* and the rhetorical *Lucrece*'.[4]

The best case against Shakespeare's authorship of the poem is Mackail's. He argues (p. 63) that its vocabulary is non-Shakespearian; that 'the style and evolution of the poem'

> must be set down as not characteristically Shakespearian, and in some respects as characteristically un-Shakespearian. A certain laboriousness, a certain cramped, gritty, discontinuous quality, affects it subtly but vitally throughout.

The author, unlike Shakespeare, fumbles at the beginning of the poem, and 'its preciosity, its strained rhetoric, its parade of learned words' would suit the Rival Poet as characterized by Shakespeare.

Very little has been written about the poem during the last thirty years, and it may therefore be worth while to re-open the question of the authorship of the poem, to examine the validity of the arguments put forward by Mackail and Robertson, and to attempt a reassessment of the poem, irrespective of its authorship.

The vocabulary of the poem is certainly unusual, though the parade of learned words is no more obvious than in *Troilus and Cressida*. There are some fifty words in the poem which are not found elsewhere in Shakespeare's works.[5] Fifteen of these are compound epithets: some of these are compounds of noun and participle (e.g., *heaven-hued, maiden-tongued, skill-contending, heart-wished*); others are compounds of two adjectives, or of adjectives with participles (e.g., *comely-distant, deep-green, deep-brained, sad-tuned, strong-bonded*). Another group of words is formed by the addition of pre-fixes (e.g., *encrimsoned, enswathed, impleached, unapproved, unshorn, enpatron*); others are formed by the addition of suffixes (e.g., *phraseless, termless, fastly, weepingly, acture, extincture*); others again are verbs coined from nouns or adjectives (e.g., *sheaved, sistering, lover'd, pensiv'd, livery*); some are comparatively common words which Shakespeare did not happen to use again (e.g., *beaded* − if this is the correct reading − *blusterer, consecrations, maund, laundering*);

and a few are the ink-horn terms which are most frequent in *Troilus and Cressida* (e.g., *annexions, congest, fluxive*). Some of these words are apparently coinages: at least the Oxford Dictionary does not give prior instances of their use. These include *acture, encrimsoned, enswathed, impleached, unapproved, unexperient, invised,*[6] *annexions, lovered* and *laundering*.

The presence of so many 'un-Shakespearian' words is not, however a decisive argument against his authorship; for all Shakespeare's plays contain words he did not use more than once, some of which he probably coined for the immediate purpose. The words listed above are similar to words used by Shakespeare: *annexment* and *enacture* in *Hamlet, pleached* in *Much Ado about Nothing, crimsoned* in *Julius Caesar*; and if *sister* as a verb occurs only in a possibly non-Shakespearian part of *Pericles,* he used *husband* as a verb in *King Lear.* There are, moreover, a number of words in 'A Lover's Complaint' used once only in Shakespeare's other works: *cautel* in *Hamlet, dialogue* as a verb in *Timon of Athens, pelleted* in *Antony and Cleopatra, commix* in *Cymbeline* and *reword* in *Hamlet.* Clearly the unusual words in 'A Lover's Complaint' are of the kind which Shakespeare would coin or borrow.

Since Hart's studies in Shakespeare's vocabulary,[7] it has been accepted by most critics who have given the matter their attention that the presence of words not used elsewhere by Shakespeare cannot be used to disprove his authorship of a play. In his later plays, at least, he used a previously unused word every ten or fourteen lines on an average, and a word new to our literature (on the evidence of *O.E.D.*) every eighteen to twenty-eight lines. In works of which Shakespeare was the part author — *Edward III* and *The Two Noble Kinsmen* — he used new words about twice as frequently as his collaborators.[8] There are 329 lines in 'A Lover's Complaint', so that one would expect to find in it at least twenty-three, and possibly as many as thirty-three, words not previously used by Shakespeare, and about fifteen words which are not known to have appeared in print before. As the poem is short, it would be unwise to lay much stress on the exact figures. In fact the number of unused words, and of words used with a different meaning, is considerably more than thirty-three, but the newly coined words number about fourteen. As the poem has been dated as early as 1585, and as late as 1603, precision is impossible in either case.

These figures do not, of course, prove that Shakespeare wrote the poem; but at least they throw doubt on the view that because of its vocabulary he could not have written it.

If we turn from vocabulary to wider questions of style, there may seem, at first sight, to be more substance in Mackail's arguments. No one could deny that there are very weak lines and clumsy expressions in the poem. Mackail cites as examples of feebleness:

> Whereon the thought might think sometime it saw . . . (10)

> What's sweet to do, to do will aptly find . . . (88)

> For on his visage was in little drawn
> What largeness thinks in Paradise was sawn.[9] (90)

Although such lines are manifestly weak, they are not weaker than numerous lines in Shakespeare's acknowledged works; and even if the lines were too bad for Shakespeare, there are others too good for some unknown poetaster, and, perhaps, too good even for Chapman. As Mackail admits (p. 62):

> There are more than a few passages in the poem which are like Shakespeare at his best, and of which one would say at first sight that no one but Shakespeare could have written them, so wonderfully do they combine his effortless power and his incomparable sweetness.

Although Mackail disagrees, it is surely easier to believe that Shakespeare wrote a poem with a number of feeble lines — some explicable by textual corruption or lack of revision — than that some other poet, having steeped himself in Shakespeare's poems and sonnets, succeeded at times in equalling his models.

Sir Edmund Chambers goes so far as to admit that Robertson's argument for Chapman's authorship of the poem are 'more plausible than some of his ascriptions to that writer'.[10] This, however, is not saying very much. Robertson relies a good deal on Mackail's essay, and he fastens on the suggestion that the poem was written by the Rival Poet. He seeks to show that the words used in the poem have the same meaning and accentuation as when they are used by Chapman, but not as when used elsewhere by Shakespeare. His first example is *authorized*:

> His rudeness so with his authoriz'd youth . . .   (104)
>
> Authoriz'd by her grandam.   (*Macbeth* III. iv. 65)
>
> Authorizing thy trespass with compare . . .   (Sonnet 35)

He suggests unwarrantably that the accentuation of the word in *Macbeth* is different from that in the other lines, though in all three the accent is on the second syllable; and, somewhat embarrassed by the sonnet accentuation, he suggests that this sonnet is either not Shakespeare's, or else written by Shakespeare in imitation of Chapman. His second example is:

> He had the dialect and different skill . . .   (125)
>
> In her youth
> There is a prone and speechless dialect
> Such as move men.   (*M.M.* I. ii. 188)

In both passages, as Robertson admits, the meaning of *dialect* is 'persuasive skill', so that the Chapman parallels he gives are largely irrelevant.

More significant are the words which occur both in 'A Lover's Complaint' and in Chapman's works, but not elsewhere in Shakespeare's. Chapman does use *maund*, *affectedly*, *sawn*, *forbod*, *pallid*, and *charmed* (in the sense of 'exercising charm'); but we may observe that *maund* is not rare, that *affectedly* is a word that any poet might have coined from *affected*, that *sawn* is not used by Chapman in the sense of 'sown' but only in the modern sense, that *forbod* is used in

Lucrece (though most editors emend to *forbade*), that *pallid* is used by Spenser, and that in any case it is not certain that the *palyd* of the first edition means *pallid*. Robertson gives other examples, but they can mostly be ignored. Some words used in 'A Lover's Complaint' can be interpreted in a different way; others listed by Robertson are used by Shakespeare as well as by Chapman; many are not precisely paralleled in Chapman's work – *acture*, for example, being nearer to Shakespeare's *enacture* than to Chapman's *facture*; and one word, *invise*, occurs only in 'The Contention of Phillis and Flora', a poem which is no longer ascribed to Chapman.

But the strongest argument against Robertson is that by using the same methods he brings himself to believe that Chapman collaborated with Shakespeare in at least thirteen of his acknowledged plays. If we refuse to accept the argument that Chapman had a hand in *Troilus and Cressida* and *Julius Caesar*, our low opinion of 'A Lover's Complaint' should not permit us to acquiesce in Robertson's ascription of the poem to Chapman.

[2]

Every one of Shakespeare's works has internal links with others. If, for example, *Troilus and Cressida* had been published anonymously, it would have been easy to demonstrate Shakespeare's authorship by its links with *Lucrece* and the Sonnets, with *Romeo and Juliet* and *Hamlet*. Even plays to which Shakespeare contributed a few scenes only – *Sir Thomas More* and *The Two Noble Kinsmen* – have multiple links with his known works. If, therefore, Shakespeare wrote 'A Lover's Complaint', we should expect to find parallels in it with his known works. Editors have pointed out a number of these but without, apparently, realizing their full significance. The following parallels may be offered as examples.

The forsaken lover is described in the first stanza as

Storming her world with sorrow's wind and rain.

In the storm scene of *King Lear*, the Gentleman tells Kent that the King

Strives in his little world of man to out-storm[11]
The to-and-fro conflicting wind and rain.

This parallel may, indeed, be regarded as suspect because its validity partly depends on a plausible emendation. More significant is the parallel between the third stanza and a passage in *Antony and Cleopatra*:

Oft did she heave her napkin to her eyne,
Which on it had conceited characters,
Laund'ring the silken figures in the brine
That seasoned woe had pelleted in tears.

So Cleopatra, replying to Antony's accusation that she is cold-hearted toward him (III. xiii. 158), exclaims:

Ah, dear, if I be so,
From my cold heart let heaven engender hail,
And poison it in the source, and the first stone
Drop in my neck; as it determines, so
Dissolve my life! The next Cæsarion smite!
Till by degrees the memory of my womb,
Together with my brave Egyptians all,
By the discandying of this pelleted storm,
Lie graveless . . .

Shakespeare does not use the word pelleted except in these two passages. In the poem, the tears are the pellets of sorrow; in the play, Cleopatra's frozen tears, turned to hail, are the pellets of her grief. Steevens says that *pellet* was 'the ancient culinary term for a *forced meat ball*', and it was also an heraldic term. The heraldic associations are certainly not present in Cleopatra's speech. Hailstones may properly be spoken of as a 'pelleted storm' – a storm of pellets – but it looks as though the more complicated imagery of *Antony and Cleopatra* was suggested by the lines of the poem, linked, perhaps, with the later lines:

> That not a heart which is his level came
> Could scape the hail of his all-hurting aim.

The play was performed before the poem was printed, so that Shakespeare must have had access to the manuscript. It may be added that on at least four occasions he uses the idea of salt tears acting as seasoning:

> Seasoning the earth with show'rs of silver brine   (*Luc.* 796)

> With eye-offending brine. All this to season
> A brother's dead love.   (*T.N.* I. i. 30–31)

> How much salt water thrown away in waste,
> To season love!   (*R.J.* II. iii. 72)

> 'Tis the best brine a maiden can season her praise in.
>   (*A.W.* I. i. 55)

     The most interesting parallels, however, are with *Hamlet*. Both Laertes and Polonius warn Ophelia against Hamlet, whose attentions, they assume, are as dishonourable as those of the handsome seducer of 'A Lover's Complaint'. Hamlet was the 'observed of all observers', as the seducer was

> one by nature's outwards so commended
> That maidens' eyes stuck over all his face.   (80)

Laertes tells his sister that Hamlet may love her now,

> And now no soil nor cautel doth besmirch
> The virtue of his will.   (I. iii. 15)

It has been suggested that Shakespeare borrowed the word 'cautel' from Henry Swinburne's *Briefe Treatise of Testaments and Last Willes*;[12] but the word is also used in 'A Lover's Complaint', though not elsewhere in Shakespeare's works. Laertes warns Ophelia that she may suffer loss of honour

> If with too credent ear you list his songs,
> Or lose your heart, or your chaste treasure open
> To his unmaster'd importunity.   (I. iii. 30–31)

This is precisely what happens to the heroine of 'A Lover's Complaint'. The seducer urges her to lend

> soft audience to my sweet design,
> And credent soul to that strong-bonded oath.   (278)

Shakespeare uses the word 'credent' on two other occasions,[13] and in each case he associates it with fornication or adultery. Ophelia tells her father that Hamlet has 'made many tenders of his affection' and 'given countenance to his speech' with 'almost all the holy vows of heaven'. Polonius retorts that 'when the blood burns', the 'soul lends the tongue vows'. So in 'A Lover's Complaint', the seducer shows the girl the presents he has received from his former victims:

> Lo, all these trophies of affections hot,
> Of pensiv'd and subdu'd desires the tender.   (218–19)

Earlier in the poem, he urges the maid not to be afraid of his 'holy vows' (179). Polonius finally tells Ophelia not to believe Hamlet's vows:

> for they are brokers,
> Not of that dye which their investments show,
> But mere implorators of unholy suits,
> Breathing like sanctified and pious bonds[14]
> The better to beguile.   (I. iii. 127–31)

So the forsaken lover was aware beforehand of the seducer's evil reputation:

> For further I could say 'This man's untrue',
> And knew the patterns of his foul beguiling;
> Heard where his plants in others' orchards grew;
> Saw how deceits were gilded in his smiling;
> Knew vows were ever broken to defiling;
> Thought characters and words merely but art,
> And bastards of his foul adulterate heart.   (169 ff.)

The seducer afterwards tells of the nun, 'or sister *sanctified*', who had fallen in love with him; and he urges the maiden to believe his 'strong-bonded' oath (279). Ophelia, finally, is urged by Hamlet to get to a nunnery, which recalls the most spectacular of the seducer's conquests; and she is dragged to a muddy death. The heroine of the poem throws her presents in the stream, 'Bidding them find their sepulchres in mud'.

Although the word *broker* was frequently used as a synonym for pimp,[15] and although the subject of seduction would almost inevitably involve the use of some of the words common to the two passages, the links between them would appear to be strong enough for us to assume that one passage was influenced by the other. Several explanations are theoretically possible:

(1) Shakespeare might have read 'A Lover's Complaint' in manuscript before he wrote *Hamlet* – that is, between 1593 and 1601.

(2) Both Shakespeare and the author of the poem might have been influenced by a corresponding scene in the Ur-*Hamlet* (if there was one).

(3) The author of the poem might have written it after the publication of *Hamlet*, and before the entering of the *Sonnets* in May, 1609.

(4) 'A Lover's Complaint' might have been written by a friend of Shakespeare's, who had access to his manuscripts.

(5) Both works may have been written by Shakespeare.

Any of these explanations is possible, but only the last is at all probable.[16]

[3]

The publication of the poem with an authentic text of the Sonnets – a text which may, indeed, be printed from Shakespeare's manuscript,[17] though not, presumably, with his

permission – is strong *prima facie* evidence for his authorship
of the poem. Although Sir Sidney Lee thought that the
publication was comparable with that of *A Passionate Pilgrim*,
and although Mackail believed that some of the sonnets were
spurious, it is obvious that even if we were doubtful about
the authorship of a few of the later sonnets, the collection was
not an anthology by various hands. Lee had some hard things
to say about the careless printing, though many of the alleged
misprints look more like a conscientious following of auth-
orial spelling.[18] As the volume was already of a respectable
size without additional matter, the publisher had no need to
pad it out with a poem by another writer; and the name
'William Shake-speare' is repeated after the title 'A Louers
complaint'. It must be assumed, therefore, without strong
evidence to the contrary, that the poem was indeed by
Shakespeare; and this is the assumption that is made in the
remainder of this essay.[19]

As the poem is written in the seven-line stanza of *Lucrece*,
it should probably be dated after *Venus and Adonis* and not,
as some have surmized, as early as 1585; and as *Lucrece* was
apparently the 'graver labour' promised in the dedication to
the earlier poem, 'A Lover's Complant' was probably written
after *Lucrece*. It has some links with the Sonnets and more
significant links with plays written after 1600 than with
those written before. It is possible, therefore, that it was
written about the turn of the century. Some have dated it
after 1601 because of supposed echoes of Holland's Pliny;[20]
but the parallels are not necessarily with the translation, so
that they cannot be used to date the poem. Perhaps it represents a first draft which Shakespeare intended to revise – one
would expect the reverend man of stanza 9 to offer the lady
good advice after her story – or which he regarded as too
slight to publish by itself. He was sufficiently busy between
1601 and 1609 for him to have had little leisure for non-
dramatic poetry; and he must have realized that the poem
was small beer compared with *Hamlet* or *King Lear*. When
he published *Venus and Adonis* he could speak of it as the

first heir of his invention, his earlier plays being as yet un-
published, and not regarded as serious literature; but, a dec-
ade later, he was recognized as the best dramatist of his time,
and he had less need to publish non-dramatic poetry.

By the time the Sonnets were published, the vogue for
sonneteering, started by Sidney, was already over. Drayton
added a few sonnets to his collection after 1605, and one or
two younger poets continued to write in the idiom of the past
age; but parody, overproduction and Donne's new style had
combined to make the love-sonnet unfashionable. In the
same way, 'A Lover's Complaint' belonged to a class of poem
which had been popular in the 'nineties and even before.
Some 'complaints', including those in The *Mirror for Magistrates*, are put into the mouths of historical figures. Lodge's
'Complaint of Elstred' (1593) and Daniel's 'Complaint of
Rosamond' (1592) are of this kind – the latter being in the
same stanza form as 'A Lover's Complaint', and both being
published with sonnet sequences. Other complaints are
spoken by mythological or allegorical characters – for instance, The *Lamentation of Troy for the Death of Hector* (1594),
and Barnfield's 'The Complaint of Chastitie' (1574) and
'The Complaint of Poetrie' (1598).

Shakespeare's poem is unusual in that it is concerned with
a fictional character in a modern, though pastoral, setting.
The first eight stanzas describe the behaviour of the deserted
woman, as observed by the poet from a hill. She is asked by
'a reverend man that graz'd his cattle nigh', who had formerly lived in the city, 'the grounds and motives of her
woe'. The remainder of the poem consists of the woman's
story of how she was seduced, and during this tale we are
not reminded at all of the initial observer, and only once of
the aged man. Within the story is a long speech of the
seducer, filling fifteen stanzas. Knowing that the woman is
aware of his promiscuity, he cheerfully admits his conduct,
but (like Juan in *Man and Superman*) he excuses himself by
claiming that he was solicited by the woman in each case,
that he was never before in love, and that he was guilty of

'errors of the blood, none of the mind'. He shows the valuable presents he has received from his lovers and offers them to the first woman, as he claims, that he has really loved. He argues, oddly, that his former lovers are anxious that she should capitulate, not because they wish her to be as frail as they themselves have been, but because they want to be happy in his happiness. But the woman is not won by his arguments. She had fallen in love with him before he began to woo, and she is overcome not by his words but by his tears which made her pity him and believe his 'holy vows'. She confesses at the end of the poem that he was so beautiful, and so good an actor, that his tears and blushes

> Would yet again betray the fore-betrayed,
> And new pervert a reconciled maid.

The underlying theme of the poem was a favourite one of Shakespeare's, the difficulty of distinguishing between appearance and reality. The heroine of the poem knows the seducer's evil reputation, but this knowledge does not save her. The theme is expressed, as in *Much Ado about Nothing*, by clothing imagery.[21] The seducer's chin was like 'unshorn velvet'; his rudeness

> Did livery falseness in a pride of truth;   (105)

and, in the penultimate stanza,

> Thus merely with the garment of a grace
> The naked and concealed fiend he cover'd,
> That th' unexperient gave the tempter place,
> Which, like a cherubin, above them hover'd.

Here the seducer is compared to a fiend, as Satan, under the distorting influence of sexual desire, appeared to be a cherub. The effect of this double image, linked by the ambiguous *tempter*, is to associate the seducer and Satan, so that the woman in her fall becomes a second Eve.

The largest group of images, however, is taken from war and these express the battle between the sexes. The aim o

the villain-hero is to make the woman surrender without
marriage; the conscious aim of the heroine is to preserve her
chastity, and, unconsciously, to conquer the man by per-
suading him to marry her, his former conquests adding to
the glory of her victory. Her straw hat – 'a platted hive of
straw' – 'fortified her visage from the sun'. Her eyes

> their carriage ride
> As they did batt'ry to the spheres intend.   (22)

She shielded her honour 'with safest distance'. Stories of the
man's licentiousness were a protection to her:

> Experience for me many bulwarks builded.   (152)

She compares her honour to a besieged city:

> And long upon these terms I held my city,
> Till thus he gan besiege me.

The seducer compares the pearls and rubies given him by
his victims to their grief and blushes:

> Effects of terror and dear modesty,
> Encamp'd in hearts, but fighting outwardly.   (202)

The woman who became a nun,

> The scars of battle scapeth by the flight.   (244)

The man tells the heroine, in reference to his previous
victims:

> I strong o'er them, and you o'er me being strong,
> Must for your victory us all congest.   (257)

The man boasts that his parts assailed the nun's eyes, or else
that her eyes, attracted by his beauty, assailed her heart. The
man assures the heroine that 'Love's arms are peace'; he
tells her that his very victims urge her

> To leave the batt'ry that you make 'gainst mine
>   (277)

H

Finally, the heroine declares that

> not a heart which in his level came
> Could scape the hail of his all-hurting aim.   (309)

There are indications, however, that the seducer is not entirely hypocritical, and that he, like the heroine, is in some sense a victim. His account of the nun's passion for him, though designed to weaken the heroine's resistance, expresses what seems to be a genuine wonder at the power of love, which overturns morality and religion:

> Religious love put out Religion's eye . . .
>
> My parts had power to charm a sacred nun,
> Who disciplin'd, ay, dieted in grace,
> Believ'd her eyes, when they t'assail begun,
> All vows and consecrations giving place.
> O most potential love! vow, bond, nor space
> In thee hath neither sting, knot, nor confine,
> For thou art all, and all things else are thine.
>
> When thou impressest, what are precepts worth
> Of stale example? When thou wilt inflame
> How coldly those impediments stand forth,
> Of wealth, of filial fear, law, kindred, fame!
> Love's arms are peace, 'gainst rule, 'gainst sense,
>   'gainst shame,
> And sweetens, in the suffering pangs it bears,
> The aloes of all forces, shocks and fears.   (250 ff.)

The last three lines of this stanza are an example of the kind of weakness which has made critics reluctant to admit Shakespeare's responsibility for the poem. It seems probable that it represents a first, or at least an early, draft. Shakespeare had abandoned the forceful clarity of *Venus and Adonis* and *Lucrece*, and he was striving, not always successfully, toward the complexity of his mature dramatic verse.

Yet the number of such confused passages is small, and they are far outweighed by the numerous brilliant lines and well composed stanzas:

> . . . but spite of heaven's fell rage,
> Some beauty peep'd through lattice of sear'd age.   (13)

> Laund'ring the silken figures in the brine,
> That season'd woe had pelleted in tears.   (17)

> But ah! who ever shun'd by precedent
> The destin'd ill she must her self assay,
> Or forc'd examples 'gainst her own content
> To put the by-past perils in her way?   (155)

> Oh, father, what a hell of witchcraft lies
> In the small orb of one particular tear!   (288)

> He preach'd pure maid, and prais'd cold chastity. (315)

It is difficult to agree with Mr Rylands that the poem is a masterpiece, even though it has masterly things in it. But the comparative failures of a great poet are often of singular interest. In 'A Lover's Complaint' Shakespeare was hampered at times by the stanza form – perhaps because he had abandoned rhyme for some years, except for particular dramatic purposes. He was hampered, too, we may suspect, by the genre of the complaint, in which we see everything through one character's eyes. Above all, his unrivalled linguistic daring was temporarily out of control, perhaps under the influence of bad models – Chapman, Marston and Markham. A fear of tameness – and a number of lines are flat indeed – led him sometimes into the opposite vice of rhetorical inflation. The poem is inferior in most ways to Shakespeare's other narrative poems, and it is inferior to the best of the sonnets; but it is not without its own special flavour, and it adds something to the total impression we have of Shakespeare as a poet.

Notes

Chapter 1

1. *Life of Samuel Johnson*, ed. G. B. Hill (Oxford, 1934), III, 376.
2. Florence E. Hardy, *Life of Thomas Hardy* (London, 1962), p. 341.
3. *Life and Letters of Anton Tchekhov*, trans. and ed. S. S. Koteliansky and Philip Tomlinson (London, 1925), pp. 36, 38.
4. E. Martin Browne, *The Making of T. S. Eliot's Plays* (Cambridge, 1969).
5. *The Artistry of Shakespeare's Prose* (London, 1968).
6. *Shakespeare Survey 23* (Cambridge, 1970), pp. 39–48.
7. One can observe something of the same kind in Marlowe, though in a more condensed form: his most flexible dramatic verse – Faustus's last speech – comes just after the wonderful prose in the scene with the scholars.
8. See Chapter 7.
9. 'The Diabolic Images in *Othello*', *Shakespeare Survey 5* (Cambridge, 1952), pp. 62–80.
10. 'Seem' and its derivatives were used by Shakespeare nearly 500 times.
11. *Shakespeare the Dramatist* (London, 1961), p. 18.
12. *Samlede Verker*, XVII (Oslo, 1946), 73; *ibid.*, XV (Oslo, 1930), 48.
13. '*Landscape*' and '*Silence*' (London, 1969), pp. 29–30.
14. S. T. Coleridge, *Shakespearean Criticism*, ed. T. M. Raysor (London, 1960, II, 85; *Letters*, ed. E. H. Coleridge (London, 1895), I, 372.
15. *Letters*, ed. M. B. Forman (Oxford, 1935), p. 288.
16. *Lectures on the English Poets* (London, 1922), pp. 47–50.
17. *Shakespeare the Craftsman* (London, 1969).

18. T. S. Eliot, *Four Quartets* (London, 1949), p. 22.
19. W. B. Yeats, *Collected Poems* (New York, 1950), p. 391.
20. III. 312.

Chapter 2

1. Blake remarked that the lines are Theseus' opinion, not Shakespeare's, 'You might as well quote Satan's blasphemies from Milton and give them as Milton's opinions'. A. Thaler, *Shakespeare and Sir Philip Sidney* (1947), compares several passages from Sidney's *Defence*:

> the poet . . . from Dante his heaven to his hell, under . . . his pen . . . the imagination and judging power . . . figured forth by the speaking picture of poesy . . . forms such as never were in nature . . . The poets give names . . . to make their picture the more lively.

2. In all the recent productions I have seen, Cinna has been lynched on the stage; and the horror is perhaps in this case legitimate and is not merely an attempt to show that Shakespeare was a forerunner of the Theatre of Cruelty. We need not suppose, as has been suggested, that the murder of a poet gives special satisfaction to an English audience, or even that the director is symbolically presenting his own butchery of the poet whose plays he 'adapts'.

3. No edition I have seen does this. Shakespeare alters the couplet though the general drift is the same; but it could be argued that he means it to be the bad poet's own rather than a quotation. This is supported by Brutus' 'jigging fools'. (Cf. Marlowe's 'jigging veins of rhyming mother wits'.)

4. J. Middleton Murry, *Countries of the Mind*, Second Series (London, 1931), p. 97, argued that Shakespeare was thinking of his own dedications to Southampton. The evidence, however, is slight.

5. Alexander, on the strength of the penultimate line of this passage, emends *wax* to *tax* in the Poet's speech. But Shakespeare was presumably thinking of wax tablets and E. A. Armstrong associates it with two Icarus passages.

6. Thaler, *Shakespeare and Sir Philip Sidney*, has shown that Shakespeare knew *The Defence of Poesy*, echoing Sidney's phrases in Menenius' fable, recalling perhaps his description of tragedy in

the disease imagery of *Hamlet* and the effect of tragedy on tyrants in the prince's words on 'guilty creatures sitting at a play', and probably replying good-humouredly to Sidney's views on the unities through the mouth of Time in *The Winter's Tale*. It seems likely therefore, that the references to poetry as feigning or lying allude to Sidney's refutation of the view that all poets were liars.

7. It would, perhaps, be possible for the Poet and Painter to be on the stage during these scenes, waiting for a suitable opportunity to approach.

8. Soon after I had completed this essay, I came across a chapter with the same title in *Shakespeare and Common Sense* by Edwin R. Hunter (Boston, 1954). Inevitably we cover much of the same ground, though with a very different emphasis. Mr Hunter's conclusion is that Shakespeare saw 'no reason for avoiding this comic and sceptical treatment of his own art . . . Shakespeare thought too highly of poetry to have thought of its needing defenders, and he is just the sort of humorous man who does not mind having the jest come up occasionally against himself and his kind'.

Chapter 3

1. Professor Stamn, in whose *festschrift* this essay first appeared, has written admirably on Shaw's attitude to Shakespeare.
2. Wilson, *op. cit.*, p. 55.
3. Henderson, *Bernard Shaw: Man of the Century*.
4. *Our Theatres*, Preface.
5. Wilson, p. 213.
6. *Ibid.*, p. 54.
7. *Ibid.*, p. 5.
8. *Ibid.*, p. 231.
9. *Ibid.*, p. 229.
10. *Ibid.*, p. 5.
11. *Ibid.*, p. 226.
12. *Ibid.*, p. 236.
13. *Prefaces* (1934), p. 178.
14. West, *Shaw on Theatre*, p. 62.
15. *Ibid.*, p. 132.

16. *Ibid.*, p. 132–3.
17. Henderson, p. 887.
18. West, p. 268.
19. *Ibid.*, p. 294.
20. Wilson, p. 241–2.
21. *Ibid.*, p. 125.
22. *Ibid.*, p. 178.
23. *Ibid.*, p. 128.
24. *Ibid.*, p. 248.
25. *Ibid.*, p. 159.
26. *Ibid.*, p. 246.
27. *Ibid.*, p. 44.
28. *Ibid.*, p. 25.
29. *Ibid.*, p. 250, 4, 79, 12, 194–5.
30. *Ibid.*, p. 7.
31. *Ibid.*, p. 5.
32. *Ibid.*, p. 9.
33. *Ibid.*, p. 9.
34. *Ibid.*, p. 142.
35. *Ibid.*, p. 15.
36. *Ibid.*, p. 33.
37. *Ibid.*, p. 16.
38. *Ibid.*, p. 159–60.
39. *Ibid.*, p. 127–8.
40. *Ibid.*, p. 134–5.
41. West, p. 222–4.
42. *Ibid.*, p. 89.
43. *Ibid.*, p. 266.
44. Wilson, p. 52.
45. *Ibid.*, p. 50.
46. West, p. 160.
47. Wilson, p. 257.
48. *Ibid.*, p. 269.
49. *Ibid.*, p. 96.
50. West, p. 130.
51. Wilson, p. xvii.
52. *Ibid.*, p. 213.
53. Henderson, p. 746.

Chapter 4

1. J. Dryden, *Of Dramatic Poesy and other Critical Essays* (ed. 1962), I, 173.
2. *Ibid.*, I, 257.
3. i.e. reject.
4. J. Dryden, *Works*, ed. Scott and Saintsbury, VI, 349.
5. W. Davenant, cited in the *Furness Variorum*, p. 515.
6. Cited in D. Nichol Smith, *Shakespeare Criticism* (1916), p. 48.
7. *Ibid.*, p. 69.
8. *Ibid.*, p. 72.
9. *Ibid.*, p. 92.
10. Cited Whiter, *op. cit.*, p. 64.
11. *Ibid.*, p. 65.
12. *Ibid.*, pp. 71, 73.
13. *Ibid.*, pp. 69–71.
14. *Timon*, IV. iii. 222; Whiter, *op. cit.*, p. 81.
15. *Ibid.*, pp. 84, 87, 83.
16. For this I was indebted to G. A. Over. His edition of Whiter, revised by Mary Bell, was published in 1967.
17. Cf. E. E. Kellett and Caroline Spurgeon discussed below.
18. *Op. cit.*, p. 124. *R.J.*, I. iv. 107; V. iii. 111.
19. See n. 16, above.
20. *Op. cit.*, p. 254. Whiter does not cite the Geneva version, as given here, nor does he refer to the adjacent text.
21. *Op. cit.*, p. 124.
22. See n. 17, above.
23. See n. 16, above.
24. Coleridge, *op. cit.* (ed. 1921), p. 169.
25. H. Elwin, *op. cit.*, pp. iii, ix, x, xvii.
26. *N.S.S. Trans.* 1877–9, pp. 385–405.
27. *Ibid.*, p. 365.
28. *Ibid.*, 1887–92, p. 24*. The paper was written as a doctoral thesis for Strasburg University, and a copy of it has been traced by Terence Spencer.
29. *Ibid.*, pp. 397–427.
30. *Southern Cross* apparently ceased publication in 1901; but Kolbe speaks of his essay on *Julius Caesar* as having been written 'some thirty years ago'. Elsewhere he speaks of an incident in his childhood sixty years before the time of his writing.

31. F. C. Kolbe, *op. cit.*, pp. 87, 95, 71, 3 ff., 145–6.
32. E.g. W. Empson and Brents Stirling.
33. *Suggestions* (1923), pp. 57–78.
34. *The Tempest*, II. i. 242.
35. Cf. also Chapter 9 below.
36. *Leading Motives in the Imagery of Shakespeare's Tragedies.*
37. *Op. cit.*, pp. 200 ff.
38. *Elizabethan and Metaphysical Imagery* (ed. 1961), pp. 254, 420.
39. *Shakespeare Survey 4* (1951), p. 20, and *Penguin New Writing*, No. 28 (1946).
40. For *Richard II* see Richard D. Altick's article, *P.M.L.A.* (1947), pp. 339–65.
41. *Op. cit.* (ed. 1963), p. 203.
42. K. Muir, *Shakespeare as Collaborator* (1960), p. 118. Although I refer to words separated by fifty lines, the cluster is complete without.
43. W. R. Keast, 'Imagery and Meaning in the Interpretation of *King Lear*', *Modern Philology*, XLVII (1950).
44. *Ibid.*
45. Charney's later book, *Style in Hamlet* (1969) should also be mentioned.
46. See n. 38 above, Helen Gardner, *The Business of Criticism* (1959), p. 132, and Roland M. Frye, *Shakespeare and Christian Doctrine* (1963). Frye thinks that Knight and his followers 'have contributed very little of any real worth to the understanding of Shakespeare'.
47. L. C. Knights' later attitude can be seen in *Some Shakespearian Themes* (1959) and *An Approach to Hamlet* (1960).
48. See, for example, *Shakespeare's Poetics*, by Russell A. Fraser (1962), and *Shakespeare's Derived Imagery* (1953), by John E. Hankins.
49. Cf. James L. Jackson, *Shakespeare Quarterly*, I (1950), p. 260.
50. E.g. S. L. Bethell's article, *Shakespeare Survey 5* (1952).
51. *The Development of Shakespeare's Imagery* (1951), p. 231.
52. See Chapter 8 below.

Chapter 5

1. *P.M.L.A.*, LXII (1947).
2. E. A. Armstrong, *Shakespeare's Imagination* (1946).
3. *Shakespeare's Imagery*, p. 230.
4. *D.U.J.* (1935), pp. 44–75.
5. *Shakespeare: A Survey* (1925), p. 20.
6. C. Spurgeon declares that there is no iterative image in the play.
7. H. Elwin, *Shakespeare Restored* (1853).
8. *Shakespere's Small Latine and Lesse Greek* (1944), ii, 472–8.
9. Except for a reference to the burden of child-bearing.
10. *The Problem of Henry VIII Reopened* (1949); *Studies in Bibliography*, VIII–XV (1959–62).
11. *Shakespeare as Collaborator* (1960).
12. See p. 61 above.

Chapter 6

1. See p. 79 above.
2. I have not yet seen a production of the play in which Romeo puts on a disguise when he leaves Juliet to go to Mantua.
3. Cf. *Shakespeare's Derived Imagery* (1953).
4. Miss Spurgeon rightly pointed out that the idea of the imagery of light and fire may be derived from Arthur Brooke's poem; but she did not quote Brooke's most suggestive image:

> What epitaph more worth, or half so excellent,
> To consecrate my memory, could any man invent
> As this our mutual and most piteous sacrifice
> Of life, set light for love?

The lines are spoken by Romeus just before his suicide. There are more than a score of light and fire images in Brooke's poem; some referring to love, and others to the feud between the two families. See ll. 35, 49, 87, 143, 173, 209, 228, 239, 434, 487, 508, 956, 978, 1157, 1465, 1726, 2787.
5. I see no reason to doubt Shakespeare's authorship.
6. In his excellent edition (1964) G. W. Williams prefers the reading *suit* for the last word of this passage. I am unconvinced by his arguments.

7. The lines I have omitted from this speech possibly echo Sonnet 85 in *Astrophel and Stella*, Cf. K. Muir, *Shakespeare's Sources I* (1957), p. 29.

8. Brooke, in spite of his moralizing epistle to the reader, in which he underlines the guilt of the lovers, stresses over and over again the workings of Fate. Fortune is mentioned 35 times; there are five references to fate or the Fates; and one line (1328) is close in spirit to two of Romeo's:

> He cried out, with open mouth, against the stars above.

9. ll. 211–12, 335, 799–808, 1361–78, 1514–26, Cf. K. Muir *N.Q.* June 1956, p. 241.

10. A few lines later Juliet says her 'bounty is as boundless as the sea'.

Chapter 7

1. *Shakespeare's Imagery* (1935), p. 318.
2. *The Development of Shakespeare's Imagery* (1951), p. 113.
3. A. Thaler, *Shakespeare and Sir Philip Sidney* (1947), p. 7.
4. *Hamlet Father and Son* (1955), p. 38.
5. Cf. J. Dover Wilson, *What Happens in Hamlet* (1935), p. 309.
6. *S.Q.* V (1954), pp. 167–76.
7. *The Imperial Theme* (ed. 1951), p. 96.
8. There is something, but not enough, to be said for Theobald's emendation of *bonds* to *bawds*, as this fits with the later association of 'devotion's visage and pious action' with the harlot's cheek. See Thomas Clayton's article, in *Shakespeare Studies*, II (1966), pp. 59–94.
9. See Anne Righter, *Shakespeare and the Idea of the Play* (1962), and G. Wilson Knight, *The Wheel of Fire* (1949), Chapter XV.
10. See K. Muir, 'The Dramatic Function of Anachronism', *Proceedings of the Leeds Philosophical and Literary Society* (1951).
11. C. Spurgeon classifies these under more than one heading. My view is confirmed by Maurice Charney in *Style in Hamlet*.
12. IV. vii. 21; V. ii. 235.

Chapter 8

1. *Shakespeare the Dramatist* (1961), p. 37.
2. *Fortnightly Review* (1910), pp. 696 ff.
3. E.g. G. Wilson Knight, *The Imperial Theme* (ed. 1951), p. 148.
4. F. C. Kolbe, *Shakespeare's Way* (1930), pp. 21–2.
5. Ed. *Macbeth* (1951), p. xxxiii.
6. *Tennessee Studies* (1960), pp. 97–100.
7. I. iii. 19–21.
8. *Shakespeare* (1936).
9. *Shakespeare Survey 4*, p. 40.
10. *The Royal Play of Macbeth* (1950), pp. 388–91.
11. *The Business of Criticism* (1957), pp. 61 ff.
12. See Glynne Wickham's article in *Shakespeare Survey 19*.
13. H. L. Rogers, *R.E.S.* (1965), p. 44, argues that the tailor would be linked in people's minds with Father Garnet; but this theory involves a later date for *Macbeth* than most critics would accept.
14. David E. Jones, *The Plays of T. S. Eliot* (1960), p. 17.
15. *Penguin New Writing*, No. 3, pp. 115–26.
16. This theme has been discussed by G. Wilson Knight, *The Imperial Theme*, by L. C. Knights, *Explorations*, among others.
17. *Dramatic Providence in Macbeth* (1950), p. 228
18. See M. M. Mahood, *Shakespeare's Word-Play* (1957).
19. *The Winter's Tale* (1947), pp. 126–7.

Chapter 9

1. L. C. Knights, *Some Shakespearian Themes* (1959), p. 149; G. Wilson Knight, *The Imperial Theme* (ed. 1951), pp. 199 ff.; Edwin Wilson, *Shaw on Shakespeare* (1961), p. 213; L. L. Schücking, *Character Problems in Shakespeare's Plays* (1922), p. 133; J. F. Danby, *Poets on Fortune's Hill* (1952), pp. 125–51; Ernest Schanzer, *Shakespear's Problem Plays* (1963).
2. The following discussion was in proof before the publication of Maurice Charney's book, *Shakespeare's Roman Plays* (1961). He makes many of the same points; but he also stresses the way in which the imagery is used to underline the contrast between Egypt and Rome, the hotness and idleness of Egypt being set

against the relative coldness and industry of Rome, as Cleopatra is contrasted with Octavia.

3. Leslie Hotson, *Shakespeare's Sonnets Dated* (1944), p. 10, argues that the 'terrene moon' is Antony's fleet. This seems very unlikely.

4. J. Middleton Murry, *Shakespeare* (1936), pp. 350 ff., argued that the theme of the play is Royalty and Loyalty. Although there is only one direct reference to loyalty in the course of the play, we may agree that Shakespeare is displaying those qualities in Antony and Cleopatra, which arouse the devoted service of their followers.

5. Michael Lloyd, *Shakespeare Survey 12*, pp. 88 ff., suggested that Shakespeare had been reading Plutarch's essay on Isis.

Chapter 10

1. *Characters of Shakespeare's Plays* (ed. London, 1902), p. 357.
2. Cited in New Variorum Edition, ed. H. E. Rollins (Philadelphia, 1938), p. 474.
3. Cited in New Variorum Edition, p. 467.
4. See pp. 142–55.
5. *English Literature in the Sixteenth Century Excluding Drama* (Oxford, 1954), p. 449.
6. *Shakespeare Survey 15* (Cambridge, 1962), pp. 62 ff.
7. Christopher Butler and Alastair Fowler in an article in *Shakespeare 1564–1964* ed. Edward A. Bloom (1964), pp. 125 ff., argue that the number symbolism in *Venus and Adonis* suggests Southampton's age of 20. 'For the summation of the substantive series is 28,800, the number of minutes in twenty days . . . the "little time" of Southampton's twenty summers'.
8. Golding adds:

> And that it is a foolishness to striue against the thing
> Which God before determineth to passe in time to bring.
> And last of all, *Adonis* death dooth shew, that manhood striues
> Against fore-warning, though men see the perill of their liues.

9.
> Sweet Adon darst not glaunce thine eye
>   N'oseres vous, mon bel amy,
> Vpon thy Venus that must die,
>   Je vous en prie, pitie me . . .

> In Cypres sat fayre Venus by a Fount,
> Wanton Adonis toying on her knee:
> She kist the wag, her darling of accompt,
> The boie gan blush, which when his louer see,
>   She smild, and told him loue might challenge debt
>   And he was young and might be wanton yet.

10. T. W. Baldwin, *The Literary Genetics of Shakespeare's Poems and Sonnets* (Urbana, 1950), Chapter 1.
11. *The Third Party* (1592), Sig. M3ᵛ.
12. *Elizabethan Love Conventions* (California, 1933), p. 285.
13. *Op. cit.*, p. 73.
14. Cf. Erasmus, *Epistles:* 'seeing it lieth in your handes to keepe that house from decay . . . every man should well and truly husband his own'.
15. III. iii. 115 ff.
16. *S.E.L..* I (1961), p. 5. Cf. *The Early Shakespeare* by the same author.
17. 'Venus Agonistes', *University of Colerado Studies* IV (1953), pp. 52–66.
18. Marston's *Metamorphosis of Pygmalion's Image* represents the *genre* at its worst — whether it was intended seriously or as a parody — in which the sensuousness degenerated into bawdy unqualified by wit.
19.   His eies did glister blud and fire: right dreadfull was to see
       His brawned necke, right dredfull was his haire which
                                               grew as thicke
       With pricking points as one of them could well by other
                                               sticke.
       And like a front of armed Pikes set close in battel ray
       The sturdie bristles on his back stoode staring vp alway.

   Brooke in the poem which was the source of *Romeo and Juliet* has an imitation of this passage which Shakespeare had read.

       His bristles stiffe upright upon his backe doth set,
       And in his fomy mouth, his sharp and crooked tuskes doth
                                               whet:
       Or as a Lyon wylde that rampeth in his rage.

This is Shakespeare's description:

> Whose tushes never sheathed he whetteth still,
> Like to a mortal butcher bent to kill.

> On his bow-*backe*, he hath a *battell set*,
> Of *bristly pikes* that euer threat his foes,
> His *eyes* like glow-wormes *shine*, when he doth fret
> His snout digs sepulchers where ere he goes,
>   Being mou'd he strikes, what ere is in his way,
>   And whom he strikes, his *crooked tushes* slay.
> His *brawnie* sides with *hairie bristles* armed,
> Are better proofe then thy speares point can enter,
> His short *thick necke* cannot be easily harmed,
> Being irefull, on the *lyon* he will venter . . .

20. *Op. cit.*, p. 71.

Chapter 11

1. T. W. Baldwin, *The Literary Genetics of Shakespeare's Poems and Sonnets* (1950) p. 118.
2. Baldwin, *op. cit.*, p. 136.
3. Baldwin, *op. cit.*, p. 133.
4. R. K. Root, *Classical Mythology in Shakespeare* (1903), p. 35.
5. *A Specimen of a Commentary* (1794), p. 136.
6. IV. v. 224–6.
7. *Lucrece*, ll. 138–9, 421–2, 699–700, 703–4.
8. Tr. Rolfe Humphries.
9. *Shakespeare Survey 15*, p. 94.

Chapter 12

1. J. M. Robertson, *Shakespeare and Chapman* (London, 1917).
2. John M. Murry, *Countries of the Mind*, 2nd ser. (London, 1931), p. 115.
3. In *Essays and Studies of the English Association*, III, 51 ff.
4. H. Granville-Barker and G. B. Harrison, *Companion to Shakespeare Studies* (Cambridge, Eng., 1934), pp. 102–3. The views of Malone, Swinburne, Butler and J. D. Wilson are cited in the New Variorum edition.

5. Mackail lists thirty, together with sixteen words used in a different sense by Shakespeare; but he does not mention the compound epithets, and his list is not complete. Since Mackail wrote his essay, Robert Gittings has suggested (*Shakespeare's Rival*, London, 1960) that the Rival Poet was Gervase Markham. He uses many unusual words. In *Devorax*, for example, his vocabulary includes *gadge*, *globy*, *invoke*(n), *intold*, *insearchable*, *ornefy*, *spelder*, *unrecurable*, *unconjoined*, *unavoid*, *valeyd*, and such compounds as *honor-loosing*, *helpe-attayning*, *thin-leau'd*, *poyson-painted*, *clowd-fashond*, *golden-spurd*, *demy-god-like*, *marish-shaken*. But, apart from a few stanzas formerly ascribed to Marlowe, the general level of the poem is low, and it contains some absurd lines, e.g., 'Stoning to death these shadowes with my teares'. This Rival Poet, at least, could not have written 'A Lover's Complaint'.

M. P. Jackson, in a pamphlet written independently of this article (University of Auckland Bulletin, 1965), lists all the uncommon words used in the poem, and shows that it contains 49 words not elsewhere used by Shakespeare, and 25 'main-words' which were new in 1609 when the poem was published. These figures, when compared with the Hart vocabulary tests (see n. 7 below) support Shakespeare's authorship of the poem.

As there are many more links with Shakespeare's later plays than with his early plays and poems it looks as though *A Lover's Complaint* was written in the seventeenth century. Mr Jackson points out a number of parallels with Shakespeare's mature plays, the most striking being 'unconstrained gyves' (242); 'gyves, Desired more than constrained' (*Cymb.*, V. iv. 14) and 'Maidens' eyes stuck over all his face' (81); 'the eyes . . . of men . . . / That numberless upon me stuck' (*Tim.*, IV. iii. 261); 'millions of false eyes / Are stuck upon thee' (*M.M.*, IV. i. 59). Mr Jackson also shows that there are examples in the poem of Shakespeare's habit of fusing apparently diverse images by means of submerged puns (e.g. ll. 22–5, where Shakespeare uses balls in the double sense of eye-balls and cannon-balls). Mr Jackson believes from the clumsiness of some lines that Shakespeare left the poem unfinished or unrevised.

6. See above, p. 209.

7. Alfred Hart, *Shakespeare and the Homilies* (Melbourne, 1934), *passim*.

8. Cf. K. Muir, *Shakespeare as Collaborator* (London, 1960), pp. 13, 101–2.

9. Mackail comments on the last of these lines:

> . . . it is not un-Shakespearian; it is a real case of what I called the shorthand notation of Shakespeare's later manner. But of course the point is that (1) Shakespeare does not use this highly compressed shorthand in his poems; and (2) where he does use it, his use of it is masterly.

To which one could retort that if five or ten years separated *Lucrece* and 'A Lover's Complaint', one would expect some difference of style; that Shakespeare's use of such shorthand notation in the plays is not always masterly; and that, in any case, the line may well be textually corrupt.

10. *William Shakespeare* (Oxford, 1930), I, 550.

11. *out-storm* Steevens; *out-scorne* Q; *om.* F.

12. W. L. Ruston, *Shakespeare's Testamentary Language* (London, 1869). Cf. K. Muir, *NQ*, CCII (1957). 285–6.

13. *M.M.*, IV. iv. 29; *W.T.*, I. ii. 142.

14. Some editors emend unnecessarily to *bawds*.

15. Pandarus, for instance, is called a broker.

16. The following parallels may be added: they are not given in the New Variorum. The idea of a battery of sighs (277) occurs also in *3 Henry VI*, III. i. 37; the idea of the eyes being glazed by tears (286) appears also in *Richard II*, II. ii. 16; the inundation of tears (290) appears twice (*K.J.*, V. ii. 48; *R.J.*, IV. i. 12); and the contrast between a false jewel and its rich setting (153) occurs in *Richard III*, V. iii. 250. *Henry VI* and *King John* had not yet been published.

17. The printing of the line (Sonnet 129) 'Made In pursut and in possession so' may be explained by the theory that Shakespeare originally wrote 'In pursut and in possession so', and that he inserted 'Made' without altering the capital letter of the next word.

18. E.g. *tottered* (26), *chrusht* (63), *could* (94), *mynuits* (14), *hower* (126), *inhearce* (86), *pibled* (60).

19. Thorpe also acquired the MS of Marlowe's translation of Lucan, and he published three plays by Chapman and four works by Ben Jonson.

20. W. J. Craig and C. K. Pooler. There are, in fact, no indisputable

verbal echoes of Holland's translation; the author of the poem could have read the original; and the information about precious stones was in any case available elsewhere. The relevant lines are:

> The diamond – why 'twas beautiful and hard,
> Whereto his invis'd properties did tend;
> The deep-green em'rald, in whose fresh regard
> Weak sights their sickly radiance do amend;
> The heaven-hu'd sapphire and the opal blend
> With objects manifold.

Holland, pp. 610–20, speaks of the wonderful 'Hardnesse of a Diamant'; of the 'Emeraud' which surpasseth other things in pleasant verdure 'be they never so greene' and 'if the sight hath beene wearied and dimmed' this 'stone doth refresh and restore it againe'; and of 'Borea, like unto the morning skie . . . Sapphires are likewise sometime blew.'

21. Cf. F. C. Kolbe, *Shakespeare's Way* (1930), p. 87.

Index of Names

Index of Works by Shakespeare